Jean Jacques Rousseau

Political Writings

Containing

The Social Contract
Considerations on the Government
of Poland
Constitutional Project for Corsica, Part I

Translated and edited by

Frederick Watkins

T0308913

The University of Wisconsin Press

Published 1986

The University of Wisconsin Press
114 North Murray Street
Madison, Wisconsin 53715

First Wisconsin printing
Originally published in The Nelson Philosophical Texts series
Raymond Klibansky, General Editor

Printed in the United States of America

Library of Congress Cataloging-in-Publication Data

Rousseau, Jean Jacques, 1712–1778.
Rousseau, political writings.
Reprint. Originally published: Edinburgh ; New York :
Nelson, 1953.
Originally published in series: The Nelson
philosophical texts. With new foreword by
Patrick Riley. Bibliography: pp. xl–lii
1. Political science—Collected works. 2. Social
contract—Collected works. I. Watkins, Frederick
Mundell, 1910–   . II. Title.
JC179.R7   1986   320   86-7749
ISBN 0-299-11094-X

POLITICAL WRITINGS

CONTENTS

Foreword by Patrick Riley ix

Editor's Introduction xvii

Editorial Note xliii

Chronological Table xlvii

Bibliographical Note xlviii

THE SOCIAL CONTRACT

BOOK I : THE STATE OF NATURE, THE CIVIL STATE AND THE ESSENTIAL CONDITIONS OF THE COMPACT

I : The Subject of the First Book . . 3

II : The First Societies 4

III : The Right of the Strongest . . . 6

IV : Slavery 8

V : That we must always go back to a First
Convention 13

VI : The Social Compact 14

VII : The Sovereign 17

VIII : The Civil State 19

IX : Real Property 21

BOOK II : LEGISLATION

I : That Sovereignty is inalienable . . 25

II : That Sovereignty is indivisible . . 26

III : Whether the General Will is subject to
Error 28

IV : The Limits of Sovereign Power . . 30

v :	The Right of Life and Death	35
vi :	Law	37
vii :	The Legislator	41
viii :	The People	46
ix :	The same continued	48
x :	The same continued	51
xi :	The various Systems of Legislation	54
xii :	The various Types of Law	57

BOOK III : POLITICAL LAWS

i :	Government in general	59
ii :	The Constituent Principle of the various Forms of Government	66
iii :	The Classification of Governments	69
iv :	Democracy	71
v :	Aristocracy	73
vi :	Monarchy	76
vii :	Mixed Governments	82
viii :	That no Form of Government is suitable to all Countries	84
ix :	The Signs of a good Government	90
x :	The Abuse of Government and its Tendency to degenerate	92
xi :	The Death of the Body Politic	96
xii :	How the Sovereign Authority is maintained	98
xiii :	The same continued	99
xiv :	The same continued	101

xv : Deputies or Representatives .   .   .   102

xvi : That the Establishment of Government is
not a Contract   106

xvii : The Establishment of Government   .   108

xviii: Means of forestalling Usurpations of
Government   109

BOOK IV : MEANS OF STRENGTHENING THE CONSTITUTION

i : That the General Will is indestructible .   113

ii : Voting Procedures   115

iii : Elections   119

iv : The Roman Assemblies   .   .   .   121

v : The Tribunate   134

vi : Dictatorship   136

vii : The Censorship   140

viii : Civil Religion   142

ix : Conclusion   155

CONSIDERATIONS ON THE GOVERNMENT OF POLAND

i : The Nature of the Problem .   .   .   159

ii : The Spirit of the Institutions of Antiquity   162

iii : Application   167

iv : Education   176

v : The Radical Defect   181

vi : The Question of the Three Orders .   .   183

vii : Means of maintaining the Constitution .   187

CONTENTS

VIII : The King 206
  IX : Specific Causes of Anarchy . . . 212
   X : Administration 219
  XI : The Economic System 223
 XII : The Military System 236
XIII : Plan for a Sequence of Official Promotions
       embracing all Members of the Govern-
       ment 245
 XIV : The Election of Kings 257
  XV : Conclusion 267

CONSTITUTIONAL PROJECT FOR CORSICA

Foreword 277
Part I 279

FOREWORD

There is no need to "recommend" the writings of Jean Jacques Rousseau: the greatest of all critics of inequality, the purest social contract theorist of the eighteenth century (and simultaneously the deepest critic of contractarianism after Hume), the greatest writer on civic education after Plato, the most perceptive understander of mastery and slavery after Aristotle and before Hegel, the finest critic of Hobbes, the most important predecessor of Kant, the most accomplished didactic novelist between Richardson and Tolstoy, the greatest confessor since St. Augustine, the author of paradoxes ("the general will is always right" but "not enlightened") that continue to fascinate or infuriate.

What recommends and urges republication of Frederick Watkins' 1953 edition of Rousseau's *Political Writings*, however, is that it contains incomparably the finest English translation of Rousseau's greatest political treatise, *The Social Contract*—in a version that combines accuracy with a very rare preservation of much of Rousseau's eloquence and elegance—as well as the best translation of the late and important *Government of Poland*, and the only translation to date of the unpublished fragment, *Constitutional Project for Corsica*. Watkins' "Introduction" to his edition, moreover, while very controversial, has the great merit of encompassing the *complexity* of Rousseau's thought, of refusing to make him merely a post-Lockean or a proto-Robespierrean.

Watkins, indeed, argues that Rousseau's chief merit as a political theorist is to acknowledge and preserve social complexity, rather than to present logical, "rational"

solutions to social problems (à la Bentham)—that Rousseau, for example, never successfully fused (in a coherent "system") the personal autonomy and the educative
authority which he equally valued, but that he saw (and
refrained from suppressing or simplifying) more facets
of social life than any other modern thinker. Rousseau's
"intuitive" grasp of complexity, for Watkins, is worth
more than a unified, systematic coherence grounded in
a one-sided, threadbare *explicandum* (such as "maxi-
mized satisfaction").

It is true, nonetheless, that Watkins' "Introduction"
bears every mark of the year in which it was written:
1951. The psychologism, the insistence that Rousseau's
work is the reflection or rationalization of the case of a
"tragic social misfit," the notion that Rousseau's vibration between extreme independence ("particularity") and
yearning for social integration ("generality") both produces and accounts for the "liberal" and "totalitarian"
aspects of his thought (not to mention the constant stress
on liberalism, totalitarianism and "constitutionalism"
themselves)—all of these are echoes of the 1950s, though
superior and intelligent echoes. It is despite these rather
restricting 'fifties categories that Watkins says valuable
things about Rousseau—about the problems of defin-
ing the "general will," about Rousseau's anticosmopoli-
tanism (particularly in *Poland*), about the "miraculous"
mission of Rousseau's Great Legislator, who helps a
people to "find" its general will.

There is no "necessity," indeed, to view Rousseau as a
tragic "case" vacillating incoherently between the anti-
thetical extremes of "liberalism" and "totalitarianism,"
whose thought is merely psychologically (never logically) unified, whose philosophy is simply a bundle of
raisons que la raison ne connaît point. One can, in fact, view

Rousseau as being quite clear about several social "models of perfection"—to recall Judith Shklar's phrase—which are not, of course, simultaneously realizable, but which are independently defensible (and independently defended): a Golden Age of Spartan civic virtue and general will (*Social Contract* and *Economie Politique*); a Stoic independence made possible by limiting one's desires to match one's powers (*Emile*); an "exemplary" life (Rousseau's own) which does little good but is at least "honest" and refrains from harm (*Confessions* and *Rêveries*); a more or less "Swiss" extended family life which is midway between individual isolation and "Roman" community (*La Nouvelle Héloise* and *Letter to d'Alembert*). Watkins is right about the complexity of Rousseau's social theory, without necessarily being right that that complexity merely echoes Rousseau's own "case"—a liberal/totalitarian bipolarity. Rousseau's complexity is more complex than that.

If 'fifties psychologism and a concern with "liberalism" vs. "totalitarianism" sometimes restrict the value of some parts of Watkins' "Introduction," there are other parts which are done to a turn. Rousseau, in a celebrated passage from *The Social Contract* (II,6) that Watkins helpfully illuminates, says that while the "general will" of a sovereign people is "always right," it is not always enlightened or capable—there may be a large and lamentable gap between the people's moral entitlement to make the fundamental, general laws under which it will live for all future time, and the people's capacity to recognize "necessity," to unite "understanding" with "will," so that finally the general will will be as enlightened as it was always right. This "understanding," this "enlightenment," he argues, must be supplied—at the beginning of civic time, when men have not yet been denatured, transformed into civic beings who think of themselves as "part of a greater whole"—by a Great Legislator, a Numa or Moses or Lycurgus who "persuades without convincing" and helps the people "find" the general will that it is seeking. On this very point Watkins brings out perfectly the utopianism (or alternatively the ultimate pessimism) of Rousseau's political thought: Rousseau, he says, "constantly emphasized" the notion that "the appearance of a genuine legislator is an event so rare as to be truly miraculous. Since the moments when men are willing to listen to a legislator are equally rare, [Rousseau's] hopes of reformation depended on the occurrence of a double miracle" (p. xxxiii).

That shapely formulation has something of Rousseau's own grace and economy of style. More contestable, though worth reading, is Watkins' interpretation of the "general will" itself—which he rightly calls "the central concept of [Rousseau's] political theory," though he seems not to recognize that Rousseau inherited *volonté générale* from the seventeenth-century French theology of Pascal, Malebranche, and Fénelon, who had wondered whether God has a "general will" to save "all men," or, à la Calvin, a mere "particular will" to save the "elect." One can see instantly why these seventeenth-century theological terms (which had been given a more secular, political meaning by Bayle and Montesquieu) would be attractive to Rousseau, who was at once the inheritor of demi-Lockean ideas of voluntary contractarianism and of quasi-Platonic notions of civic education. After all, the two "terms" of *volonté générale*—"will" and "generality"—represent two of the main strands in Rousseau's thought. "Generality" stands, *inter alia,* for the rule of law, for civic education which draws us "out of ourselves" and toward the general (or common) good, for the non-particularist citizen-virtues of Sparta and republican Rome. And the notion of "will" stands for his conviction that "civil association is the most voluntary act in the world," that "to deprive your will of all freedom is to deprive your actions of all morality." And if one could (through the educative efforts of Numa or Lycurgus) "generalize" the will, so that it "elects" only law, citizenship, and the common good, and avoids "willful" self-love, then one would have a general will in Rousseau's special sense: the general will one has "as a citizen."

Watkins sees very clearly the tension between *volonté* and *généralité* in Rousseau's thought; after all, is every kind of educative "generalizing" consistent with (really) "willing"? But he puts this tension down, characteristically, to Rousseau's "tragic" vibration between isolation and community. More important, while he sees correctly that Rousseau's general will is "another version of the old proposition that social harmony depends on the maintenance of general rules of sociability at the expense of selfish impulses" (p. xxiv), he tends to assimilate Rousseau's general will overmuch to Kant's "categorical imperative."

Why is such an overassimilation of the *citoyen de Génève* to the *Weltbürger* Kant not as fully warranted as Watkins believes? Simply because of the difference between *generality* and *universality*. Rousseau's rejection of any reason-ordained *morale universelle* in the "First Version" of *The Social Contract* rules out Kantianism in advance, since the "categorical imperative" of the *Grundlegung* is both rational and universal. Rousseau's "generality,"—in which each denatured citizen wills the general good of his own *polis,* but not the universal good of a true *cosmopolis*—indeed becomes sharper if one contrasts Rousseaueanism with the thought of Kant, viewed as the perfect representative of German rationalistic universalism ("I am never to act otherwise than so that I could also will that my maxim should become a universal law . . . reason extorts from me immediate respect for such [universal] legislation"), and with that of William Blake, seen as a typical representative of English ethical "empiricism":

> He who would do good to another
> Must do it in Minute Particulars;
> General good is the plea
> Of the scoundrel, hypocrite and flatterer.

The discovery of an *ethos* that rises above "minute particulars," that moves toward universality but has its reasons for not building *on* reason, and for drawing up short at a more modest "generality"; the advocacy of a kind of willing which is more than egoistic and selfish and *particulière* but less than a Kantian, universal, "higher" will—that is the distinctive contribution to political and moral thought made by Rousseau, who "socialized" the general will bequeathed to him by his French theological predecessors. (Watkins acknowledges that Rousseau is more "politan," so to speak, than "cosmopolitan," and laments that Rousseau's "integral nationalism" kept him from embracing a universal, Kantian "eternal peace" between all "republics." Rousseau's politanism, of course, is at its clearest in *Poland,* which Watkins translated with such fidelity and grace.)

By now it will be clear that, however one may disagree with this or that strand of Watkins' interpretation of Rousseau, he brings up the central questions and difficulties, always preserving Rousseau's complexity. One could say of Watkins what he said of Rousseau: that if he is not always right, he invariably sees what is important and refuses to oversimplify in the interest of a too easily bought "unity" or "coherence." The traits that

Watkins most admired in Rousseau were his own greatest strengths as well.

Patrick Riley

Madison, Wisconsin
January, 1986

INTRODUCTION

ALTHOUGH nearly two centuries have passed since the publication of the *Social Contract*, Rousseau still holds his place as one of the most stimulating and controversial of political theorists. The continuing interest of his work comes from the fact that the problem to which he addressed himself has been recognised in ever increasing measure as the crucial issue of modern politics. In the middle of the eighteenth century, social conditions were, or at least appeared to be, comparatively stable. This made it possible for most of Rousseau's contemporaries to take the existence of society for granted, and to focus their attention on the relations between society and government. For Rousseau, however, the basic problem was to secure the voluntary integration of individual and social action. In the twentieth century, with its unprecedentedly rapid social changes, this problem has become peculiarly acute. Liberals and totalitarians, in their respective ways, are equally preoccupied with the task of causing people to identify their individual interests with collective institutions. As a highly gifted pioneer in this particular field of investigation, Rousseau is still capable of throwing revealing light on the problems of twentieth-century politics. General recognition of the importance of his work has not led, however, to any corresponding agreement as to the nature of his influence. For many authoritarians, Rousseau is the evil spirit of the modern world, a reckless libertarian whose siren voice has lured successive generations along the path of undisciplined individualism and self-indulgence. An increasing number of liberals regard him, on the contrary, as the prophet of all that is most distasteful in the individual-destroying excesses of totalitarian government. Diametrically opposed as these interpretations are, both can be supported by a judicious selection of quotations from Rousseau's own writings. After some two hundred years of continuous study Rousseau still continues, therefore, to be one of the most bitterly controversial figures in the history of political thought. This stands as a tribute both to the importance and to the complexity of his approach to the problem of politics.

The difficulty of interpreting him arises, in my opinion, from the fact that most students insist on crediting him with a degree of logical consistency which is not in fact characteristic of his writings. The true nature of his work can be appreciated only if the reader recognises from the beginning that its underlying unity is psychological rather than logical in character. The nature of the human mind is such that people generally begin by making a number of mutually exclusive demands upon the universe. They want to be both loved and feared, both co-operative and autonomous. With increasing experience the logical incompatibility of many of these demands becomes apparent, and an attempt is made to reconcile them in some sort of consistent system. Political theorists are for the most part men with a highly developed logical faculty. In the interest of consistency, they are apt to abstract from the complex unity of human nature some particular psychological trait, and to follow it to its logical conclusion at the expense of every other aspect of experience. Hobbes with his emphasis on the fear of death, and Bentham with his vision of man as a hedonistic calculating-machine, are extreme examples of this tendency.

Rousseau was an entirely different sort of person, and the strengths and weaknesses of his thought are correspondingly distinct from those of most political theorists. Though endowed by nature with no great gifts of analytical clarity, he perceived the political and social motivations of men with uncommon intuitive insight. Because of the contradictions inherent in his own personality, he found it necessary to make room in his political theory for psychological complexities unknown to the systematic constructions of more strictly logical thinkers. Since he himself was unable to reduce his thought to a logically consistent whole, it is futile to impose a system upon him by following any one of his several insights to its logical conclusions. The value of his work lies in the fact not that he was able to resolve, but that he was able to perceive, some of the basic perplexities and contradictions of modern political life. Any useful interpretation of his writings must begin, therefore, with an understanding of the psychological factors which enabled him to take so comprehensive a view of the problem of politics.

The basic feature of Rousseau's personal experience, which goes far to explain the direction of his political thought, is the fact that nature and circumstances had conspired to make him a tragic social misfit. Born with an unstable temperament which led, in the closing years of his life, to actual paranoia, he was a man who, even under the most favourable circumstances, would have found no little difficulty in meeting the requirements of normal social life. Unfortunately the circumstances of his early years were such as to aggravate the problem. The career to which he was destined by family tradition, and for which family precept and example ought to have prepared him, was that of a skilled workman in the sober and God-fearing city of

Geneva. By the death of his mother and the desertion of his father he was early abandoned, however, to the well-intentioned but rather casual care of relatives who showed no great skill in imposing an effective discipline upon so difficult a child. The result was that, after a series of unhappy apprenticeships, he ran away and spent the formative years of youth and early manhood in a life of indolent and irresponsible vagabondage. In the long run native talent triumphed over faulty training, and won him an enviable place in the literary and intellectual circles of Paris. For a person of his temperament, however, it was then far too late to acquire the necessary modicum of social skills required for the enjoyment of success. The art of getting along happily with other people was one that he never succeeded in mastering. To the distress of his many faithful and influential friends, shyness and suspicion led him to prefer a life of self-imposed isolation. Thus Rousseau was, to a positively pathological degree, a man cut off from the normal pleasures of social life. For him the conflict between society and the individual was no cold theoretical problem, but a matter of tragic personal experience. This was the immediate source of that passionate interest in social and political questions which formed so large a part of his total life and work.

In view of the nature of his interest, it is psychologically by no means surprising to discover that Rousseau's attitude toward society was basically ambivalent. When people suffer a profoundly frustrating experience, their attitude toward the source of their difficulties is apt to be inextricably compounded of attraction and repulsion. In his reaction to the tragedy of social frustration, Rousseau followed the classic pattern. When he remembered the discomforts of social life, his only thought was to escape; but when he considered the loneliness of his isolation, he yearned for society with all the passion of unrequited love. This led him to adopt two logically incompatible, but psychologically complementary, points of view. He felt, on the one hand, that society, in so far as it runs counter to the will of the individual, is an unmitigated evil. This finds expression in the liberal aspect of his thought, with its extreme emphasis on the subordination of social action to the requirements of the individual. But he also felt, on the other hand, that social action was the highest form of individual satisfaction, and that no price would be too high to pay for the creation and maintenance of a society in which the desires of the individual were so perfectly adjusted to the requirements of the group that there could be no possible conflict between them. This finds expression in the totalitarian aspect of his thought, with its extreme emphasis on the value of social discipline. Although the first aspect is more prominent in his non-political writings, and the second in his political works, both are important throughout. Without an appreciation of this psychological ambivalence, the significance of his thought can hardly be understood.

A second feature of Rousseau's personal background, which also needs to be kept in mind, is the fact that he was Swiss. Considering that Geneva was the scene of his earliest frustrations, and the first of the many societies from which he fled, it may seem surprising that he should have retained any great affection for his native land. But early experiences, especially when unpleasant, are apt to exert a powerfully formative influence. Later successes in other lands could never wholly quench Rousseau's feeling of guilt for his youthful failure in Geneva. A pathetic desire to re-establish himself in the eyes of his fellow-citizens is visible, for example, in the dedication of the *Discourse on the Origin of Inequality*, with its fulsome praise of Geneva's worthy magistrates. Unlike the majority of his contemporaries, who were fully reconciled to the absolutist realities of eighteenth-century politics, and pinned their hopes on enlightened despotism, Rousseau never abandoned the republican ideals of his native city. His extensive acquaintance with the writings of classical antiquity likewise helped to strengthen him in the view that a small, compact community run by a politically active citizen body was the only acceptable form of government. An idealised version of Geneva, reinforced by the classical tradition of the ancient city state, was the foundation of his whole conception of politics.

Rousseau's devotion to the republican ideal was further strengthened by yet another aspect of his Genevan heritage, the Calvinist tradition. Since he himself was far from being an orthodox Calvinist, this element in his thought is often overlooked. But the spirit of Calvin, though already much relaxed and secularised, was an all-pervasive force in the Geneva of Rousseau's youth, and there is much in his later writings which becomes intelligible only in the light of that early influence. From the point of view of politics, the most important characteristic of Calvinism is its emphasis on inner-worldly asceticism. The ideal Calvinist society was a community of saints, austerely and tirelessly devoted to the task of ensuring that God's will be done on earth as it is in heaven. The good life for them was a life not of worldly pleasure but of strict simplicity and unremitting duty. Although the theological foundations of this way of life, even in Geneva, had been greatly weakened by the end of the seventeenth century, the sober and puritanical habits it had engendered continued long thereafter to dominate the Genevan atmosphere. This was the air that Rousseau breathed in his earliest years, and it remained as one of the major influences on his subsequent thought.

Without some knowledge of this background it is hard to appreciate the intensely moralistic character of Rousseau's political writings. The widespread illusion that he was an immoralist is largely due to the fact that many of those who have commented on his work have been Catholics or other non-Calvinists who were unable or unwilling to recognise the moral character of an essentially Calvinist position.

The Calvinist influence is most clearly shown, perhaps, in his rejection of hedonism. At a time when most of his contemporaries were appealing to the pleasure-pain principle as a basis for social and political reform, Rousseau inveighed against the evils of luxury and pleasure with all the fervour of an old-style presbyterian elder. When lax Genevans actually suggested that a theatre be established in their godly city, the expatriate's rage knew no bounds.[1] Alienation from his native land, and from the principles of Calvinist orthodoxy, did nothing to modify his devotion to the ascetic Calvinist ideal of plain living and hard work.

Asceticism was not, however, the most important aspect of the Calvinist tradition, nor was it the one which had the deepest influence on the development of Rousseau's political thought. The essence of the Calvinist heritage consists in a peculiar form of moral activism, of which puritanism is no more than a super-ficial manifestation. This activism is the product of a psychological ambivalence which is curiously parallel to

[1] See the *Letter to M. d'Alembert*. It is perhaps worth noting in this connexion that Rousseau's own first great success in Paris was with an opera, *Le Devin du village*. Bad conscience may have had something to do with the virulence of his subsequent hostility towards the stage.

the ambivalence of Rousseau's own attitude toward
society. Logically speaking, the Calvinist doctrine of
predestination might have been expected to lead to an
extreme form of individualism, and to the mystical
withdrawal of all true believers from worldly preoccupa-
tions. If the elect are chosen directly by God, and if
the church is unable to improve the other-worldly
prospects either of saints or of sinners, there would seem
to be no reasonable motive for social action on the part
of Calvinists. The inner tension which resulted from
their faith was such, however, that they in fact became
the most fanatical of social reformers. Contemplating
the awful majesty of an omnipotent and inflexible God,
many lived under the shadow of a constant dread that
they might not in fact be among the chosen saints.
The only way for such people to show that they were
on God's side, and thus presumably of the elect, was to
work unceasingly for the accomplishment of God's will
on earth. In the case of those other, and more fortunate Calvinists who felt sure of their own election,
awe and gratitude led to a similar sense of obligation.
God willed that all men, saints and sinners alike, should
lead lives of sober austerity. To establish the rule of
the saints, and to repress the wickedness of sinners, was
therefore an all-important duty. Thus the attitude of
the Calvinists toward the world, like Rousseau's attitude
toward society, was basically ambivalent. As individuals
enjoying the free gift of God's grace, they loathed the
world as a place of sin and corruption; as saints dedicated to the greater glory of God, they could not rest
until they had made the world their own. This last
could be accomplished only by energetic and concerted
action. In spite of its individualistic premises, therefore,
Calvinism everywhere pressed toward the establishment
of theocracies which were virtually totalitarian in their

insistence on social discipline. Intense moral activism was its ultimate political consequence.

This aspect of the Calvinist tradition is reflected in the moral activism which permeates the whole of Rousseau's political thought. It is true that he rejected the aristocratic implications of Calvinist orthodoxy, with its sharp distinction between the elect, who bear the responsibility of ruling, and the damned, who have only to obey. His repudiation of the doctrine of original sin left no room for any such distinction. The rejection of Calvinist theology, however, did not lead him to abandon, but rather to intensify and universalise, the Calvinist political ethic. Classical antiquity provided him with the example of a society in which the assumption of political responsibilities was regarded not as a duty assumed by the chosen few for the greater glory of God, but as a natural condition of human perfection. Rousseau's respect for the ancient philosophers helped, therefore, to reinforce his inherited belief in the principle of moral activism, and encouraged him to reaffirm it on a purely secular and humanistic basis. The resulting merger of classical and of Calvinist influences gave rise to an attitude of moral strenuousness which is one of the most distinctive features of his political theory, and serves above all else to distinguish his work from that of most of his contemporaries. The latter, though likewise under the influence of classical humanism, were willing to accept any form of government, however despotic, which seemed capable of achieving desirable results. For Rousseau no government, however efficient, was morally justified unless it rested on the active participation of all its citizens. Political life, in his view, was an unremitting struggle to subdue selfish impulses in the interest of the common good. No man was a fully developed moral being unless he participated in this struggle. All this is a reaffirmation, in humanistic terms, of the Calvinist tradition of moral activism. Rousseau's ideal state is a secular kingdom of saints, which differs from its prototype in that the duty of political action is no longer confined to the elect, but is transformed into a general burden on the conscience of all mankind.

The moralistic core of his thought is nowhere more clearly demonstrated than in his curiously ambivalent attitude toward the state of nature. This is one of the points on which his work is most readily open to misinterpretation. Rousseau is often regarded as an admirer of the ' noble savage ', and it is true that he paints a rather idyllic picture of the pre-political condition of man. In many cases, however, his praise of the primitive has reference not to the state of nature, but to such early political societies as Rome or Sparta. And in the *Social Contract*, at least, he is perfectly explicit in stating that the transition from the state of nature to civil society is a necessary forward step in the history of mankind. The reasons he advances in support of this proposition are of a characteristically moral kind. In the state of nature man's contact with his fellow men is so infrequent and discontinuous that mere instinct is a sufficient guide to conduct. Without the experience of organised social life, he has no occasion to discipline his natural appetites in the interest of common action. Thus reason and morality do not exist in the state of nature; they are products of civil society. But man without reason and morality is no man at all; he is simply a beast. The civil state is necessary, therefore, to the full development of men, and even though the corruptions to which it is subject may make life far more wretched than it was in the state of nature, this must be accepted as one of the risks implicit in the assumption of moral responsibilities. The civil state may be unpleasant, but it provides an indispensable occasion for the development of a sense of duty. This is the moral ground, characteristically austere and anti-hedonist, on which Rousseau tries to demonstrate the superiority of society to the state of nature.

If the civil state is to be justified on these grounds, however, political life must be so organised as to provide men with an opportunity for the assertion of moral responsibility. This is the main significance of Rousseau's theory of the general will. Although this is the central concept of his political theory, its exact meaning is never clearly defined by the author himself, and the resulting obscurities leave room for many legitimate differences of interpretation. Rousseau's general purpose in introducing it is, however, clear. His own frustrated desire to participate in social life had left him with the feeling that the primary purpose of society was to provide its members with an occasion for voluntary social action. This feeling was reinforced by the inherited Calvinist belief that the good life was a life of conscious moral action. Personal experience and Calvinist background both led to the conclusion that the only legitimate form of government is one which rests on the continuous moral participation of all men. There can be no moral responsibility for acts which do not proceed from the will of the acting agent. In asserting that every citizen must participate in the formation of a general will, and that this general will is the sole legitimate source of political action, Rousseau was stating his conviction that the only justification of society is to provide an opportunity for the moral self-development of men.

The extreme to which he carried the principle of moral responsibility is shown with particular clarity in his curious treatment of the problem of contract. For several centuries before his time, the opponents of political absolutism, inspired by such medieval precedents as Magna Carta, had been relying on various forms of contract, social or governmental, to safeguard the rights of individuals. Rousseau followed this tradition to the extent of calling his major political work the *Social Contract*, and of using the term to designate the primary act of association necessary to the creation of a legitimate political order. The idea of contract was actually incompatible, however, with the moral implications of the general will. It was therefore modified to the point of extinction in Rousseau's political system. The difficulty was that a contract, if it is to have any significance at all, must be capable of obliging men to act against their will. If I promise today to do something tomorrow, it is in recognition of the fact that when tomorrow comes I may wish, and may even feel morally bound, to do something quite different. Contractual obligations are therefore incompatible with continuous moral responsibility, since they have the effect of confining the period of responsible action to the moment when the contract is being made. For Rousseau, however, continuous moral responsibility was the essence of political legitimacy. He was accordingly forced to reduce the contractual element in his theory to the barest possible minimum. He therefore denied that there could be any sort of contractual obligation between society and government, asserting that society was free at any time to set up any kind of government it pleased. What then of the relationship between the individual and society? Although Rousseau retained the term contract to describe this relationship, he phrased the contract itself in such a way that it ceased to be contractual in anything but name. In his version of the matter, the individual agrees to give up all his rights to the community, which means that he has no contractual claims to assert against it. The community, on the other hand, can make use of these rights only in accordance with the general will, in the formation of which each individual participates. In other words, the specific rights and duties of the individual are determined not by the terms of the social contract itself, but by the continuing moral consensus of the individuals who are parties to it. But a promise to do tomorrow what you want to do tomorrow imposes no obligation on the will. By putting the matter in this form, Rousseau postulated a social contract which was not in fact a contract. To have done otherwise would have been to impair the integrity of his principle that continuous moral responsibility is the basis of political legitimacy.

Rousseau's desire to preserve the individual as a morally responsible agent gave rise, however, to a difficult political problem. If he had been a pure individualist, it would have been easy for him to adopt an anarchist position and assert with Godwin and others that society should be maintained on a basis of pure consent. But Rousseau was too much concerned with the maintenance of social order, and too keenly aware of the obstacles to social action, to adopt so unrealistic a solution. Although his concept of the general will was designed to protect the moral freedom of the individual, he recognised that individuals in a state of perfect freedom might well commit acts incompatible with the existence of society. If society is a necessary condition for the exercise of human freedom, it follows that socially disruptive behaviour must be repressed in the interest of freedom itself. Rousseau accepted this conclusion. As he himself said, in a well-known passage, men must be forced to be free. But if the legitimacy of coercion is recognised, what becomes of the attempt to eliminate personal frustration and to maximise moral responsibility? Can an individual who is being coerced remain in any meaningful sense of the term a responsible moral agent? This is the crucial issue of Rousseau's political thought.

His own solution of the problem is contained in his distinction between the general and the particular will. Although this all-important distinction is nowhere clearly defined, its general tenor emerges in the course of his writings. Rousseau in this connexion is clearly referring to the psychological fact that men, in defiance of logic, are capable of willing simultaneously two or more mutually incompatible ends. The desire to have cake and eat it too is as old as human nature. The same principle applies to the relationship of the individual to the community. In so far as the individual shares the purposes, and is thus a morally responsible member, of any social group, he wills that the life and activity of that group should be effectively preserved. Individuals who share a common or general will of this sort constitute a single voluntary community; individuals who do not share it are no part of the community, and remain unbound by any sort of moral obligation. When Rousseau says, therefore, that it is only in accordance with the general will that men can be forced to be free, he is maintaining the essentially individualist proposition that a man can only be bound by decisions with which he himself is in moral agreement. But a man is not merely a citizen; he is also a private individual, with interests and purposes of his own. The private or particular will which directs him toward these latter objects may well come in conflict with the general will which he shares with other members of his group. A

xxxi EDITOR'S INTRODUCTION

man who believes, for example, that tax evasion or murder are incompatible with the public interest may still be tempted for private reasons to file dishonest tax returns or to eliminate an unattractive wife. Although the application of coercive sanctions under such circumstances is undoubtedly frustrating to the particular will of the individual concerned, the event may be described in a very real sense as an expression of his own moral judgment. By distinguishing, therefore, between the general and the particular will, Rousseau is able to combine individual responsibility and social coercion within his political system.

Though expressed in rather novel terms, this aspect of Rousseau's thought is by no means wholly original. It places him, indeed, in the tradition of ethical rationalism which proceeds from the Stoic idea of natural law to the Kantian categorical imperative. The basic principle of the rationalist school is that the human mind, by a process of generalisation, is capable of discovering the basic rules of human sociability. Experience shows, so the argument runs, that there are certain forms of self-assertion which, by running counter to the like self-assertion of others, lead to social conflict, and thus to the negation of man's desire for peaceful association with his fellows. Reason enables men to maximise their social satisfactions by teaching them to make only such demands as prove to be compatible with the like demands of others. Rational morality consists, therefore, in the formulation of generally applicable rules of conduct, and in the repression of all selfish impulses which run counter to those rules. Rousseau's statement of the relationship of the general to the particular will is essentially a restatement of this well-known position. It is true that the rationalistic element is somewhat obscured by his emphasis on will. When he says that the general will is always right, it is not immediately clear whether he means that it is right because it is general, or general because it is right. Emphasis on the former possibility has led many interpreters to see Rousseau as an apostle of pure moral relativism. This interpretation is hard to reconcile, however, with his repeated statements that the general will is not the will of all, and that the decisions of a social group, even when unanimous, have no necessary claim to rightness. Something more than consensus is clearly implied in Rousseau's concept of the general will. Conformity to the rationally discoverable conditions of human sociability is also required. This rational element is particularly clear in his treatment of the legislator, as we shall see hereafter. It is also implicit in his rigorous insistence that the general will can only be expressed in the form of general legislation. Thus his concept of the general will belongs in the main stream of Western rationalism, and is closely related, as Kant himself felt, to the principle of the categorical imperative. His subordination of the particular to the general will is just another version of the old proposition that social harmony depends on the maintenance of general rules of sociability at the expense of selfish impulses.

The real novelty of Rousseau's theory is his attempt to apply the principles of natural morality to the determination of political legitimacy. In this attempt he was by no means wholly successful. The difficulty, as usual, was to find a reliable point of contact between abstract moral principles and concrete political institutions. Many medieval thinkers tried to solve the problem by appealing to the institutions of an infallible church as an agency for the enforcement of natural law. Rousseau needed, but was unable to discover, an equally authoritative exponent of the general will. It is true that his general principles led him to a number of negative conclusions. Since the purpose of the state was to provide men with an opportunity for the exercise of political responsibility, it followed that there could be no valid expression of the general will without the personal participation of the entire citizen body. No part of the whole, not even a representative assembly, could be relied upon for this purpose, and if circumstances arose, as in Poland, where representative institutions were unavoidable, their value would be directly proportional to the rigour with which they were subjected to the control of the electorate. All this sounds very much like a plea for direct popular democracy, and Rousseau is often presented as an exponent of absolute majority rule. He himself was too conscious of the difficulty of the problem, however, to commit himself to the proposition that a majority of the electorate, or any other determinate political institution, was necessarily capable of expressing the general will. His repeated statements, in the *Social Contract* and elsewhere, that bare majorities should be used only for relatively minor or unusually pressing decisions, and that larger majorities, up to and even including unanimity, might be required for more important acts of legislation, are a sufficient proof that he placed no unlimited confidence in the justice of majority decisions. Even a unanimous decision might, in his view, be mistaken as to the true interests of society, and thus no proper expression of the general will. His theory ends, therefore, with the rather unsatisfactory conclusion that no government is legitimate unless it rests on the general will, and that there is no reliable way of telling what the general will may be. By following his principles it is possible to say that a given government is not, but never that it is, legitimate.

With all its weaknesses, however, Rousseau's concept of the general will deserves to rank as a basic contribution to the theory of constitutional government. The very fact, indeed, that he failed to institutionalise it is one of its chief virtues. The institutions of constitutional democracy, like those of any other living form of government, are constantly changing in response to fresh experience. If Rousseau had insisted on ascribing final legitimacy to any particular type of political machinery, his work would soon have been hopelessly dated. This has actually been the fate of those few specific conclusions, such as the rejection of representative institutions, which do emerge from his writings. The lasting value of his concept of the general will is that it sets forth, however obscurely, the basic and frequently forgotten principles which alone can explain the institutions and usages of constitutional democracy. For the modern constitutionalist, as for Rousseau, respect for the moral responsibility of individual citizens is the foundation of all political legitimacy. Coercion is justified only in so far as it is based on some sort of general agreement. Constitutional government assumes that all the citizens of a particular state, no matter how divided they may be in their personal opinions, are so firmly agreed in their desire to share a common political existence that they are willing to repress their particular views in the interest of common action. The skill of constitutional statesmanship consists in limiting the demands of collective action to the area of actual or potential agreement. If this proves impossible, minority groups may come to feel that the values of the community are less important to them than the particular interests they are asked to sacrifice on its behalf. When this happens, there ceases to be any constitutionally legitimate basis for coercion, and a proper constitutional government must either relax its demands in such a way as to win back the disaffected minority, or else recognise the right of the latter to set themselves up as an independent political society. The repeal of national prohibition in America, and the abandonment of post-Civil-War attempts to impose racial equality on the Southern United States, are characteristic examples of the first approach ; the second is well illustrated by the separation of Norway from Sweden by mutual agreement, and by the progressive elimination of compulsory ties within the British Commonwealth. Such episodes can only be justified on the principle, first set forth by Rousseau, that no coercion is legitimate unless it is based on a general will. And just as Rousseau himself was unable to discover any reliable means of identifying the general will, modern constitutionalists have likewise been forced in practice to admit that the general will is, in the last analysis, an extra-legal force. Although bills of rights and other institutional devices may help to keep constitutional governments from overstepping the limits of common agreement, they can never provide any final answer to the problem. Even the American process of constitutional amendment, which goes to uncommon lengths in its attempt to safeguard minority interests, has not always been successful in preventing the legal adoption of measures which proved to be unacceptable. Constitutionalism, in the last analysis, is a moral principle, an appeal to the individual conscience. Moral principles can never be wholly embodied in, but must always serve as an external check upon, political institutions. The greatness of Rousseau as a constitutional theorist rests on his profound feeling for this all-important fact.

Now that the liberal aspect of Rousseau's thought has been considered, we must turn our attention to the totalitarian aspect. For him, as for most totalitarians, extreme pessimism was the basis for an ultimate rejection of constitutional principles. A thorough and consistent liberal must believe not only that ordinary people ought to assume responsibility for their own political destinies, but also that they are able, on the basis of their own reason and experience, to maintain social order. Although Rousseau was enough of an individualist to accede to the first of these propositions, his view of human nature was too pessimistic to allow him to accept the second. His attitude here is closely parallel, indeed, to that of orthodox Calvinism. For the Calvinist, unredeemed human nature is hopelessly corrupt and sinful. The maintenance of a decent human society depends, therefore, on the intervention of divine grace, as embodied in the rule of the saints. While Rousseau rejected the idea of original sin, and believed in the natural goodness of man, his view of the social capacities of ordinary men was equally despairing. In his theory natural circumstances and social traditions took the place of sin as the source of an almost universal corruption against which the unaided reason of the unenlightened could never hope to prevail. No amount of effort or good will could enable men living in an unfavourable geographical environment, or under unsatisfactory economic and social conditions, to create a good political system. Even under the most favourable circumstances, moreover, simple people could not by themselves hope to discover workable institutions. Only a man of outstanding moral and intellectual attainments would be capable of such an achievement. Rousseau rather fancied himself in this role, and the major part of his political writing is actually devoted to an investigation of the geographic, social, economic and other conditions necessary for the establishment of a successful political order. In this aspect of his work he clearly belongs in the tradition of those who, like Plato, Machiavelli and Marx, have looked to social science for the liberation and instruction of mankind. Just as the Calvinists felt that sinful men were helpless without the intervention of the elect, Rousseau believed that ignorant men were helpless without the aid of a scientifically competent élite. The totalitarian aspect of his thought is derived from this conviction.

The resulting mixture of liberal and authoritarian principles is curiously exemplified in Rousseau's theory of the legislator. The idea itself is derived in part from Plato's theory of the philosopher-king, and in part from the experience of such historical or semi-historical figures as Moses, Numa, Lycurgus and Calvin. Like his prototypes, Rousseau's legislator was a person of outstanding moral and intellectual genius. His function was to perceive the optimum conditions of sociability as they existed at a given time and place, and to devise institutions which would enable men to live accordingly. He was unlike the philosopher-king or a modern dictator, however, in that he was supposed to refrain entirely from the use of coercive power. For all his pessimism as to the political creativeness of ordinary men, Rousseau was too firmly wedded to the principle of individual responsibility to admit the legitimacy of pure coercion under any circumstances whatsoever. He therefore insisted that the legislator, though justified in using lies and other forms of deception for the attainment of his purposes, would have to persuade rather than force ordinary people to accept his proposals. Enlightened leadership rather than enlightened despotism was Rousseau's solution to the problem of transcending the moral and intellectual limitations of ordinary men.

The institutions to be accepted on this basis were, however, strictly totalitarian in character. This fact is made sufficiently clear in the *Social Contract*, and is strongly underlined in the essays on Poland and Corsica. As a political scientist, though not as a political philosopher, Rousseau's principal claim to fame rests, indeed, on his skill in discovering most of the basic principles and practices of what later came to be known as integral nationalism. Since ordinary men by their own efforts were incapable of appreciating the rational needs of society, the task of Rousseau's all-wise legislator was to remove every conceivable temptation to antisocial action. This called for the minimisation of private interests and activities, and for the complete absorption of the individual in the collective life of the state. All forms of private association were to be discouraged as inimical to the general will. Private property likewise was a danger, and ought in principle to be abolished; since that seemed impracticable, the duty of the legislator was to regulate it in such a way that economic rivalries would never emerge to distract men from their common allegiance. Private religion, though grudgingly admitted as one of the unfortunate consequences of Christianity, was to be kept rigidly subordinate to a civil profession of faith. Rousseau even believed that private amusements were destructive of social unity, and should therefore be replaced by an endless series of public games and ceremonies. Although he recognised that no single pattern of life would be appropriate to all times and places, and that the legislator would have to modify his proposals in the light of particular circumstances and prejudices, the over-all purpose is clear. It is to create a citizen body so firmly habituated to the requirements of collective action that the natural impulse to individual selfishness will be minimised. Such is the essentially totalitarian outcome of Rousseau's distrust of ordinary human nature.

For Rousseau, as for all proponents of integral nationalism, the ultimate effect of this pessimism was to destroy all hope of achieving any comprehensive form of human sociability. This stands in marked contrast to the liberal position. If human beings are capable, through their own experience, of discovering rational grounds for co-operation, there is no reason why the area of voluntary social action should not be indefinitely extended. Thus a liberal faith in the inherent rationality of men encourages the hope of attaining ever wider forms of social collaboration. Kant's vision of eternal peace through world federation is the classic statement of this particular aspect of the liberal ideal. That Rousseau himself, in his more liberal moments, was somewhat attracted by this line of thought is shown by his friendly though critical discussion of the Abbé de Saint-Pierre's proposal for the federation of Europe, and by the federal elements he incorporated in his own plans for the governments of Poland and Corsica. He tells us that the *Social Contract* was originally intended to include an extensive discussion of the problem of federalism, and there is some evidence that a part of this work, now lost, was actually completed. It is easy to see, however, why he never succeeded in getting it ready for publication, for the fact is that the totalitarian aspects of his thought were logically incompatible with the very idea of federalism. Federalism involves the supposition that men are capable of owing loyalty simultaneously to two or more units of political action. This was one of the things that the totalitarian Rousseau could never admit. If men's irrational selfishness was such that they could not be trusted to form private associations within a single state, how could they possibly be expected to form member states within a wider confederation? As a proper totalitarian, Rousseau believed that man's anti-social tendencies could be overcome only by inspiring him with an irrational and all-absorptive devotion to the institutions of a particular state. Complete uniformity is most readily obtained in a small society completely cut off from contact with the outside world. Rousseau was therefore an outspoken enemy of all cosmopolitan tendencies, and emphasised the importance of giving a people manners and customs so completely distinctive that it would be impossible for them to communicate with outsiders. Economic autarky and cultural isolation were as dear to him as to any modern dictator. But if the formation of an operative general will depends on total dedication to the interests of a particular state, it is hard to see how there could be any bonds, other than those of conquest and coercion, to unite the members of several such states in a larger political whole. Since Rousseau, unlike modern dictators, rejected coercion as a basis of legitimate authority, he was left with no effective means of achieving anything beyond the narrowest forms of political co-operation.

In terms of its own objectives, Rousseau's political thought was a failure. This was inevitable in view of the conflicting liberal and totalitarian assumptions on which it was based. As a liberal, Rousseau was unwilling to admit any element of coercion that would in the slightest degree detract from the moral responsibility of the individual. This made it impossible for him to accept any practicable form of élitist authoritarianism. As a totalitarian pessimist, on the other hand, he was unable to believe in the creative potentialities of ordinary individuals. The result was to leave him with little more to offer than a political ideal which,

xl

as he himself was the first to see, was virtually un-realisable. At a time when city states like Geneva were already a hopeless anachronism, and the whole trend of politics lay in the direction of larger political units, he believed that the possibilities of legitimate government were inversely proportional to the size of states. Living in the early stages of an industrial and commercial revolution that was already beginning to transform Europe from a rural to an urban economy, he felt that political virtue was incompatible with any but the simplest agrarian societies. Discouragement under these circumstances was unavoidable, and the final outcome of Rousseau's investigations was to leave him with a profound conviction that mankind was doomed to a future of progressive corruption and decay. It is true that there were certain regions on the periphery of Europe where conditions were not yet entirely hope-less. In Poland and, above all, in Corsica, he thought that there were people who still retained enough of the primitive virtues to offer a promising field of action for a properly qualified legislator. In one brief and isolated passage of the *Social Contract* he also held forth the dim and tenuous hope that other peoples might, in some future revolutionary crisis, be sufficiently shaken from their evil ways to accept true principles of legislation. He constantly emphasised, however, that the appearance of a genuine legislator is an event so rare as to be truly miraculous. Since the moments when men are willing to listen to a legislator are equally rare, his hopes of reformation depended on the occurrence of a double miracle. And even if, in defiance of the laws of prob-ability, a legislator did in fact succeed in establishing a legitimate political system, the inevitable processes of time and decay would ultimately undo his work. Con-servative pessimism was the end result, therefore, of

Rousseau's political writing. Old-established institutions, for all their imperfections, are the product of a past which was simpler and less corrupt than the present. To abolish such institutions in the hope of finding anything better is to take an irresponsible risk. Except in the rarest cases, therefore, Rousseau's advice was that peoples should cleave to their existing traditions. In its final outcome his theory is rather more conservative, and far less hopeful, than the traditionalism of Edmund Burke.

Rousseau's failure to solve the problem of political legitimacy should not be allowed to blind us, however, to the peculiar merits of his approach to the problems of politics. It is all too easy to achieve logical consistency at the expense of experience. Most of the fallacies of contemporary political controversy are due to this very fact. Starting from the proposition that man is a rational animal, and following it to its extreme conclusions, liberals are apt, as in many of the current plans for world federalism, to underestimate the difficulties of voluntary co-operation. By leading men to expect unrealisable prodigies of non-coercive action, such theories can only lead to disillusionment and to an unnecessary denigration of the actual achievements of constitutional government. An equally logical system, based on the assumption that man is essentially irrational, leads to totalitarian coercion and to the needless destruction of liberal values. The highest type of political theorist is one who is able to appreciate human nature in its manifold aspects, and to create a system without doing violence to any phase of human experience. Although Rousseau had few gifts as a systematic thinker, he had an extraordinary range of political insight, and an even more extraordinary courage in refusing to sacrifice any part of that insight in the interest of superficial consistency.

That is why, after some two hundred years, he still retains an honourable place as one of the most stimulating figures in the history of political thought.

Editorial Note

The most important document for the study of Rousseau's political theory is the *Social Contract*, first published in 1762. Because of its largely theoretical and abstract character, however, it gives a rather one-sided impression of the nature and scope of the author's interests in this field. This difficulty can best be remedied by considering it in conjunction with two other works, the *Considerations on the Government of Poland* and the *Constitutional Project for Corsica*. Neither of these writings was published during the author's lifetime, and the second is no more than a fragmentary and unfinished sketch. But in spite of their manifest inferiority to the *Social Contract*, they are important for the light they throw on the more famous work. Both are attempts by the author himself to apply his abstract theoretical principles to the solution of concrete political problems. This forced him to deal, far more fully than in the *Social Contract* itself, with the practical implications of his political theory. The result is to clarify the theory itself in many important particulars.

The more rewarding of these secondary works is the *Considerations on the Government of Poland*. Completed in 1772, it is one of the last of Rousseau's productions, and may be taken as representing his final position in the field of politics. The circumstances which led to its composition were peculiarly challenging. The Republic of Poland was on the eve of the first of the three partitions which led, in the period between 1772 and 1795, to the disappearance of that country from the map of

Europe. This tragic phase in the life of a once powerful people had begun in 1764 with the election, under Russian pressure, of Stanislas Poniatowski, a former lover of Catherine the Great, to the recently vacated throne of Poland. For a time it seemed that Poland was about to be absorbed, without effective protest, by the expanding Russian Empire. Russia became involved, however, in a war with Turkey. This gave the Poles a final opportunity for resistance. Anticipating the event, the landowners of Podolia, following the old Polish custom of direct political action, banded together in 1768 to form the Confederation of Bar, an *ad hoc* organisation dedicated to the reassertion of Polish independence. In spite of Russia's military intervention on behalf of its puppet government, the influence of the Confederation increased, and in 1769 it was able to convene an assembly with representatives from every section of the Republic. Recognising that extensive reforms would be needed if Poland was to survive as a modern state, this assembly included among its acts a resolution that foreign political theorists be asked to lend their advice. Count Wielhorski, one of the members, was commissioned to approach Rousseau on the matter. Although Rousseau had always been sceptical as to the possibility of reforming a corrupt society, he could not resist the appeal of a people engaged in a life and death struggle against despotism. On the basis of information on Polish conditions supplied to him by Count Wielhorski, he accordingly undertook to suggest means whereby the healthier elements of the Polish national tradition might be strengthened and a truly viable republic established. The *Considerations on the Government of Poland*, a manuscript intended not for publication but for private circulation among leaders of the reformist party, was the outcome of this undertaking. It is interesting as a serious and sustained attempt to apply the principles of the *Social Contract* under conditions which Rousseau himself, though he tried to put up a brave front, was bound to regard as relatively unpromising.

The *Constitutional Project for Corsica* was the outcome of a similar appeal for practical assistance in an even more desperate struggle against despotism. In 1735 the people of Corsica, long a cruelly exploited colonial dependency of the Republic of Genoa, had rebelled against their masters, and driven them from most of the island. Although Genoese rule was restored in 1748 by foreign intervention, the rebellion was resumed in 1752, and soon found an uncommonly gifted leader in the person of Pasquale Paoli. The successful resistance of this spirited and primitive people aroused the admiration of Rousseau. In 1762 he had, in the *Social Contract*, expressed the opinion that Corsica, alone among the lands of Europe, was ripe for the services of a true legislator. Two years later a distinguished Corsican soldier in the French service, Buttafuoco, acting perhaps as agent for Paoli, requested that Rousseau himself should undertake the work of drafting a constitution for the new republic. On the condition that he be supplied with the fullest possible information on the local situation of Corsica, Rousseau accepted the proposal. Unfortunately this was the precise moment when the popular and official persecution of Rousseau, occasioned by the public furore surrounding the publication of the *Social Contract* and other works, was reaching its climax. Although he found time in 1765, in one of his places of all-too-temporary exile, to make a substantial beginning, he never had the leisure to complete the undertaking. After 1768, when France bought the island from Genoa and suppressed the rebellion, there was no further ground to hope for the establishment of a Corsican republic, and the work was abandoned as an unfinished fragment among the author's unpublished papers. Unsatisfactory as its present state may be, however, the *Constitutional Project for Corsica* is significant as Rousseau's only attempt to apply the principles of the *Social Contract* in a social and political context which he himself regarded as being virtually ideal. As far as it goes, it provides the clearest possible demonstration of the practical implications of his political thought.

The purpose of the present edition is to make these works available, in English translation, in a form convenient for the use of students. The *Social Contract* and the *Considerations on the Government of Poland* are presented in their entirety. Of the *Constitutional Project for Corsica*, Part I, which forms a fairly continuous whole, is given complete; Part II, which consists only of scattered fragments, has been omitted. In preparing the translations the editor has relied on the French text as established in C. E. Vaughan, *The Political Writings of Jean Jacques Rousseau* (Cambridge, 1915, 2 vols.). All footnotes, unless expressly attributed to the editor, are by Rousseau.

The editor wishes to acknowledge a profound debt of gratitude to his colleague, Miss Norah M. Lenoir of McGill University, who generously undertook the task of comparing the translation with the original texts, and eliminated many of the inaccuracies of the original manuscript. Since her advice was not always followed, the editor himself must assume responsibility for whatever flaws remain in the final version.

F.W.

McGill University,
Montreal, *1951*.

CHRONOLOGICAL TABLE OF ROUSSEAU'S LIFE AND WRITINGS

1712, 28 June.   Born in Geneva.

1728–41   Wanderings and casual employment in Italy, France and Switzerland.

1741–62   Chiefly in Paris and its environs.
1742, *Dissertation sur la musique moderne.* 1743–4, in Venice as secretary to the French Embassy. 1745, *Les Muses galantes.* 1749, articles on music in the *Encyclopédie. Essai sur l'origine des langues.* 1751, *Discours sur les sciences et les arts.* 1752, *Narcisse. Le Devin du village.* 1753, *Lettre sur la musique française.* 1754, visit to Geneva. 1755, *Discours sur l'inégalité.* Article on " Economie politique ", *Encyclopédie.* 1758. *Lettre à M. d'Alembert.* 1761. *La nouvelle Héloïse. La paix perpétuelle. Polysynodie.* 1762, *Du contrat social. Emile.*

1762–67   In exile, chiefly in Switzerland and England.
1762–65, in Neuchâtel. 1762, *Lettre à M. de Beaumont.* 1764, *Lettres écrites de la montagne.* 1765, *Projet pour la Corse* (unpublished). 1766–67, in England. Quarrel with Hume.

1767–78   In France, chiefly in Paris.
1767, *Dictionnaire de la musique.* 1772, *Considérations sur le gouvernement de Pologne* (unpublished). 1778, *Rêveries du promeneur solitaire. Les confessions* (published 1781–90).

1778, 2 July.   Died in Ermenonville.

BIBLIOGRAPHICAL NOTE

THE literature on Rousseau in general, and on his political thought in particular, is so voluminous that it would be neither possible nor desirable, within the framework of the present volume, to attempt anything in the way of a comprehensive bibliography. The following suggestions are intended merely as an aid to those students who may wish some preliminary guidance in the field.

The best critical text of the political writings of Rousseau is to be found in the Vaughan edition, to which reference has already been made. In addition to its exhaustive discussion of the early editions and manuscripts, this valuable work also contains a useful commentary on Rousseau's political thought.

The political aspects of Rousseau cannot be fully understood without some knowledge of his general background and influence. Though in some respects outmoded by subsequent scholarship, John Morley, *Rousseau* (2nd ed. London, 1883, 2 vols.) still retains its place as the best biography available in English. A particularly useful discussion of Rousseau's intellectual background is to be found in C. W. Hendel, *Jean-Jacques Rousseau, Moralist* (London and N.Y., 1934). To this should be added two important works recently published by Robert Derathé, *Le Rationalisme de J.-J. Rousseau* (Paris, 1948) and *Jean-Jacques Rousseau et la science politique de son temps* (Paris, 1950). Both Hendel and Derathé lay considerable emphasis, as does the present editor, on the close relationship between Rousseau's thought and the rationalistic traditions of

Western ethical and political thought. For a contrary view see Irving Babbitt, *Rousseau and Romanticism* (Boston, 1919).

A brief but penetrating study of the main currents of eighteenth-century thought, with some consideration of Rousseau's anomalous position among his contemporaries, is to be found in Carl Becker, *The Heavenly City of the Eighteenth-century Philosophers* (New Haven, 1932). Ernst Cassirer, *Rousseau, Kant, Goethe* (Princeton, 1945), throws interesting light on the relationship between Rousseau and Kant.

Some discussion of Rousseau's political ideas, and of their place in the main currents of Western theory, is to be found in all the general histories of political thought. For this kind of treatment see G. H. Sabine, *A History of Political Theory* (2nd. ed. New York, 1950) and F. M. Watkins, *The Political Tradition of the West: A Study in the Development of Modern Liberalism* (Cambridge, Mass., 1948).

There are also a number of books on special topics which devote a substantial amount of attention to Rousseau. Among the more notable are Otto Gierke, *Natural Law and the Theory of Society: 1500 to 1800* (Cambridge, 1934, 2 vols.) and J. W. Gough, *The Social Contract: A Critical Study of its Development* (Oxford, 1936). The subject of Rousseau's contribution to modern nationalism is discussed in Hans Kohn, *The Idea of Nationalism: A Study in its Origins and Background* (New York, 1944). For his ideas on international organisation, see C. J. Friedrich, *Inevitable Peace* (Cambridge, Mass., 1948). On the difficult question of interpreting Rousseau's concept of the general will, the editor still knows of no work that is more helpful than T. H. Green, *Lectures on the Principles of Political Obligation* (London and New York, 1895).

Of the studies more strictly limited to the analysis of Rousseau's political thought, particularly worthy of mention are Alfred Cobban, *Rousseau and the Modern State* (London, 1934), A. M. Osborn, *Rousseau and Burke: A Study of the Idea of Liberty in Eighteenth-century Political Thought* (New York, 1940), and E. H. Wright, *The Meaning of Rousseau* (London, 1929).

THE
SOCIAL CONTRACT

OR

PRINCIPLES OF POLITICAL RIGHT

—Foederis æquas
dicamus leges.
Virgil, *Aen.*, XI.321

First published
1762

FOREWORD

This little treatise is an extract from a more extensive work which I began some time ago without considering my abilities, and have long since abandoned. Of the various fragments which might have been taken from the part already written, this is the most considerable, and strikes me as being the least unworthy of being offered to the public. The rest has been destroyed.

BOOK I

IT is my purpose to inquire whether it is possible for
there to be any legitimate and certain rule of administration in civil society, taking men as they are and laws
as they may be. In this inquiry I shall endeavour at
all times to ally the obligations of law and right with
the requirements of interest, in order that justice and
utility may never be disjoined.

I shall enter upon my subject without demonstrating
its importance. It may be asked whether I am a prince
or legislator to be writing on politics. I answer that I
am not, and that that is the very reason why I am
writing on them. If I were a prince or legislator, I
should not waste my time saying what ought to be
done; I should do it, or be silent.

Since I am by birth the citizen of a free state, and a
member of the sovereign, my right to vote in that state,
no matter how little influence my voice may have in
public affairs, is enough to make it my duty to study
them. And whenever I reflect on governments, how
happy I am to find that my investigations always give
me new reasons for loving that of my own country!

CHAPTER I

THE SUBJECT OF THE FIRST BOOK

MAN is born free, and everywhere he is in chains.
One thinks himself master of others, but is himself
the greater slave. How did this change take place?

I do not know. What can render it legitimate? I believe I can answer this question.

If I were to consider nothing but force and its effects, I should say: ' As long as a people is compelled to obey, and does so, it does well; as soon as it can shake off the yoke, and does so, it does even better; for in recovering its liberty on the same grounds on which it was stolen away, it either is right in resuming it, or was wrongly deprived in the first place.' But the social order is a sacred right which serves as the basis for all others. And yet this right does not come from nature; thus it is founded on conventions. The problem is to know what these conventions are. Before considering this question, I must prove the points I have just been making.

Chapter II

THE FIRST SOCIETIES

THE most ancient of all societies, and the only natural one, is that of the family. But children remain bound to their father only so long as they need him for their own self-preservation. The moment this need ceases, the natural bond is dissolved. The children are exempted from the obedience they owed their father, the father from the cares he owed his children, and all alike return to a state of independence. If they continue together, their connexion is no longer natural, but voluntary; and the family itself is maintained by convention only.

This common liberty is a consequence of the nature of man. Self-preservation is the first law of human nature, our first cares are those we owe ourselves; and as soon as a man has reached the age of reason, he

4

becomes the sole judge of the means appropriate to his own self-preservation, and thus his own master.

The family may be taken, therefore, as the prototype of political societies; the ruler represents the father, the people the children; and since all are free and equal by birth, they will not alienate their liberty except in their own interest. The only difference is that, in the family, the love the father bears his children repays him for the care he gives them; while, in the state, the pleasure of ruling takes the place of the love that the ruler does not have for his peoples.

Grotius denies that all human power is established for the benefit of the governed, and cites slavery as an example. His regular method of reasoning is to keep arguing from fact to right.[1] A more logical method might be used, but none more favourable to tyrants.

According to Grotius, therefore, it is doubtful whether the human race belongs to a hundred-odd men, or those men to the human race; all through his book he seems to incline to the former opinion. This is also the sentiment of Hobbes. And so we see the human species divided into herds of cattle, each with its own ruler, who watches over it in order to devour it.

As the nature of the shepherd is superior to that of his flock, so also is the nature of the rulers or shepherds of men superior to that of their peoples. Such was the reasoning, according to Philo, of the Emperor Caligula, who from this analogy concluded, logically enough, that kings were gods, or else that their peoples were beasts.

Caligula's reasoning comes to the same thing as that of Hobbes and Grotius. Aristotle, before them all, had

[1] ' Learned studies of public law are often nothing more than the history of ancient abuses; and it is a useless infatuation to spend too much time and effort studying them ' (*Treatise on the Interests of France in Relation to her Neighbours*, by the Marquis d'Argenson).

also said that men are not naturally equal, but that some are born for slavery, and others for dominion.

Aristotle was right, but he mistook the effect for the cause. Nothing is more certain than that every man born in slavery is born for slavery. Slaves in their chains lose everything, even the desire to leave them; they love their servitude as the companions of Ulysses loved their brutishness.[1] If there are slaves by nature, therefore, it is because there have been slaves against nature. Force made the first slaves, and their cowardice has perpetuated them.

I have said nothing of King Adam or of the Emperor Noah, father of three great monarchs, who, like the children of Saturn, with whom some have tried to identify them, divided the universe between them. I hope that my moderation will be properly appreciated; for as the direct descendant of one of these princes, and perhaps in the senior line, how do I know that, if titles were verified, I would not find myself the legitimate king of the human race? Be that as it may, there can be no doubt that Adam was sovereign of the world, just as Robinson Crusoe was sovereign of his island, so long as he was its sole inhabitant; and the great advantage of this empire was that the monarch, secure on his throne, had neither rebellions, nor wars, nor conspirators to fear.

CHAPTER III

THE RIGHT OF THE STRONGEST

THE strongest is never strong enough to be always the master, unless he transforms his might into right, and

[1] See a short treatise by Plutarch, entitled *That Animals reason.*

obedience into duty. Hence the right of the strongest, a 'right' which looks like an ironical pleasantry, but in fact is a well-established principle. But will no one ever tell us what this word means? Force is a form of physical power; I am at a loss to see how it can produce any moral consequences. To yield to force is an act of necessity, not of will; at the very most it is an act of prudence. In what sense can it be a duty?

Let us for a moment take this alleged right for granted. I say that it leads to nothing but a meaningless farrago of nonsense. For if it is might that makes right, the effect changes with the cause and any might which exceeds the first inherits its right. As soon as you are able to disobey with impunity, you can do so legitimately; and since the strongest is always right, to become the strongest is all that matters. But what kind of a right is it that expires when might ceases? If we must obey by force, we have no need to obey by duty; and if we are no longer forced to obey, we are no longer obliged to do so. Thus we see that the word *right* adds nothing to might; in this context it is absolutely meaningless.

'Obey the powers that be.' If this means 'Yield to force,' the precept is good but superfluous; I warrant that it will never be violated. All power comes from God, I admit, but so does all illness; does that mean we are forbidden to call a doctor? If a brigand surprises me in a dark forest, am I not only forced to give my purse, but also obliged in conscience to let him have it, though able to withhold it? For the pistol in his hand is, after all, a form of power.

Let us agree, then, that might does not make right, and that we are obliged to obey none but legitimate powers. Thus we keep coming back to my original question.

7

Chapter IV

SLAVERY

Since no man has natural authority over his fellow men, and since might in no sense makes right, conventions remain as the basis of all legitimate authority among men.

If an individual, says Grotius, can alienate his liberty and enslave himself to a master, why should not a whole people be able to alienate its liberty and subject itself to a king? There are many ambiguous words here that call for explanation; but let us confine our attention to the word *alienate*. To alienate is to give or sell. Now a man who enslaves himself to another does not give himself away; he sells himself, at the very least, for his subsistence. But why does a people sell itself? Far from providing his subjects with their subsistence, a king derives his own wholly from them; and as Rabelais says, a king does not live on a pittance. Do the subjects, then, give their persons on condition that their goods be taken too? I cannot see what they have left to preserve.

You will say that the despot guarantees civil tranquillity to his subjects. So be it; but what does it profit them if the wars his ambition brings upon them, if his insatiable greed, if the oppressions of his ministers, make them more desolate than their own dissensions would have done? What does it profit them, if this very tranquillity is one of their misfortunes? Men also live tranquilly in dungeons; is that enough to make prisoners content? The Greeks pent up in the cave of the Cyclops lived tranquilly, while awaiting their turn to be devoured.

8

To say that a man gives himself gratuitously is to say something absurd and inconceivable; an act of this sort is illegal and void, for the simple reason that the man who performs it is not in his right mind. To say the same thing of a whole people is to postulate a people of madmen, and madness does not make right.

Even if it were possible for each man to alienate himself, he would not be able to alienate his children; by birth they are men, and free; their liberty belongs to them, and they alone have the right to dispose of it. Before they have reached the age of reason, their father may, in their name, lay down conditions for their preservation and well-being, but he cannot give them irrevocably and unconditionally; for such a gift is contrary to the purposes of nature, and exceeds the rights of paternity. For an arbitrary government to be legitimate, therefore, it would be necessary for the people of each generation to be able to accept or reject it; but then the government would no longer be arbitrary.

To renounce your liberty is to renounce your very quality of manhood; it is to renounce not only the rights, but even the duties of humanity. There can be no possible compensation for anyone who renounces everything. Such a renunciation is incompatible with the nature of man; and to deprive your will of all freedom is to deprive your actions of all morality. Finally, a convention which stipulates absolute authority on the one hand, and unlimited obedience on the other, is vain and contradictory. Is it not clear that you are under no obligation whatsoever to a person of whom you have the right to demand everything? And does not this unilateral and unequal stipulation in itself render the act null and void? For what claim could my slave have against me, when he himself, and all

9

that belongs to him, is mine? His rights belong to me, and to say that they can be asserted against me is nonsense.

Grotius and the rest use war as yet another basis for the alleged right of slavery. Since the conqueror, according to them, has the right to kill the vanquished, the latter may buy back his life at the cost of his liberty; and this convention is all the more legitimate in that it is advantageous to both parties.

But it is clear that this alleged right to kill the vanquished is in no sense a result of the state of war. Men are not natural enemies, for the simple reason that, while living in their original independence, they have no mutual relations sufficiently stable to constitute either a state of peace or a state of war. It is the relationship between things, not men, that constitutes war; and since the state of war cannot arise from relations purely between persons, but only from relations involving things, private warfare, or the war of man against man, can exist neither in the state of nature, where there is no settled property, nor in the social state, where everything is subject to law.

Individual combats, duels and encounters are insufficient to constitute a state of any kind; and as for the private wars authorised by the Establishments of King Louis IX of France, and suspended by the Peace of God, they were abuses of feudalism, an absurd system if ever there was one, contrary to the principles of natural law and to all good polity.

Thus war is a relationship not between man and man but between state and state, a relationship in which individuals are enemies only incidentally, not as men, or even as citizens,[1] but as soldiers; not as members of

[1] The Romans, who understood and respected the laws of war better than any nation on earth, carried their scruples in this

their native country, but as its defenders. Finally, the only enemies a state can have are other states, not men; for as between things of diverse nature, no true relationship can be established.

This principle is also in conformity with the established precepts of all ages, and with the constant practice of all civilised peoples. Declarations of war are a notification not so much to the powers as to their subjects. The foreigner, whether he be a king, a private individual, or a people, who plunders, kills or detains subjects without declaring war on their prince, is not an enemy but a brigand. Even in time of war, though a just prince in enemy territory may well seize all public property, he respects the persons and goods of private individuals; he respects the rights on which his own are founded. Since the purpose of war is to destroy the enemy state, you have a right to kill its defenders as long as they are bearing arms; but as soon as they lay down their arms and surrender, they cease to be enemies, or instruments of the enemy, and once again become mere men, whom we no longer have a right to kill. Sometimes it is possible to kill a state without killing a single one of its members; but war

---

matter to such a point that no citizen was allowed to serve as a volunteer without being expressly engaged against the enemy, a particular enemy designated by name. When a legion in which Cato the Younger was receiving his first military experience under Popilius was re-formed, Cato the Elder wrote to Popilius that if he wanted his son to continue serving under him, he would have to have him take a new military oath because, the first having been annulled, he was no longer able to bear arms against the enemy. And the same Cato wrote his son to be very careful not to appear in battle until he had taken this new oath. I know that the siege of Clusium and other particular instances could be cited against me; but what I am citing is law and custom. The Romans were the people who least often transgressed their laws; and their laws were better than those of any other people.

confers no right that is not necessary to its purpose. These principles are not those of Grotius; they are not founded on the authority of poets; but they are derived from the nature of things, and founded on reason.

As to the right of conquest, it has no other foundation than the law of the strongest. If war does not give the victor the right to massacre conquered peoples, this non-existent right cannot be the basis of a right to enslave them. It is only when we cannot enslave an enemy that we have the right to kill him; thus the right to enslave him does not arise from that right, and it is an iniquitous bargain to make him buy his life, to which we have no right, at the price of his liberty. In basing the right of life and death on the right of slavery, and the right of slavery on the right of life and death, is it not clear that we are falling into a vicious circle?

And even if this horrible right of universal massacre be granted, I say that a slave taken in war (or a conquered people) is under no obligation whatsoever to his master except to obey him as long as he is forced to do so. In taking an equivalent for his life, the victor has done him no favour; instead of killing him to no purpose, he has killed him usefully. Far, then, from having acquired any authority over him in addition to force, the master still remains in a state of war with the slave; their relationship itself is a result of that state; and the exercise of the right of war presupposes that there has been no treaty of peace. They have made a convention, to be sure; but this convention, far from ending the state of war, presupposes its continuation.

Thus, in whatever light we may consider the matter, the right of slavery is null, not only because it is illegitimate, but also because it is absurd and meaningless. The words *slavery* and *right* are contradictory; the one excludes the other. The following speech, whether made by one individual to another, or by an individual to a people, would in either case be equally ridiculous: ' I enter into an agreement with you, wholly at your expense and to my profit, which I shall honour as long as it pleases me, and which you will honour as long as I think proper.'

Chapter V

THAT WE MUST ALWAYS GO BACK TO A FIRST CONVENTION

If I were to grant everything I have thus far refuted, the abettors of despotism would be no better off. There will always be a great difference between subjecting a multitude and ruling a society. If scattered individuals, in however great numbers, are successively enslaved to a single man, I see in them nothing more than a master and his slaves, I do not see a people and its ruler. It may be an aggregation, but not an association; there is no commonwealth, no body politic there. The master, even though he may have enslaved half the world, remains a mere individual; his interest, distinct from that of the rest, remains but a private interest. As soon as he dies, his empire is left scattered and disconnected, just as an oak-tree crumbles and falls into a heap of ashes after it has been consumed by fire.

A people, says Grotius, can give itself to a king. According to Grotius, therefore, a people is already a people before it thus gives itself. The very gift is a civil act; it presupposes a public deliberation. So before we examine the act whereby a people elects a king, it would be well to examine the one whereby a people becomes a people; for this act, being necessarily prior to the other, is the true foundation of society.

If there were no prior convention, indeed, and unless the election were unanimous, what would be the obligation of the minority to submit to the will of the majority? And what gives a hundred who want a master the right to speak for ten who do not? The law of majority rule itself is a conventional institution, and presupposes unanimity on one occasion at least.

Chapter VI

THE SOCIAL COMPACT

LET us assume that men have reached the point where the obstacles to their self-preservation in the state of nature are too great to be overcome by the forces each individual is capable of exerting to maintain himself in that state. This original state can then no longer continue; and the human race would perish if it did not change its mode of existence.

Now, since men cannot engender new forces, but can only combine and direct those already in existence, their only means of self-preservation is to form by aggregation a sum of forces capable of overcoming all obstacles, to place these forces under common direction, and to make them act in concert.

This sum of forces can only arise from the concurrence of many; but the force and liberty of each man being the primary instruments of his own self-preservation, how can he pledge them without harming himself and neglecting the cares he owes his own person? This problem, in relation to my subject, may be expressed in the following terms: ' To find a form of association which defends and protects the person and property of each member with the whole force of the community, and where each, while joining with all the rest, still obeys no one but himself, and remains as free as before.' This is the fundamental problem to which the social contract provides the answer.

The clauses of this contract are so completely determined by the nature of the act that the slightest modification would render them null and void; so that, though they may never have been formally declared, they are everywhere the same, everywhere tacitly admitted and recognised, until the moment when the violation of the social compact causes each individual to recover his original rights, and to resume his natural liberty as he loses the conventional liberty for which he renounced it.

These clauses, rightly understood, can be reduced to the following only: the total alienation of each member, with all his rights, to the community as a whole. For, in the first place, since each gives himself entirely, the condition is equal for all; and since the condition is equal for all, it is in the interest of no one to make it burdensome to the rest.

Furthermore, since the alienation is made without reservations, the union is as perfect as possible, and no member has anything more to ask. For if the individuals retained certain rights, each, in the absence of any common superior capable of judging between him and the public, would be his own judge in certain matters, and would soon claim to be so in all; the state of nature would continue, and the association would necessarily become tyrannical or meaningless.

Finally, each individual, by giving himself to all, gives himself to no one; and since there is no member over whom you do not acquire the same rights that you give him over yourself, you gain the equivalent of all you lose, and greater force to preserve what you have.

If the social compact is stripped to its essentials, therefore, you will find that it can be reduced to the following terms: ' Each of us puts in common his person and all his powers under the supreme direction of the general will; and in our corporate capacity we receive each member as an indivisible part of the whole.'

In place of the private and particular person of each of the contracting parties, this act of association immediately produces an artificial and collective body, made up of as many members as there are voices in the assembly, and receiving from this same act its unity, its collective personality, its life and its will.   The public person thus formed by the union of all the rest was formerly known as a *city*,[1] and is now called a *republic* or *body politic*;   when passive it is known to its members as the *state*, when active as the *sovereign*, and as a *power* when it is being compared with its fellows. The members are known collectively as the *people* ;   and

[1] The true meaning of this word has been almost entirely lost in modern times;   most people mistake a town for a city, and a householder for a citizen.   They do not know that houses make a town, but citizens a city.   This same error once cost the Carthaginians dear.   I have never read that the title of *cives* was ever given to the subjects of any prince, not even to the ancient Macedonians nor, in our own day, to the English, although they are closer to liberty than all others.   Only the French assume the name of citizens casually, because they have no true idea of its meaning, as a glance at their dictionaries will show;   if it were not for this ignorance their usurpation of the title would convict them of lèse-majesté. To them this name expresses a quality, not a right.   When Bodin tried to speak of the citizens and burghers of Geneva, he made the gross blunder of mistaking the one for the other.   M. d'Alembert did not make the same mistake, and in his article on *Geneva* he has properly distinguished between the four classes of men (or five, if you count mere foreigners) who reside in our city, only two of which constitute the Republic.   No other French author, to my knowledge, has understood the meaning of the word *citizen.*

individually they are called, as participants in the sovereign authority, *citizens*, and, as men owing obedience to the laws of the state, *subjects*. But these terms are often confused and mistaken for one another; it is enough to be able to distinguish between them when they are used with absolute accuracy.

Chapter VII

THE SOVEREIGN

FROM the formula already given, it can be seen that the act of association involves a reciprocal engagement between the public and its individual members, and that each individual, by contracting, so to speak, with himself, finds himself under the following two-fold obligation: as a member of the sovereign to the individual members, and as a member of the state to the sovereign. But the principle of civil law which states that no one can make binding commitments to himself is not applicable in this case; for there is a great difference between assuming obligations towards yourself, and doing so toward a whole of which you are a part.

It is also to be observed that public deliberation which, because of the two-fold nature of their relationship, is able to obligate all subjects toward the sovereign, cannot, for the opposite reason, obligate the sovereign toward itself; and that in consequence it is contrary to the nature of the body politic for the sovereign to bind itself by a law it cannot break. Since its relationships can only be conceived under a single aspect, it remains in the position of an individual contracting with himself; from which it follows that there is not, and cannot be, any sort of fundamental law binding

17

on the body of the people, not even the social contract. This does not mean that this body cannot perfectly well assume obligations toward others in so far as they do not deviate from this contract; for in relation to foreigners, it becomes a simple entity, an individual.

But the body politic or sovereign, since it owes its being solely to the sanctity of the contract, can never bind itself, even to foreigners, to do anything derogatory to this original act, such as to alienate some part of itself or to subject itself to another sovereign. To violate the act by which it exists would be to destroy itself; and that which is nothing produces nothing.

From the moment when a multitude is thus united as a body, no one of its members can be offended without attacking the body itself; still less can the body be offended without affecting its members. Thus duty and interest alike oblige the two contracting parties to assist one another; and the same individuals should try to combine all the advantages which depend on both aspects of this twofold relationship.

Now the sovereign, being composed merely of the individuals who are its members, has and can have no interest contrary to theirs; consequently the sovereign power has no need to guarantee the rights of its subjects, since it is impossible for the body to want to harm all its members; and we shall see later that it cannot harm any particular individual. The sovereign, by the very fact that it exists, is always everything it ought to be.

The same is not true, however, of the relation of the subjects to the sovereign; in spite of their common interests, there would be no assurance that they would fulfil their obligations unless means were found to guarantee their fidelity.

Actually each individual may, as a man, have a private will contrary to, or divergent from, the general will he has as a citizen. His particular interest may speak to him quite differently from the common interest; his existence, being naturally absolute and independent, may make him envisage his debt to the common cause as a gratuitous contribution, the loss of which will be less harmful to others than the payment is burdensome to himself; and regarding the artificial person of the state as a fictitious being, because it is not a man, he would like to enjoy the rights of a citizen without fulfilling the duties of a subject, an injustice which, if it became progressive, would be the ruin of the body politic.

In order, therefore, that the social compact may not be a meaningless formality, it includes the tacit agreement, which alone can give force to the rest, that anyone who refuses to obey the general will shall be forced to do so by the whole body; which means nothing more or less than that he will be forced to be free. For this is the condition which, by giving each citizen to his country, guarantees him against any form of personal dependence; it is the secret and the driving force of the political mechanism; and it alone gives legitimacy to civil obligations, which otherwise would be absurd, tyrannical, and subject to the gravest abuses.

Chapter VIII

THE CIVIL STATE

This passage from the natural to the civil state produces a very remarkable change in man, substituting justice for instinct as the guide to his conduct, and giving his actions the morality they previously lacked. Then only is it that the voice of duty takes the place of physical impulse, and law the place of appetite; and that man, who until then has thought only of himself, finds himself compelled to act on other principles, and to consult his reason before listening to his inclinations. Although in this state he loses many of his natural advantages, he gains so many in return, his faculties are exercised and developed, his ideas are broadened, his sentiments ennobled and his whole soul elevated to such an extent that if the abuses of this new condition did not often degrade him beneath his former state, he ought unceasingly to bless the happy moment which wrested him forever from it, and turned him from a stupid and limited animal into an intelligent being and a man.

Let us draw up the balance sheet in terms readily capable of comparison. What man loses by the social contract is his natural liberty, and an unlimited right to everything he wants and is capable of getting; what he gains is civil liberty, and the ownership of all he possesses. In order to make no mistake as to the balance of profit and loss, we must clearly distinguish between natural liberty, which has no other limit than the might of the individual, and civil liberty, which is limited by the general will; and between possession, which results merely from force or from the right of the first occupier, and property, which can only be founded on a positive title.

To the foregoing we might add that, along with the civil state, man acquires moral liberty, which alone makes him truly master of himself; for the impulse of mere appetite is slavery, and obedience to self-imposed law is liberty. But I have already said more than enough under this head, and the philosophic meaning of the word *liberty* is not my present subject.

Chapter IX

REAL PROPERTY

EACH member of the community gives himself to it at the moment of its creation, giving himself as he then finds himself, together with all his powers, of which his possessions are a part. This does not mean that, by this act, possession changes its nature as it changes hands, and that it becomes property on being transferred to the sovereign. But just as the might of the city is incomparably greater than that of an individual, so also is public possession in fact stronger and more irrevocable than private possession, without being more legitimate, at least from the point of view of foreigners. For the state, in relation to its members, is the master of all their possessions under the social contract, which serves, within the state, as the basis of all rights; but in relation to other powers, it is master only by the right of the first occupier, a right which it derives from its members.

The right of the first occupier, though more real than that of the strongest, does not become a true right until after the establishment of the right of property. Every man has a natural right to everything he needs; but the positive act which makes him the owner of a particular piece of property excludes him from all the rest. His share having been allotted, he should restrict himself to it, and has no further right to the common store. That is why the right of the first occupier, so weak in the state of nature, is respected by all civilised men. In this you are respecting not so much the things that belong to others, as the things that do not belong to you.

Generally speaking, to justify the right of the first occupier to a given piece of land, the following conditions must be fulfilled: first, the land must not yet be occupied by anyone; second, no more should be occupied than is needed for subsistence; third, possession must be taken not by an empty ceremony, but by work and tillage, the only signs of property which, in the absence of juridical titles, ought to be respected by others.

In granting the right of the first occupier to the claims of need and labour, are we not actually extending it as far as it is capable of going? Can this right remain unlimited? Is it enough to set foot on common ground in order to claim forthwith to be its master? Is it enough to be able for a moment to exclude others by force, in order to deprive them forever of the right to return? How can a man or a people, without culpable usurpation, seize and deprive the whole human race of an immense territory, thus preventing other men from enjoying that residence and subsistence which nature gives to all in common? When Nuñez Balboa, standing on the seashore, took possession of the South Seas and all South America in the name of the crown of Castile, was this enough to dispossess all the inhabitants and to exclude all other princes? If so, such ceremonies were rather unnecessarily reduplicated; and the Catholic King, sitting in his own room, needed to do no more than take possession of the whole universe at a single stroke, subsequently excluding from his empire any regions already in the possession of other princes.

It is easy to see how the combined and contiguous lands of individuals become the public territory, and how the right of sovereignty, extending from the subjects to the lands they occupy, becomes at once real and personal; and this places the possessors in a state

22

of greater dependence than before, and makes their very resources the warrants of their fidelity, an advantage which does not seem to have been clearly sensed by the monarchs of antiquity, who, in calling themselves simply kings of the Persians, Scythians, or Macedonians, seemed to regard themselves as rulers of men rather than as masters of the country. Their modern counterparts more shrewdly call themselves kings of France, Spain, England, etc. By holding the territory thus, they are quite sure of holding its inhabitants.

The singular feature of this alienation is that the community, far from despoiling individuals of the possessions it accepts from them, does no more than confirm them in legitimate possession, changing usurpation into a genuine right, and use into property. Since the possessors are then considered as depositaries of the commonwealth, and since their rights are respected by all members of the state and maintained against foreigners with all its strength, it follows that, by a cession advantageous to the public and still more so to themselves, they may be said to have acquired all that they have given, a paradox easily explained by the distinction between the rights of proprietor and sovereign in the same property, as we shall see hereafter.

It may also happen that men begin to unite before they have any possessions, subsequently acquiring a territory sufficient for all, and either use it in common or else divide it between them, equally or in proportions fixed by the sovereign. No matter how this acquisition is made, the right of each individual over his own property is always subordinate to the right of the community over all; otherwise there would be no substance to the social bond, nor any real force in the exercise of sovereignty.

I shall conclude this chapter and book with the following remark, which should serve as the basis of the whole social system: instead of destroying natural equality, the fundamental compact, on the contrary, substitutes moral and legal equality for such physical inequalities as nature may have created among men; and different as they may be in physical or intellectual powers, they all become equal by convention and in the eyes of the law.[1]

[1] Under bad governments, this equality is merely apparent and illusory; it serves only to maintain the poor man in his poverty, and the rich man in his usurpation. As a matter of fact, laws are always useful to those who have property, and harmful to those who have nothing. It follows, therefore, that the social state is advantageous to men only in so far as they all have something, and no one has any more than he needs.

BOOK II

CHAPTER I

THAT SOVEREIGNTY IS INALIENABLE

THE first and most important consequence of the principles thus far established is that the general will alone can direct the forces of the state in accordance with the purpose for which it was created, namely, the common good. For if the opposition of private interests made the establishment of societies necessary, it is the agreement of those same interests that made it possible. It is what these several interests have in common that constitutes the social bond; and if there were no point on which all of them were in agreement, there could be no society. Now it is exclusively on the basis of this common interest that society must be governed.

I say, therefore, that since sovereignty is nothing but the exercise of the general will, it can never be alienated; and that the sovereign, which is only a collective being, can be represented by itself only. Power may well be transferred, but will cannot.

As a matter of fact, if it is not impossible for a particular will to agree with the general will on some specific point, at least it is impossible for that agreement to be constant and durable; for the particular will tends by its very nature to partiality, and the general will to equality. Even if this agreement did remain constant, it would be the result not of skill but of chance, and it would be even more impossible to guarantee that it would continue to do so. The sovereign may well say: ' At the present moment I want what that particular individual wants, or at least what he says he wants.' But it cannot say: ' What that individual wants tomorrow, I too shall want '; since it is absurd for the will to bind itself for the future, and impossible for any willing being to consent to anything contrary to its own welfare. If, therefore, the people promises simply to obey, it dissolves itself by that very act, and ceases to be a people. As soon as there is a master, there is no longer a sovereign; and from that moment the body politic is destroyed.

This does not mean that the commands of rulers may not be taken as expressions of the general will, as long as the sovereign is free to oppose them and fails to do so. In such a case the consent of the people is to be presumed from universal silence. This will be explained more fully hereafter.

Chapter II

THAT SOVEREIGNTY IS INDIVISIBLE

SOVEREIGNTY is indivisible for the same reason that it is inalienable. For the will either is or is not general; [1] it is the will either of the whole body of the people, or of a part only. In the first case, the declaration of that will is an act of sovereignty and constitutes law. In the second, it is only a particular will, or an act of magistracy; at most, it is no more than a decree.

But our political theorists, since they are unable to

[1] For a will to be general it is not always necessary that it should be unanimous; but it is necessary that all the voices should be counted, for any formal exclusion breaks the generality.

divide sovereignty in principle, divide it in its objects. They divide it into force and will, into legislative and executive powers, into rights of taxation, justice and war, into domestic and foreign affairs; sometimes they jumble all these parts together, and sometimes they separate them. They make of the sovereign a fantastic creature composed of bits and pieces; it is as if they were making a man out of several bodies, one made up entirely of eyes, another of arms, another of feet. It is said that Japanese conjurers cut a child to pieces before the eyes of the audience; then, throwing all the members one by one into the air, they cause the child to fall back again, alive and perfectly reassembled. The conjuring tricks of our political theorists are much the same; after having dismembered the social body with a dexterity worthy of professional mountebanks, they reassemble the pieces without our knowing how.

This error comes from having arrived at no clear conception of the nature of sovereign authority, and from having mistaken as parts of that authority mere emanations from it. Thus, for example, the acts of declaring war and making peace have been regarded as acts of sovereignty, which is not the case; for neither of these acts is a law, but only an application of law to a particular case, as we shall clearly see when the precise meaning of the word *law* is defined.

If we were to study the other divisions in the same way, we should find that whenever we think we see sovereignty divided, we are mistaken; that the rights which are taken for parts of sovereignty are all subordinate to it, and always presuppose the existence of a supreme will which these rights merely put into execution.

It would be hard to exaggerate the obscurity which this lack of precision has cast over the judgments of

writers on public law when they have tried, on the
basis of the principles thus established, to determine
the respective rights of kings and peoples. Anyone
can see how, in the third and fourth chapters of the
first book of Grotius, this learned man and his translator Barbeyrac were entangled and hampered by their
sophistries, fearful lest they might say too much or too
little in accordance with their principles, and shock the
interests they had to reconcile. Grotius, a refugee in
France, dissatisfied with his own country and trying to
pay court to Louis XIII, to whom his book is dedicated,
spares no effort to despoil peoples of all their rights and
to invest kings with them as skilfully as possible. This
would also have been quite to the taste of Barbeyrac,
who dedicated his translation to King George I of
England. But unfortunately the expulsion of James II,
which he calls abdication, forced him to make reservations, to quibble and to beat around the bush, in order
not to make a usurper out of William. If these two
authors had adopted correct principles, all these difficulties would have disappeared, and they would
always have been consistent; but, sad to say, they
would have spoken the truth, and paid court to the
people only. Now truth does not lead to fortune; and
the people bestows neither ambassadorships, professor-
ships nor pensions.

Chapter III

WHETHER THE GENERAL WILL IS SUBJECT TO ERROR

From the preceding it follows that the general will is
always right, and always tends to the public good; but

it does not follow that the deliberations of the people will always have the same rectitude. We always desire our own good, but we do not always recognise it. You cannot corrupt the people, but you can often deceive it; and it is then only that it seems to will something bad.

There is often a great difference between the will of all and the general will; the latter looks only to the common interest, while the former looks to private interest, and is simply a sum of particular wills. But if you cancel out from these same wills all the mutually destructive pluses and minuses,[1] the general will remains as the sum of the differences.

If the people were sufficiently well-informed, and if in their deliberations the citizens held no communication with one another, the general will would always result from the large number of small differences, and the deliberations would always be good. But when cliques and partial associations are formed at the expense of the whole, the will of each of these associations becomes general with reference to its members, and particular with reference to the state; then it can no longer be said that there are as many voters as there are individuals, but only as many as there are associations. The differences become less numerous, and give a less general result. Finally, when one of these associations becomes large enough to prevail over all the rest, the result is no longer a sum of small differences,

[1] ' Each interest,' says the Marquis d'Argenson, ' has different principles. The agreement of two particular interests is created by opposition to the interests of a third party.' He might have added that the agreement of all interests is created by opposition to the interest of each individual. If there were no distinct interests, the common interest would scarcely be felt, since it would never encounter obstacles; everything would go by itself, and politics would cease to be an art.

but one single difference. Then there is no longer a general will, and the opinion which prevails is only a private opinion.

If the general will is to be well expressed, therefore, it is important that there should be no partial society in the state, and that each citizen should have personal opinions only; [1] such was the unique and sublime system instituted by the great Lycurgus. And if there are partial societies, their number must be multiplied and provision made against their inequality, as by Solon, Numa and Servius. These precautions are the only effective means of ensuring that the general will always will be enlightened, and that the people will make no mistakes.

Chapter IV

THE LIMITS OF SOVEREIGN POWER

IF the state or city is merely an artificial person whose life consists in the union of its members, and if the most important of its cares is for its own self-preservation, it must have some universal and compelling force to move and dispose each part in the manner most appropriate to the whole. Just as nature gives each man absolute power over all his members, the social compact gives the body politic absolute power over all its own parts; and as I have said, it is this same power which, when

[1] ' It is a fact,' says Machiavelli, ' that some divisions are harmful and some beneficial to republics; the harmful ones are those which are accompanied by sects and partisanship, the beneficial those which are accompanied by neither. Since the founder of a republic cannot provide that there will be no enmities within it, he must therefore provide at least that there will be no sects.' *History of Florence*, BOOK VII.

directed by the general will, bears the name of sovereignty.

But in addition to the public person, we have also to consider the private persons who compose it, and whose life and liberty are naturally independent of it. The problem is, therefore, to distinguish clearly between the respective rights of the citizens and of the sovereign; [1] and between the duties the former must fulfil in their capacity as subjects, and the natural rights they must enjoy in their capacity as men.

It is agreed that, under the social compact, what each individual alienates is that part only of his power, goods and liberty which the community needs for its own use; but it must also be agreed that the sovereign alone is judge of that need.

All the services a citizen can render the state are owed to it as soon as the sovereign requests them; but the sovereign, for its part, cannot burden the subjects with any restraints which are useless to the community. It cannot even desire to do so; for under the law of reason, no less than under the law of nature, no effect is produced without a cause.

The engagements which bind us to the social body are obligatory only because they are mutual; and their nature is such that, in fulfilling them, we cannot work for others without also working for ourselves. Why is the general will always right, and why do all constantly will the happiness of each, unless it is because there is no one who fails to appropriate the word ' each ' to himself, and to think of himself when voting for all? Which proves that equality of right, and the idea of

[1] Attentive readers, please do not hasten to accuse me of inconsistency at this point. Because of the poverty of the language, I have not been able to avoid verbal contradiction; but wait and see.

justice to which it gives rise, is derived from the preference each man feels for himself, and thus from the nature of man; that the general will, to be truly such, must be general in its objects as well as in its essence; that it must proceed from all and be applicable to all; and that it loses its natural rectitude when directed toward any individual and determinate object, for in that case we are judging that which is foreign to us, and thus have no true principle of equity to guide us.

As soon, indeed, as it has to do with a fact, or with a particular point of right not covered by a general and prior convention, the affair becomes contentious; it is a lawsuit where the individuals concerned and the public are the contending parties, but where I cannot see that there is any law to be followed, nor any authoritative judge. Under these circumstances it would be ridiculous to rely on an express decision of the general will, for this can only be the conclusion of one of the parties to the controversy, and thus, from the standpoint of the other party, an alien and particular will, inclined on this occasion to injustice and subject to error. Just as a particular will, therefore, cannot represent the general will, the general will likewise changes its nature when directed toward a particular object, and cannot, without ceasing to be general, pronounce on any individual or fact. When the Athenian people, for example, appointed or cashiered its rulers, awarded honours to some and imposed penalties on others, and indiscriminately performed all the acts of government through multitudes of particular decrees, then the people no longer had, properly speaking, a general will; it was no longer acting as a sovereign, but as a magistrate. This will seem to be at variance with currently accepted views; but you must leave me time to expound my own.

From this we must conclude that what makes a will general is not so much the number of voices as the common interest that unites them. For under this system each individual necessarily submits himself to the conditions he imposes on others; and this admirable union of justice and interest gives to the common deliberations a character of equity which is seen to vanish in the discussion of any particular affair, for lack of any common interest to unite and identify the rulings of the judge with the views of the litigants.

From whatever direction we approach the principle, we always reach the same conclusion, namely that the social compact establishes such a degree of equality among the citizens that they all bind themselves under the same conditions, and must all enjoy the same rights. Thus, by the nature of the compact, every act of sovereignty, that is to say every authentic act of the general will, obliges or favours all the citizens equally; which means that the sovereign is aware only of the whole body of the nation, and recognises none of its individual members. Strictly speaking, then, what is an act of sovereignty? It is not a convention made between a superior and an inferior, but one made between the body as a whole and its several members; and this convention is legitimate because it is based on the social contract, equitable because it is common to all, useful because it can have no other object than the general welfare, and secure because it is guaranteed by public force and the supreme power. As long as the subjects are bound by such conventions only, they are obedient to no one, but only to their own will; and to ask how far the rights of the sovereign and of the citizens respectively extend, is to ask to what extent the latter are able to enter into obligations toward themselves, each to all and all to each.

From this it can be seen that the sovereign power, absolute, sacred and inviolable as it is, does not and cannot go beyond the limits of general conventions, and that each individual can freely dispose of whatever goods and liberties those conventions have left to him; hence the sovereign never has a right to burden one subject more than another, for that would be a particular question to which its competence no longer extends.

Once these distinctions are granted, private individuals are so far from making any real renunciation under the social contract that their situation, as a result of that contract, is really better than before; and instead of alienating anything, they have simply and advantageously exchanged an uncertain and precarious mode of existence for one that is better and more secure; they have exchanged natural independence for liberty, the power of harming others for their own security, and their own might, which might be overcome by others, for a right which the social union makes invincible. Their very lives, which they have dedicated to the state, are continuously protected by it; and when they risk them in its defence, what more are they doing than giving them back to the donor? What are they doing that they did not do more often, and with greater danger, in the state of nature, when, in the course of inevitable combats, they defended at the risk of their lives the means of preserving them? It is true that all must fight for their country when necessary; but it is also true that no one ever has to fight for himself. On balance do we not gain by running, on behalf of that which constitutes our security, a part of the risks we would have to run the moment that means of security was withdrawn?

Chapter V

THE RIGHT OF LIFE AND DEATH

It is asked why individuals, who do not have the right to dispose of their own lives, are able to transfer to the sovereign the very right that they do not possess. This question seems hard to answer only because it is badly framed. Every man has a right to risk his own life in order to save it. Has it ever been said that a person who throws himself out of a window to escape a fire is guilty of suicide? Has this crime ever been so much as imputed to one who, knowing the danger at the time of embarkation, dies in a storm at sea?

The purpose of the social contract is to preserve the contracting parties. He who wills the end wills the means also; and these means necessarily involve certain risks, and even certain losses. He who wishes to preserve his life at the expense of others ought also when necessary to give it for their sake. Now the citizen is no longer judge of the dangers to which the law wishes him to expose himself; and if the prince has told him: ' It is expedient for the state that you should die,' he ought to die; since it is on this condition only that he has lived in security up to that moment; and his life is no longer a simple boon of nature, but a conditional gift of the state.

The death penalty inflicted on criminals may be envisaged from much the same point of view; it is in order not to fall victim to a murderer that we consent to die if we ourselves commit murder. In making this contract, far from disposing of our own lives, we are thinking only of ensuring them; nor is it to be supposed that any of the contracting parties is at the time premeditating his own hanging.

35

Furthermore, every malefactor, in attacking the laws of society, makes himself by his heinous crimes a rebel and a traitor to his country; he ceases to be a member of it by violating its laws; he even makes war upon it. Then the preservation of the state is incompatible with his own; one of the two must perish; and when the culprit is put to death, it is less as a citizen than as an enemy. The procedures of trial and judgment are the declaration and proof that he has broken the social contract, and therefore is no longer a member of the state. Now in view of the fact that he has recognised himself to be such, at least by residence if in no other way, he must be cut off from it by exile as a violator of the compact, or by death as a public enemy. For an enemy of this sort is not an artificial person, but an individual man, and in such cases the right of war is to kill the vanquished.

But, it will be said, the condemnation of a criminal is a particular act. True, and therefore this condemnation is not a function of the sovereign; it is a right the sovereign can confer without itself being able to exercise it. All my ideas hang together, but I cannot expound them all at once.

Frequent punishments, however, are always a sign of weakness or indolence on the part of the government. There is no man so bad that he cannot be made good for something. We have no right, even as an example, to put anyone to death unless it is impossible to preserve him without danger.

As to the pardoning power, or the right to exempt a culprit from the penalty prescribed by law and pronounced by the judge, this belongs exclusively to that which is above the judge and the law, namely the sovereign; and even its rights in this matter are not very clear, and the occasions for exercising them are

very rare. In a well-governed state there are few
punishments, not because there are many pardons, but
because there are few criminals; when the state is
declining, the multitude of crimes ensures their impunity.
Under the Roman Republic, neither the senate nor the
consuls tried to grant pardons; even the people did
not do so, though it sometimes revoked its own judgments. Frequent pardons proclaim that heinous crimes
will soon no longer need them; and everyone can see
where that leads. But I can feel my heart protesting
and holding back my pen; let us leave the discussion
of these matters to the just man who has never sinned,
and himself has never needed pardoning.

Chapter VI

LAW

By the social compact we have given life and being
to the body politic; we must now, by legislation, give
it movement and will. For the original act, by which
the body is formed and united, does not as yet make
any decision as to the means necessary to its preservation.

That which is good and conformable to order is such
by the nature of things, independent of human conventions. All justice comes from God, and He alone is its
source; but if we knew how to receive it from so great
a height, we should need neither government nor laws.
Undoubtedly there is a universal justice derived from
reason only; but this justice, to be admitted among us,
must be mutual. From a human standpoint, the laws
of justice are inoperative among men for lack of natural
sanctions; they are but the fortune of the wicked and
the misfortune of the just, when the latter observes

them toward everyone, and no one observes them toward him. Conventions and laws are necessary, therefore, to unite rights with duties, and to accomplish the purposes of justice. In the state of nature, where all is held in common, I owe nothing to those to whom I have promised nothing; and I recognise as belonging to others only that which is useless to me. It is otherwise in the civil state, where all rights are fixed by law.

But what, after all, is a law? As long as we are content to conceive of this word in purely metaphysical terms, we shall continue to argue without understanding one another; and when we have said what a law of nature is, we shall be no nearer to knowing what is meant by a law of the state.

I have already said that there is no general will with reference to a particular object. Now a particular object must be either inside or outside of the state. If it is outside, a will which is foreign to that object is not general with reference to it; and if it is inside the state, it is part of the state, in which case a relationship is created between the whole and the part which makes them two distinct entities, the part on the one hand, and the whole minus the part on the other. But the whole minus the part is not the whole; and as long as this relationship continues, there is no longer a whole, but two unequal parts; from which it follows that the will of the one is no longer general with reference to the other.

But when the whole people legislates for the whole people, it considers itself only; and if a relationship is then established, it is between the whole object seen from a certain point of view, and the whole object seen from another point of view, with no division of the whole. Then the substance of the enactment, like the will which enacts it, is general. It is this act which I call a law.

When I say that the object of laws is always general, I mean that the law considers subjects collectively and actions abstractly; it is never concerned with an individual man or with a particular action. Thus the law may well provide that there will be privileges, but it cannot give those privileges to anyone by name; the law may create several classes of citizens, and even lay down qualifications for membership, but it cannot designate any particular individual for admission to them; it can establish a royal government and a hereditary succession, but it cannot elect a king or appoint a royal family; in short, no function which relates to an individual object pertains in any way to the legislative power.

Once this idea is accepted, it is immediately obvious that there can be no further question of asking who has the right to make laws, for they are acts of the general will; nor whether the prince is above the laws, since he is a member of the state; nor whether the law can be unjust, since no one is unjust to himself; nor how it is possible to be at once free and subject to law, since the laws are merely registrations of our will.

It is also obvious that since the law is universal both in its will and in its object, that which any man, whoever he may be, ordains on his own authority is not a law at all. Even that which the sovereign ordains with regard to a particular object is no longer a law, but a decree; nor is it an act of sovereignty, but of magistracy.

I call a *republic*, therefore, any state which is ruled by laws, no matter what the form of its administration may be; for then the public interest alone governs, and the commonwealth is respected. Every legitimate government is republican.[1]   I shall explain hereafter what is meant by *government*.

Laws properly speaking are nothing more than the conditions of civil association.   The people subject to the laws should be their author;   only those who are forming an association have the right to determine the conditions of that society.   But how will they determine them?   Will it be by common agreement, by a sudden inspiration?   Has the body politic any organ to express its will?   Who will give it the foresight needed to formulate and publish its acts in advance?   Or how will it declare them when the need arises?   How can a blind multitude, which often does not know what it wants, since it rarely knows what is good for it, by itself execute so great and difficult a project as a system of legislation?   The people by itself always wills the good, but by itself it does not always see it.   The general will is always right, but the judgment which guides it is not always enlightened.   It must be made to see things as they are, sometimes as they ought to appear;   it must be shown the good road it is seeking, safeguarded against seduction by particular wills, given a clear view of local and temporal circumstances, and taught to weigh the attraction of immediate and palpable advantages against the danger of distant and hidden evils.   Individuals see the good they reject;   the public wills the good it does not see.   All stand equally in need of guidance.   The former must be obliged to bring their wills into conformity with their reason;   the

[1] By this word I do not mean merely an aristocracy or a democracy, but in general any government guided by the general will, whch is the law.   To be legitimate, the government must not be ideintical with, but the servant of, the sovereign;   under these conditions, even a monarchy is a republic.   This will be explained in the following book.

latter must be taught to know what it wants. Then public enlightenment will effect a union of understanding and will within the social body; then the parts will work together in perfect harmony, and the whole will achieve its greatest power. From this arises the need for a legislator.

CHAPTER VII

THE LEGISLATOR

To discover the rules of society best suited to nations would require a superior intelligence which saw all the passions of men and experienced none; which had nothing in common with our nature, and knew it thoroughly; whose happiness was independent of us, and which nevertheless was willing to concern itself with ours; and finally, one which, looking to distant glory in the course of time, would be able to work in one century and reap its reward in another.[1] It would take gods to give men laws.

The same line of reasoning which Caligula followed as a matter of fact was followed by Plato as a matter of right when he attempted, in his *Statesman*, to define the civil or royal man. But if it is true that a great ruler is a rare person, what shall we say of a great legislator? The first has only to follow the model that the second has to propose. The latter is the engineer who invents the machine, the former is only the workman who builds it and makes it run. 'At the outset of societies,' says Montesquieu, 'it is the rulers of

[1] A people does not become famous until its legislation is beginning to decline. No one knows how many centuries the Spartans enjoyed the institutions of Lycurgus before the rest of Greece paid any attention to them.

41

republics who create their institutions, and thereafter it is the institutions that mould the rulers of republics.'

Anyone who ventures to create institutions for a people must feel himself capable, so to speak, of changing human nature, transforming each individual, who in himself is a perfect and isolated whole, into part of a larger whole from which this same individual in a sense receives his life and being; he must feel capable of changing the constitution of man in order to strengthen it, and of replacing the physical and independent existence we have all received from nature with a partial and corporate existence. In short, he must deprive man of his own powers to give him powers which are foreign to him, and which he cannot use without the help of others. The more completely dead and extinguished these natural powers are, and the greater and more durable the acquired powers, the more secure and perfect also will be the new constitutional order; so that if each citizen is nothing, and can do nothing, without all the rest, and if the power acquired by the whole community is equal or superior to the sum of the natural powers of all its members, the legislative system may be said to have reached the highest attainable peak of perfection.

The legislator is in every respect an extraordinary figure in the state. His talents and his office must be equally exceptional. He is neither a magistrate nor a sovereign. His office, which constitutes the republic, has no place in its constitution. It is a special and superior function which has nothing in common with the governance of men. For if it is true that he who rules men should not rule the laws, it is equally true that he who rules the laws should not rule men. Otherwise the laws he gives would be minister to his passions, and hence would often do no more than to perpetuate his injustices; never would he be able to prevent particular or private views from impairing the sanctity of his work.

When Lycurgus gave laws to his country, he began by abdicating the kingship. It was the custom of most Greek cities to entrust the drawing-up of their laws to foreigners. The republics of modern Italy often imitated this custom; Geneva did likewise, and profited thereby.[1] Rome, in her heyday, saw all the crimes of tyranny revived in her bosom, and nearly perished, through having united legislative authority and sovereign power in the same hands.

Even the decemvirs, however, never arrogated to themselves the right to enact any law solely on their own authority. 'None of our proposals,' they told the people, 'can become law without your consent. Romans, be yourselves the authors of the laws which are to constitute your happiness.'

He who drafts the laws, therefore, has, or should have, no right to legislate; and even if the people should want to divest itself of this incommunicable right, it cannot do so, for the fundamental compact provides that individuals are bound only by the general will, and there can never be any assurance that a particular will is in conformity with the general will until it has been submitted to the free suffrage of the people. I have said this already, but it is worth repeating.

Thus in the work of legislation we find combined two apparently incompatible things: an enterprise beyond

[1] Those who think of Calvin only as a theologian are ill-acquainted with the scope of his genius. The drafting of our wise edicts, in which he played a large part, does him as much honour as his *Institutes*. No matter what changes time may effect in our religious practices, the name of this great man will never cease to be blessed as long as the love of country and liberty are not extinguished among us.

43

the powers of man, and, to carry it out, an authority that is nil.

There is still another difficulty which deserves attention. Wise men who try to speak to the mob in their own rather than in popular language cannot make themselves understood. But there are innumerable ideas which cannot be translated into the language of the people. Views which are excessively abstract, and objects which are excessively remote, are equally beyond its scope; each individual, having no taste for any plan of government other than that which bears on his own particular interests, finds it hard to perceive the advantages to be derived from the continuous sacrifices required by good laws. For a new-born people to be able to appreciate sound political principles, and to follow the fundamental rules of political necessity, the effect would have to become the cause; the social consciousness to be created by the new institutions would have to preside over the establishment of those same institutions; and men, before laws existed, would have to be as the laws themselves should make them. Since, therefore, the legislator cannot employ either force or argument, he must necessarily have recourse to another species of authority, one which can compel without violence and persuade without convincing.

That is why the founding fathers of nations have always had to resort to divine intervention, and to honour the gods for their own wisdom, in order that the people, submissive to the laws of the state as to the laws of nature, and recognising the same power at work in the formation of the city as in the creation of man, might obey freely, and wear with docility the yoke of public felicity.

This sublime reason, which is beyond the understanding of the vulgar, is that whose decisions the legislator puts in the mouth of the immortals, in order to compel by divine authority those whom human prudence could not move.[1] But it is not every man who can make the gods speak, nor gain credence when he proclaims himself their interpreter. The great soul of the legislator is the true miracle by which his mission must be justified. Anyone can engrave tablets of stone, or bribe an oracle, or train a bird to whisper in his ear, or feign secret intercourse with some divinity, or discover some other crude means of imposing on the people. A man who can do merely this may even perchance be able to bring together a troop of madmen; but he will never found an empire, and his absurd creation will not long survive him. False miracles create a passing bond; only wisdom can make it durable. The continuing existence of the Judaic law, and the law of the Child of Ishmael,[2] which for ten centuries has governed half the world, still bear witness to the greatness of the men who dictated them; and though philosophic pride, or blind party spirit, considers them to be no more than lucky impostors, the true student of politics admires in their institutions that great and powerful genius which presides over all durable creations.

From all this we should not conclude with Warburton that our politics and our religion have a common purpose; but that, in the creation of nations, the one serves as the instrument of the other.

[1] 'Truly,' says Machiavelli, ' there has never been among any people any extraordinary legislator who did not have recourse to God, since otherwise his work would not have been accepted; for there are many things which a wise man knows, but the reasons for which are not in themselves sufficiently evident to enable him to persuade others.' *Discourses on Titus Livy*, BOOK I, chap. 11.

[2] [i.e. Mohammed—TR.]

45

Chapter VIII

THE PEOPLE

JUST as an architect, before erecting a great edifice, observes and sounds out the ground to see if it can support the weight, the wise legislator does not begin by drawing up laws which are good in themselves, but first investigates whether the people for whom they are intended is capable of bearing them. That is why Plato refused to give laws to the Arcadians and the Cyrenians, knowing that both these peoples were rich, and could not bear equality. That is why Crete offered the spectacle of good laws and bad men, since Minos had merely disciplined a people full of vices.

Innumerable nations which would never have been able to support good laws have made a great name for themselves; and even those which could have stood such laws have had, out of the total period of their existence, only a very short time during which they would have been capable of receiving them. Most peoples, like men, are docile only in their youth; as they grow older they become incorrigible. Once customs are established and prejudices have taken root, it is a dangerous and futile project to try to reform them; the people cannot stand having its ills touched even for the purpose of destroying them, like stupid and cowardly invalids who tremble at the sight of the physician.

This does not mean that just as there are illnesses which throw men's heads into confusion and make them forget the past, there may not sometimes be violent epochs in the lifetime of states, during which revolutions do for peoples what certain crises do for individuals; when horror of the past takes the place of

46

oblivion, and when the state, consumed by civil wars, is reborn, so to speak, from its ashes, and recovers the vigour of youth as it leaves the arms of death. Such was Sparta in the time of Lycurgus; such was Rome after the Tarquins; and such, among us, were Holland and Switzerland after the expulsion of the tyrants.

But these events are rare; they are exceptions to be explained by the particular constitution of the state in question. They could not even occur twice among the same people; for a people can free itself when it is merely barbarous, but it can no longer do so when its civic vitality has been exhausted. In the latter case, troubles may destroy it, but revolutions cannot restore it to vigour; and as soon as its chains are broken, it breaks apart and ceases to exist. Thereafter it needs a master, not a liberator. Free peoples, remember this maxim: ' Liberty can be won, but it can never be recovered.'

Youth is not the same thing as childhood. There is with nations, as with men, a time of youth or, if you prefer, of maturity, for which we must wait before subjecting them to laws. But the maturity of a people is not always easy to recognise; and if it is anticipated, the effort is wasted. Some peoples can be disciplined from the moment of birth; others are incapable of it after ten centuries. The Russians will never have a real polity, because they were given one too soon. Peter had a gift for imitation, but he lacked true genius, the gift of creating and making everything out of nothing. Some of the things he did were good; most of them were out of place. He saw that his people were barbarous; he failed to see that they were not ripe for a polity. He tried to civilise them, when what they needed was to be hardened to warfare. His first wish was to create Germans and Englishmen, whereas he should have begun by creating Russians. He prevented his people from ever becoming what they might have been, by persuading them that they were what they were not. Thus do French schoolmasters train students to shine for a moment in childhood, and to amount to nothing thereafter. The Russian Empire sought to subjugate Europe, and will itself be subjugated. The Tartars, its subjects and neighbours, will become its masters, and our own. This revolution strikes me as inevitable. All the kings of Europe are working in concert to speed the event.

Chapter IX

THE SAME CONTINUED

JUST as nature has set limits to the height of a well-proportioned man, beyond which it creates only giants or dwarfs, so also, with regard to the ideal constitution of a state, there are limits to the extent it can attain without being either too large to be well governed or too small to be self-sufficient. In every body politic there is a *maximum* of force which it cannot exceed, and from which it often departs by growing too large. The more the social bond is stretched, the weaker it becomes; and generally speaking, a small state is proportionately stronger than a large one.

This principle can be demonstrated in a thousand different ways. In the first place, administration becomes more difficult over great distances, just as a weight becomes heavier at the end of a longer lever. It also becomes more burdensome as the chain of command is lengthened. For to begin with, each town has its own administration, for which the people pays;

each district has one, for which the people again pays; next each province, and then the larger governmental units, satrapies or vice-royalties, for which it is necessary to pay ever more dearly the higher up the scale we mount, and always at the expense of the unfortunate people; finally comes the supreme administration, which crushes everything. All these surcharges constantly exhaust the subjects; far from being better governed by all these various agencies, they are less well served than would be the case if they were subject to one only. And yet there are hardly any resources left for extraordinary emergencies; and when it is necessary to make provision for them, the state is always on the brink of ruin.

Nor is this all; not only does the government have less vigour and celerity in enforcing the laws, in preventing vexations, in correcting abuses and in forestalling those seditious attempts which may be made in distant places; but the people has less affection for its rulers, whom it never sees, for its country, which it regards as the universe, and for its fellow-citizens, most of whom are strangers. The same laws cannot suit so many diverse provinces with different customs, living in contrasting climates, and incapable of supporting the same form of government. Different laws do nothing but create trouble and confusion among people who live under the same rulers and in constant intercommunication, and thus move about and intermarry freely; and when they are subjected to alien customs, they never know whether their own patrimony is really theirs. In this crowd of mutual strangers brought together in a single capital city by a common administration, talents are hidden, virtues overlooked, and vices unpunished. The rulers, overburdened with business, see nothing for themselves; clerks govern the state. Ultimately the steps which must be taken to maintain the central authority, which so many distant officials are trying to elude or dominate, take up the whole attention of the public; nothing is left over for the welfare of the people, and little for its defence in case of need; and that is how a body which is too large for its constitution weakens and dies, crushed by its own weight.

On the other hand, the state must provide itself with some solid basis to resist the shocks it cannot help experiencing, and to support the efforts it will have to make to maintain itself. For all peoples have a sort of centrifugal force by which they constantly act against one another, and they tend, like the vortices of Descartes, to aggrandise themselves at the expense of their neighbours. Thus the weak are in danger of being quickly swallowed up; and no people has much chance of self-preservation unless it places itself in a sort of equilibrium with all the rest, which more or less equalises the pressure.

Thus it can be seen that there are reasons both for expansion and for contraction; and it is not the least of the skills of statesmanship to strike between them that balance which is most favourable to the preservation of the state. In general it may be said that the reasons for expansion, being merely external and relative, should be subordinated to those for contraction, which are internal and absolute. A strong and healthy constitution is the first thing to be sought; and the vigour born of a good government is more to be relied on than the resources provided by a large territory.

There have been states so constituted, however, that the need for conquest was a part of their very constitution, and that, in order to maintain themselves, they were forced to grow ever larger. They may have congratulated themselves on this fortunate necessity, which nevertheless showed them both the limits of their greatness and the inevitable moment of their fall.

CHAPTER X

THE SAME CONTINUED

A BODY politic can be measured in two ways, by the extent of its territory and by the number of its people; and between these two factors there is an optimum ratio which determines the proper size of the state. It is men who make the state, and it is the land which feeds men. The optimum ratio is, therefore, that the land should be sufficient to support its inhabitants, and that there should be as many inhabitants as the land can feed. It is this proportion that marks the maximum strength attainable by any given number of people. For if there is too much land, it is hard to defend, it is insufficiently cultivated, and it produces too much; this is the proximate cause of defensive wars. If there is not enough land, the state must turn to its neighbours to supplement it; this is the proximate cause of offensive wars. Any people so situated that its only choice lies between commerce and war is intrinsically weak; it is at the mercy of its neighbours and the course of events; its existence can never be anything but short and precarious. Either it conquers, and changes its position, or it is conquered, and ceases to exist. Only greatness or insignificance can enable it to remain free.

It is impossible to calculate any fixed ratio between the amount of land and the number of men which are sufficient to each other; partly because of the differences to be found in the character of the terrain, in its degree of fertility, in the nature of its products and in the influence of its climate, and partly because of the differences to be observed in the temperament of its inhabitants, some of whom consume little in a fertile country, and others much on an ungrateful soil. You must also take into account the greater or lesser fecundity of the women, other special circumstances which may make the country either favourable or unfavourable to the growth of population, and the extent to which the legislator can hope to encourage it by his new institutions; which means that the latter should base his judgment not on what he sees, but on what he foresees, and should fix his attention not so much on the existing level of the population as on the level it ought naturally to attain. Finally, there are innumerable occasions when particular local circumstances will require or permit the inclusion of more territory than would seem to be necessary. Thus you will expand considerably in a mountainous country, where the natural products, namely woods and pastures, require less labour, where experience shows that women are more fecund than in the plains, and where the mountain slopes leave little level ground, the only kind that can be counted on for vegetation. On the seacoast, on the contrary, you can contract, even in the midst of rocks and nearly barren sands, because fishing there can largely take the place of land-produce, because the inhabitants need to live closer together to ward off pirates, and because it is easier, by colonisation, to rid the country of its surplus population.

If laws are to be given to a people, there is yet another condition to be fulfilled, a condition which cannot take the place of any of the others, but without which all the rest are useless: this is the enjoyment of prosperity and peace. For the time when a state is putting itself in order is, like the time when a battalion is drawing up in formation, the moment when the body is least capable of resistance and easiest to destroy. Better resistance could be made in a period of absolute chaos than in a moment of fermentation, when everyone is concerned with his own position and not with the common danger. If a war, a famine or a rebellion occurs at this critical time, the state will inevitably be overthrown.

This is not to say that there have not been plenty of governments established during such storms; but then it is the governments themselves that destroy the state. Usurpers always stir up or make use of these troubled times to secure, under the cover of public panic, the passage of destructive laws which the people would never adopt in cold blood. The choice of the moment for legislation is one of the surest signs by which to distinguish the work of the legislator from that of the tyrant.

What people, then, is fit for legislation? One which, though already united by some common bonds of origin, interest or convention, has not yet borne the true yoke of laws; one which has no customs and no deeply-rooted superstitions; one which has no fear of being overwhelmed by sudden invasion; one which, without participating in the quarrels of its neighbours, can resist each of them by itself, or use one to repel another; one whose individual members can all know one another, and where it is not necessary to impose greater burdens on a man than a man is able to bear; one which can get along without other peoples, and without which all other peoples can get along; [1] one

[1] If one of two neighbouring peoples could not get along without the other, the situation would be very difficult for the first, and very dangerous for the second. Any wise nation, in such a case, will

which is neither rich nor poor, and can be sufficient unto itself; one, finally, which combines the firmness of an old people with the docility of a new one. What makes the work of legislation difficult is not so much the things that have to be created as the things that have to be destroyed; and what makes it so rarely successful is the impossibility of finding natural simplicity combined with social requirements. It is true that all these conditions are hard to find together. And that is why we see so few examples of well-constituted states.

In Europe there is still one country capable of legislation; this is the island of Corsica. The valour and constancy with which this worthy people has succeeded in regaining and defending its liberty well deserves that some wise man should teach it how to preserve that liberty. I have a certain presentiment that one day this small island will astonish Europe.

CHAPTER XI

THE VARIOUS SYSTEMS OF LEGISLATION

IF we investigate what precisely constitutes the greatest good of all, which ought to be the object of any system of legislation, we shall find that it comes down to two principal objects, *liberty* and *equality*: liberty, because any form of private dependence is that much force

---

very quickly bestir itself to free the other from this condition of dependence. The Republic of Thlascala, which was completely surrounded by the Mexican Empire, preferred to do without salt rather than to buy it from the Mexicans, or even to accept it from them as a gift. The wise Thlascalans saw the trap hidden beneath this generosity. They preserved their freedom; and this small state, enclosed in that great empire, became in the end the instrument of its ruin.

subtracted from the body of the state; and equality, because liberty cannot subsist without it.

I have already said what civil liberty is. With regard to equality, we must not take this word to mean that degrees of power and wealth are exactly the same; but that, so far as power is concerned, it is not great enough to permit men to resort to violence, and is never exercised otherwise than by virtue of rank and law; and that, so far as wealth is concerned, no citizen is rich enough to be able to buy another, and none so poor as to be forced to sell himself;[1] and this presupposes, on the part of the great, moderation of possessions and prestige, and on the part of the humble, moderation of avarice and envy.

This equality, people say, is a theoretical chimera which cannot exist in practice. But if the abuse is inevitable, does it follow that we ought not even to regulate it? It is precisely because the force of circumstances constantly tends to destroy equality that the force of legislation should always tend to maintain it.

But these general objects of every good legislative system must be modified in each country with reference to the local situation and the character of the inhabitants; and it is with reference to these conditions that we must assign to each people a particular legislative system which, though it may not be intrinsically the best, is best for the state for which it is intended. Is the soil, for example, ungrateful and barren, or the country

[1] Do you really want to give stability to the state? Then bring the two extremes as close as possible; tolerate neither rich men nor beggars. These two classes, which are naturally inseparable, are equally ruinous to the common welfare; from the one come the abettors of tyranny, and from the other tyrants. It is always between them that public liberty becomes an article of commerce; the one buys, and the other sells it.

too small for its inhabitants? Then turn to industry and the arts, whose products you will exchange for the foodstuffs you lack. Do you, on the contrary, occupy rich plains and fertile hillsides? In a good terrain do you need more inhabitants? Then devote your whole attention to agriculture, which causes men to multiply, and drive out the arts and crafts, which would serve merely to complete the depopulation of the country by concentrating in a limited number of places the few inhabitants it has.[1] Do you occupy an extensive and convenient seacoast? Then cover the sea with ships, cultivate commerce and navigation; your life will be brilliant and short. Does the sea at your shores lap only against cliffs that are virtually inaccessible? Then remain barbarous and ichthyophagous; it will give you a more tranquil, perhaps a better, and certainly a happier life. In short, in addition to the principles which are common to all, each people has within itself something which requires those principles to be applied in a particular way, and which makes its legislation appropriate only to itself. Thus the Hebrews in former times, and the Arabs more recently, made religion their main object, the Athenians literature, Tyre and Carthage commerce, Rhodes shipping, Sparta war, and Rome virtue. The author of the *Spirit of the Laws* has given innumerable examples of the skill with which the legislator directs his legislative system to each of these objects.

If the constitution of a state is to be really firm and enduring, the natural fitness of things must be so well observed that the laws and natural circumstances co-incide at every point, and that the former do no more,

[1] Any branch of foreign trade, as M. d'Argenson says, is hardly of more than apparent advantage to a kingdom as a whole; it may enrich certain individuals, and even certain towns; but the whole nation gains nothing thereby, and the people is no better off.

so to speak, than to guarantee, accompany and rectify the latter. But if the legislator mistakes his object and adopts a principle different from that which arises from the nature of things, if the one tends to servitude and the other to freedom, the one to wealth and the other to population, the one to peace and the other to conquest, then you will see the laws imperceptibly weaken and the constitution change; and the state will never cease being troubled until it is destroyed or altered, and invincible nature has resumed its sway.

Chapter XII

THE VARIOUS TYPES OF LAW

In setting the whole in order, and in giving the best possible form to the commonwealth, there are various relationships to be considered. First, there is the action of the body as a whole upon itself, that is to say, the relationship of the whole to the whole, or of the sovereign to the state. And this relationship is a composite of the relationships between intermediate factors, as we shall see hereafter.

The laws which regulate this relationship are called political laws, and are also known as fundamental laws, not wholly without reason if those laws are wise. For if there is only one good way of organising any given state, a people which has found that way should hold to it. But if the established order is bad, why should we regard as fundamental the laws which prevent it from being good? In any case, moreover, a people always has a right to change its laws, even the best; for if it is pleased to do itself harm, who has a right to prevent it from doing so?

57

The second relationship is that of the members with one another, or with the entire body. And this relationship ought in the first respect to be as weak, and in the second respect as strong as possible, in order that each citizen may be perfectly independent of all the rest, and extremely dependent on the city; and this is always accomplished by the same means, for it is the power of the state alone that constitutes the liberty of its members. This second relationship is the source of civil laws.

We may also consider a third kind of relationship between the individual and the law, the relationship of disobedience to penalty. And this occasions the establishment of criminal laws, which basically are not so much a particular species of law as the sanction for all the rest.

In addition to these three types of law there is a fourth, the most important of all, which is graven not in marble or bronze, but in the hearts of the citizens; which forms the real constitution of the state; which day by day acquires new strength; which revives or replaces the other laws when they grow old or are extinguished, which preserves the people in the spirit of its original institutions, and imperceptibly substitutes the force of habit for that of authority. I am speaking of manners, morals, customs and, above all, of public opinion, a factor unknown to our political theorists, but on which the success of all the rest depends; a factor with which the great legislator is secretly concerned when he seems to be thinking only of particular regulations; for the latter are only the soffit of the arch, while manners and morals, though of slower growth, are in the end its unshakable keystone.

Of these various classes, political laws, which constitute the form of the government, are the only ones relevant to my subject.

BOOK III

BEFORE speaking of the various forms of government, let us try to determine the precise meaning of this word, which has not yet been very well explained.

CHAPTER I

GOVERNMENT IN GENERAL

I WARN the reader that this chapter must be read with great care, and that I do not know the secret of making my meaning clear to anyone who will not pay attention.

Every free action is the effect of two concurrent causes: a moral cause, or the will which determines the act; and a physical cause, or the power which executes it. When I walk toward an object, it is necessary first of all that I should want to go there, and in the second place that my feet should take me there. A paralytic who wants to run, and an active man who does not, will both stay where they are. The body politic has the same motive powers; here too there is a distinction between force and will, the latter being known as *legislative power* and the former as *executive power*. Nothing in the body politic is done, or ought to be done, without the concurrence of both.

We have seen that the legislative belongs, and can only belong, to the people. On the principles already established it is easy to see, on the other hand, that the executive power cannot belong to the general public in its legislative or sovereign capacity; for this power is made up exclusively of particular acts, which are not within the province of the law, and not, therefore, within that of the sovereign, whose acts can never be anything but laws.

Thus the public force needs an agent of its own to unite it and put it into operation under the direction of the general will, to serve as a means of communication between the state and the sovereign, and to do for the collective person much the same thing as the union of body and soul does for the individual. That is the reason why a state needs to have a government; and it is a mistake to identify the government with the sovereign, to which it merely ministers.

What, then, is the government? It is an intermediary body established between the subjects and the sovereign to enable them to communicate with one another, and entrusted with the execution of law and the maintenance of liberty, both civil and political.

The members of this body are called magistrates or *kings*, that is to say, *governors;* and the body as a whole is known as the *prince*.[1] Those who maintain, therefore, that the act by which a people subjects itself to rulers is not a contract are perfectly right. It is absolutely nothing but a commission, an office in which the rulers, as mere officials of the sovereign, exercise in its name the power of which it has made them the depositaries, and which it can limit, modify or resume whenever it pleases; for the alienation of such a right

[1] Thus in Venice the college of senators is called *Most Serene Prince*, even when the doge is not present.

is incompatible with the nature of the social body, and contrary to the purpose of the association.

By *government* or supreme administration, therefore, I mean the legitimate exercise of the executive power; and the individual or group entrusted with this administration I call *prince* or *magistrate*.

It is in the government that there are found the intermediate forces whose relations constitute those of the whole with the whole, or of the sovereign with the state. This last relationship may be visualised as that between the two extremes of a continuous proportion, with the government as the geometrical mean. The government receives from the sovereign orders which it then issues to the people; and if the state is to be well balanced, the net product or power of the government, taken by itself, must be equal to the net product or power of the citizens, who are sovereigns on the one hand, and subjects on the other.

Furthermore, no one of these three terms can be altered without immediately destroying the proportion. If the sovereign tries to govern, or if the magistrate tries to make laws, or if the subjects refuse to obey, order is succeeded by disorder, force and will no longer act in concert, and the state, being dissolved, falls thereby either into despotism or anarchy. Furthermore, since there is only one geometrical mean for any given pair of extremes, there is only one good government possible in any given state. But since innumerable events may change the relations of a people, different governments may be good not only for different peoples, but also for the same people at different times.

In attempting to give an idea of the different relations which may prevail between these two extremes, I shall take as an example the number of the people, since this is one comparatively easy to express.

Let us assume that the state is composed of ten thousand citizens. The sovereign can only be considered collectively and as a body; but each particular member, in his capacity as a subject, is considered as an individual. Thus the sovereign is to the subject in the ratio of ten thousand to one; which means that each member of the state has for himself only one ten-thousandth part of the sovereign authority, although he is entirely subject to it. If the people is composed of one hundred thousand individuals, the condition of the subjects remains unchanged; and each alike is under the full authority of the laws, while his vote, reduced to one hundred-thousandth, has only one-tenth as much influence in drawing them up. Thus, since the subject always remains one, the ratio of sovereign to subject increases in direct proportion to the number of citizens. From which it follows that liberty diminishes the larger the state becomes.

When I say that the ratio increases, I mean that it departs from unity. Thus the greater the ratio is in a mathematical sense, the smaller it is in the ordinary sense of the word. In the first sense the ratio, considered according to quantity, is measured by the exponent; in the second, considered in relation to identity, it is reckoned by similarity.

Now the smaller the ratio of particular wills to the general will, that is to say, the ratio of morals and manners to law, the greater the need for coercive power. Thus the government, in order to be good, must be relatively stronger as the people is more numerous.

On the other hand, since the growth of the state gives the depositaries of public authority greater temptation and opportunity to abuse their power, the more force the government needs to restrain the people, the more does the sovereign also need to restrain the government. I am not speaking here of absolute force, but of the relative force of the various parts of the state.

From this double ratio it follows that the continuous proportion between the sovereign, the prince and the people is by no means an arbitrary idea, but a necessary consequence of the nature of the body politic. It also follows that since one of the extremes, namely the people in its capacity as subject, is fixed and represented by unity, every time the double ratio is increased or diminished, the simple ratio similarly increases or diminishes, and the middle term is consequently altered. Which shows that there is no unique and absolutely valid form of government, but that there can be as many different kinds of government as there are different sizes of state.

If you were to turn this system to ridicule and say that in order to find this geometrical mean and create the governmental body, it is merely necessary, according to me, to take the square root of the number of the people, I would answer that I am here using this number only by way of an example; that the ratios of which I speak are measured not only by the number of men, but more generally by the quantity of action, which is the combined result of many causes; and that, finally, if I borrow geometrical terms for a moment to express myself in fewer words, I am nevertheless not unaware of the fact that geometrical precision is not to be found in moral quantities.

The government is on a small scale what the body politic containing it is on a large scale. It is an artificial person endowed with certain faculties, active like the sovereign, passive like the state, and capable of being broken up on analysis into similar component parts; the relationship between these parts consequently gives rise to a new ratio; and each part in turn can be similarly subdivided, at each stage of the official hierarchy, until we finally reach an indivisible middle term, that is to say a single ruler or chief magistrate, who may be envisaged as the unity standing at the middle of this sequence between the fractional and the numerical series.

Without burdening ourselves with this multiplication of terms, let us be content to consider the government as a new body within the state, distinct from the people and from the sovereign, and occupying an intermediary position between them.

There is an essential difference between these two bodies, in that the state exists of itself, and the government exists only through the sovereign. Thus the dominant will of the prince is, or ought to be, the general will or the law exclusively; his force is but the public force concentrated in him. As soon as he tries to perform any absolute and independent act on his own authority, the bonds that hold the whole system together begin to loosen. If it finally reached the point where the particular will of the prince was more active than the will of the sovereign, and he used the public force entrusted to him to execute this particular will, the result would be to create, in a manner of speaking, two sovereigns, one *de facto* and the other *de jure;* and at that instant the social union would vanish, and the body politic would be dissolved.

Nevertheless, if the governmental body is to have a real life and existence to distinguish it from the body of the state, and if all its members are to be capable of acting in concert and fulfilling the purpose for which it was established, it must have a particular personality, a feeling shared by all its members, and a special force and will tending to its own self-preservation. This particular existence presupposes the existence of assemblies and councils, the power to deliberate and decide, and the recognition of rights, titles and privileges appertaining exclusively to the prince, and rendering the status of the magistrate honourable in proportion to its difficulty. The problem is to find means of giving this subordinate group a place within the larger whole such that it will in no wise alter the general constitution while consolidating its own; such that it will never fail to distinguish between its particular force, designed for its own self-preservation, and the public force, designed for the preservation of the state; such that, in short, it will always be ready to sacrifice the government to the people, and not the people to the government.

Furthermore, although the artificial body of the government is the product of another artificial body, and enjoys nothing more than what might be called a borrowed and subordinate existence, this does not mean that it cannot act with varying degrees of vigour or celerity; enjoying, so to speak, a more or less rugged state of health. Finally, without directly departing from the purposes for which it was established, it may deviate from them more or less, depending on the way in which it is constituted.

From all these various differences arise the various relations which ought to exist between the government and the body of the state, depending on the accidental and particular relations by which this same state is modified. For often the government which is intrinsically the best will become the most vicious, if its relations are not altered to fit the defects of the body politic to which it belongs.

Chapter II

THE CONSTITUENT PRINCIPLE OF THE VARIOUS FORMS OF GOVERNMENT

IN order to explain the general cause of these differences, we must now distinguish between the prince and the government, just as I have already distinguished between the state and the sovereign.

The body of magistrates may be composed of a larger or smaller number of members. We have already said that the ratio of sovereign to subjects is greater in proportion to the number of the people; and by an obvious analogy, we may say the same thing of the government in relation to the magistrates.

Now the total force of the government, being always that of the state, never varies; and from this it follows that the more of that force it expends on its own members, the less it has left to exert on the people as a whole.

Thus the larger the number of magistrates, the weaker the government is. Since this is a basic principle, we must try to make it clearer.

In the person of the magistrate we can distinguish three essentially different wills. First there is the will of the individual, which tends solely to his own private advantage; second, the collective will of the magistrates, which refers solely to the advantage of the prince, and may be called the corporate will, being general in relation to the government, and particular in relation to the state of which the government is a part; third, the will of the people or the sovereign will, which is general both in relation to the state, considered as the whole, and in relation to the government, considered as a part of the whole.

66

In a perfect system of legislation, the particular or individual will ought to be null, the corporate will of the government very subordinate, and the general or sovereign will consequently predominant at all times, and the sole regulator of all the others.

In the order of nature, on the contrary, these different wills become more active the more they are concentrated. Thus the general will is always the weakest, the corporate will stronger, and the particular will the strongest of all; with the result that each member of the government is first of all an individual, and then a magistrate, and then a citizen, a sequence diametrically opposite to the requirements of social order.

This means that whenever the whole government is in the hands of a single individual, the particular will and the corporate will are perfectly united, and the latter is therefore raised to the highest possible degree of intensity. Now considering that the use of force depends on the degree of will, and that the absolute quantity of force at the disposal of the government remains constant, it follows that the most active form of government is that of a single individual.

If, on the contrary, we unite the government with the legislative authority, making the sovereign a prince, and all the citizens magistrates, then the corporate will, being merged with the general will, will be no more active than the general will itself, and will leave the particular will as strong as possible. Thus the government, while still retaining the same absolute quantity of force, will have the minimum of relative or effective force.

These ratios are incontestable, and other considerations also serve to confirm them. It is obvious, for example, that each magistrate is more active in his corporate group than each citizen in the body of the nation, and hence that the particular will has much more influence on the acts of the government than on those of the sovereign; for each magistrate is almost always charged with some particular governmental function, whereas no citizen has any distinct sovereign function to set him off from any other citizen. The larger the state becomes, moreover, the greater its total strength, although the increase is not in direct proportion to the extent of the state's growth. But if the state remains the same, it does not matter how much the number of magistrates increases, for the government does not thereby acquire any real increase of strength, since its strength is the strength of the state, the quantity of which remains constant. Thus the relative strength or activity of the government diminishes, without its real or absolute strength being able to increase.

It is also clear that the transaction of business becomes slower as the number of people entrusted with it becomes greater; prudence is overemphasised at the expense of good fortune; opportunities are allowed to slip by, and by much deliberation the fruits of deliberation are often lost.

I have just shown that the government weakens as the number of magistrates increases; and I have already shown that the more numerous the people is, the more repressive force is needed. From which it follows that the ratio of magistrates to government should be in inverse proportion to the ratio of subjects to sovereign; which means that, the more the state expands, the more the government ought to contract; and thus that the number of rulers should diminish in proportion to the increase of the population.

It should be noted that I am here speaking solely about the relative strength of the government, not about its rectitude. For on the contrary, the more numerous the body of magistrates is, the more nearly does the corporate will approximate to the general will; whereas under a single magistrate this same corporate will, as I have said, is merely a particular will. Thus we gain in one direction what we lose in the other; and the skill of the legislator consists in knowing how to determine the point where the force and the will of the government, which always stand in inverse proportion, will be combined in the ratio most advantageous to the state.

Chapter III

THE CLASSIFICATION OF GOVERNMENTS

In the preceding chapter we have seen why the various species or forms of governments are distinguished according to the number of the members who compose them; it now remains to see how this classification is made.

The sovereign may, in the first place, entrust the exercise of government to the whole people, or to the majority of the people, with the result that there are more citizen-magistrates than private citizens. *Democracy* is the name given to this form of government.

It may, on the other hand, restrict the exercise of government to a small number, with the result that there are more private citizens than magistrates; and this form of government is called *aristocracy*.

Finally, it may concentrate the whole government in the hands of a single magistrate, from whom all the rest derive their power. This third form is the most common of all, and is called *monarchy* or royal government.

69

It should be observed that all these forms, or at least the first two, may exist in varying degrees, and have, indeed, considerable latitude; for democracy may either embrace the whole people, or exclude any number up to one half. Aristocracy, in turn, may include indeterminately any number from the smallest up to one half. Even monarchy may be shared to some extent. Under her constitution Sparta always had two kings; and in the Roman Empire as many as eight emperors were to be seen at one time, without it being possible to say that the Empire was divided. Thus there is a point where each form of government merges with the next, and it is obvious that, although three names only are used, government is really susceptible of as many different forms as the state has citizens.

Furthermore, since a single government can, in certain respects, be divided into a number of different parts, some administered in one way and some in another, these three forms may be combined to produce a multitude of mixed forms, each multipliable by all the simple forms.

People in all periods have spent much time arguing about the best form of government, without considering that each is the best in certain circumstances, and the worst in others.

If the number of supreme magistrates in any given state ought to be inversely proportional to the number of citizens, it follows as a general rule that democratic government is suitable to small states, aristocratic to those of medium size, and monarchical government to large states. But who can count the host of circumstances that may provide exceptions to this rule?

Chapter IV

DEMOCRACY

He who makes the law knows better than anyone else how it ought to be executed and interpreted. It would seem, therefore, that there could be no better constitution than that which unites the executive with the legislative power. But that is the very reason why this form of government is in certain respects unsatisfactory; for things which ought to be distinguished are not, and the prince and the sovereign, being but one person, constitute a government which might be said to be no government at all.

It is not good for the maker of laws to execute them, nor for the body of the people to turn its attention away from general considerations to particular objects. Nothing is more dangerous than the influence of private interests in public affairs; and the abuse of laws by the government is a lesser evil than that corruption of the legislative authority which is the inevitable result of particular opinions. When this occurs, the substance of the state changes, and all reform becomes impossible. A people which would never abuse governmental authority would not abuse independence either; a people which would always govern well would not need to be governed.

In the strict sense of the term, there never has been, and there never will be, a real democracy. It is against the order of nature for the majority to govern and for the minority to be governed. It is impossible to imagine a people remaining constantly assembled to attend to public business; and it is easy to see that committees could not be set up for this purpose without changing the form of administration.

Actually, I believe it may be laid down as a general rule that whenever the functions of government are divided between several bodies, those which are the less numerous sooner or later acquire the greater authority, if only for the reason that their greater ease in expediting business naturally leads them in that direction.

Furthermore, how many nearly incompatible things does not this form of government presuppose? It requires, first of all, a very small state, where the people can readily be assembled, and where each citizen can easily be acquainted with all the rest; second, great simplicity of manners and morals, to provide against the necessity of discussing questions which are too numerous and too difficult; it also requires great equality of rank and fortune, for otherwise equality of rights and authority could not long subsist; and finally, little or no luxury. For luxury either is the consequence of wealth, or else makes wealth necessary; it corrupts the rich and the poor alike, the first by possession and the second by covetousness; it sells out the country to effeminacy and vanity; it deprives the state of all its citizens by subjecting some to others, and all to irrational opinions.

That is why a famous author has described virtue as the fundamental principle of republics, for all these conditions could not long be met without it. But because of his failure to analyse the question properly, this great genius was often wrong, and sometimes lacking in clarity ; and he did not see that, since the sovereign authority is everywhere the same, the same fundamental principle should be characteristic of every well-constituted state, though in varying degree, to be sure, depending on the form of government.

We may add that there is no form of government so susceptible to civil wars and intestine agitations as is the democratic or popular, for there is none which tends so strongly and continuously to change its form, nor any which requires more vigilance and courage to keep it unchanged. It is under this constitution above all that the citizen must arm himself with strength and constancy, and every day of his life say from the bottom of his heart, as a virtuous palatine [1] once said in the Polish Diet, ' I prefer a dangerous liberty to quiet servitude.'

If there were a people of gods, it would govern itself democratically. So perfect a form of government is not for men.

CHAPTER V

ARISTOCRACY

In this case we have two very distinct artificial persons, the government and the sovereign; and thus we have two general wills, the one general in relation to all the citizens, the other in relation to the members of the administration only. Although the government, therefore, may well regulate its own members as it likes, it can never speak to the people otherwise than in the name of the sovereign, that is to say in the name of the people itself; a thing it must never forget.

The first societies were governed aristocratically. The heads of families deliberated together on public business. The young readily yielded to the authority of experience. Hence the words *priests*, *elders*, *senate* and *gerontes*. Even today the savages of North America are still governed in this way, and very well governed.

[1] The Palatine of Posen, father of the King of Poland, Duke of Lorraine.

But as institutional inequality began to prevail over natural inequality, wealth or power [1] was increasingly preferred to seniority, and aristocracy became elective. Finally the transmission of power, together with property, from father to son, created patrician families and thus made the government hereditary; it was then possible to be a senator at the age of twenty.

There are, therefore, three kinds of aristocracy: natural, elective and hereditary. The first is appropriate only to simple peoples; the third is the worst known form of government. The second is the best; it is aristocracy in the proper sense of the term.

This form of government has the advantage not only of distinguishing between sovereign and governmental powers, but also of choosing its members. For all the citizens, in a popular government, are born magistrates; but here the number of magistrates is small, and they only become such by election,[2] a method which turns probity, talent, experience and all the other grounds of preferment and public esteem into as many guarantors of good government.

Furthermore, it is easier for the government to assemble; affairs are better discussed, and expedited in a more orderly and diligent fashion; and the credit of the state is better maintained abroad by venerable senators than by an unknown or despised multitude.

[1] It is clear that the word *optimates*, as used by the ancients, does not mean the best, but the most powerful.

[2] It is very important to have the form of election to the magistracies regulated by law; for if it is left to the discretion of the prince, the government cannot fail to sink into hereditary aristocracy, as happened in the Republics of Venice and Berne. Thus the former of these states has long since fallen into dissolution; but the latter is preserved by the extreme wisdom of its senate, an honourable and very precarious exception.

In short, it is the best and most natural arrangement for the wisest to govern the multitude, as long as we are sure that they will rule in its interest and not in their own. There is no need to multiply authorities to no purpose, nor to have twenty thousand men do what a hundred selected men can do still better. But we cannot avoid mentioning that, under this system, the corporate interest of the government begins to direct the public power less strictly in accordance with the general will, and that there is also an inevitable tendency to exempt a part of the executive power from the rule of law.

As to the particular conditions under which this form of government is suitable, the state must not be so small, nor must the people be so simple and upright, that the execution of law follows directly from the general will, as is the case in a good democracy. Nor must the nation be so large that the rulers, scattering to govern it, will be able in their respective departments to infringe upon the sovereign, and proceed from independence to mastery.

But if aristocracy calls for somewhat fewer virtues than popular government, it also calls for others peculiar to itself, such as moderation among the rich, and contentment among the poor; for it seems that rigorous equality would be out of place in such a system; it was not even observed in Sparta.

Finally, if this form of government permits a certain inequality of fortune, it is simply in order that the administration of public affairs may in general be entrusted to those who can best afford to give all their time to it; but not, as Aristotle asserts, in order that the rich may always have the preference. On the contrary, it is important that the election of an occasional poor man should teach the people that, in the scale of human merit, there are grounds of preference more important than wealth.

CHAPTER VI

MONARCHY

So far we have considered the prince as an artificial and collective person, united by the force of law, and exercising the executive power within the state. We must now consider this power brought together in the hands of a natural person, a real man, who alone has the right to dispose of it according to law. Such a person is called a monarch or king.

Quite contrary to the other administrations, where a collective being represents an individual, in this form of government an individual represents a collective being; with the result that the artificial unity which constitutes the prince is at the same time a physical unity, in which are naturally combined all the faculties which the law unites with such difficulty in other administrations.

Thus the will of the people, and the will of the prince, and the public force of the state, and the particular force of the government, are all moved by the same lever; all the controls of the machine are in the same hand; and everything proceeds to the same goal. There are no opposing movements to cancel each other out; and it is impossible to imagine any sort of constitution in which a smaller effort will produce a greater result. Archimedes sitting quietly on the shore, and drawing a great ship with ease along the water, represents for me a skilful monarch governing his vast states from his study, and causing everything to move while himself appearing motionless.

But if no government is more vigorous, there is also none where the particular will holds greater sway and more easily dominates the rest. It is true that everything proceeds toward the same goal; but this goal is not the public felicity; and the very strength of the administration constantly works to the prejudice of the state.

Kings want to be absolute; and from afar men cry out to them that the best way to do this is to make themselves beloved of their peoples. This precept is admirable, and in some respects it is even very true. Unfortunately it will always be the laughing-stock of courts. The power which comes from the love of the people is undoubtedly the greatest of all; but it is precarious and conditional, and princes will never be satisfied with it. The best kings want to be able, if they like, to be wicked without ceasing to be master. A political sermoniser will waste his breath when he tells them that the strength of the people is their own, and that their greatest interest is, therefore, to have the people prosperous, numerous and redoubtable; they know very well that this is not true. Their personal interest is primarily that the people should be weak and wretched, and ever incapable of resisting them. I admit that if the people were always perfectly submissive, it would be in the prince's interest for it to be powerful in order that that power, which is his own, might render him redoubtable to his neighbours. But since this interest is only secondary and subordinate, and since the two assumptions are mutually exclusive, it is natural that princes should always give their preference to the precept most immediately useful to them. Samuel strongly impressed this on the Hebrews, and

77

Machiavelli has demonstrated it. While pretending to teach kings, he has been an excellent teacher of peoples. The *Prince* of Machiavelli is the book of republicans.[1]

We have found, on general grounds, that monarchy is suitable only to large states; and when we examine monarchy itself we shall see that this conclusion is again confirmed. The more numerous the public administration becomes, the more does the ratio of prince to subject diminish and approach equality, reaching the ratio of one to one, or equality itself, in democracy. This same ratio increases as the government contracts, and reaches its maximum when the government is in the hands of a single individual. The distance between the prince and the people then becomes excessive, and the state lacks bonds of union. To supply this lack, therefore, there must be intermediary orders; there must be princes, grandees and noblemen to fill them. But all that is unsuitable for a small state, which would go bankrupt supporting so many dignitaries.

But if it is hard for a large state to be well governed, it is still harder for it to be well governed by a single man; and we all know what happens when the king lets others act for him.

An essential and inevitable defect, which will always make monarchy inferior to republican government, is that in the latter the voice of the public almost never

[1] Machiavelli was a worthy man and a good citizen; but being attached to the Medici, he was forced, during the period of his country's oppression, to disguise his love of liberty. The very choice of his detestable hero is enough in itself to reveal his hidden intention; and a comparison of the principles set forth in his *Prince* with those of his *Discourses on Titus Livy* and his *History of Florence* demonstrates that this profound political theorist has so far found only superficial or corrupt interpreters. The court of Rome strictly banned his book. I can well believe it; for that is the court he most clearly depicts.

raises to the highest offices men who are not enlightened and capable, and who do not fill them with credit; whereas those who rise to the top in monarchies are usually nothing more than petty muddlers, petty rascals and petty intriguers, whose petty talents, which in courts are the passport to great office, serve only to show the public their ineptitude as soon as they are appointed. The people is much less deceived in such choices than the prince; and a man of real merit is almost as rare in a ministry as a fool at the head of a republican government. Thus when, by fortunate chance, a born ruler takes the helm of affairs in a monarchy almost ruined by all these fine fellows, people are always surprised at the resources he discovers, and an epoch is made in the history of a country.

For a monarchical state to be well governed, its size or extent would have to be tailored to fit the capacities of the ruler. It is easier to conquer than to reign. With a long enough lever, it is possible to move the world with a single finger; but to sustain it requires the shoulders of a Hercules. If a state is large, the prince is almost always too petty. And if, on the contrary, it should happen that the state is too petty for its ruler, a rare occurrence, it is still badly governed; for the ruler, thinking always of great enterprises, forgets the interests of his peoples, and by the abuse of his excessive talents makes them no less wretched than does a stupid ruler by his lack of talents. A kingdom really ought to expand or contract at the beginning of each reign, according to the prince's capacity; whereas in a republic, the talents of a senate being less variable, the state can have fixed limits without detracting from the administration.

The most perceptible disadvantage of government by a single man is the lack of that continuity of succession

79

which, in the other two forms of government, provides an unbroken bond of union. When a king dies, another is needed; elections leave dangerous gaps in the succession; they are stormy; and unless the citizens are honest and unselfish to an extent hardly possible under this form of government, intrigue and corruption will play a part in them. It is hard for one to whom the state has sold itself not to sell it in turn, and to compensate himself at the expense of the weak for the money that the powerful have extorted from him. Sooner or later, such an administration becomes wholly venal; and then the peace enjoyed under kings is worse than the disorder of interregnums.

What has been done to forestall these evils? Crowns have been made hereditary in certain families; and an order of succession has been established to eliminate all occasions for dispute at the death of kings. In other words, by substituting the disadvantages of a regency for those of an interregnum, people have preferred apparent tranquillity to wise administration, and have thought it better to risk having children, monsters or imbeciles for rulers, than to have to dispute over the choice of good kings. They have not taken into consideration the fact that, in exposing themselves to the risks of this alternative, they are making a gamble in which the odds are almost wholly against them. There was much good sense in the remark that the younger Dionysius made to his father when the latter, reproaching him for some shameful action, asked: ' Did I set you the example?' ' No,' replied the son, ' but your father was not a king.'

In the case of a man brought up to rule others, almost everything conspires to deprive him of justice and reason. Much trouble is taken, so they say, to teach young princes the art of ruling; they do not seem to profit by this education. It would be better to begin by teaching them the art of obeying. The most famous kings of history were not brought up to rule; this is a science in which we are never less accomplished than when we have learned too much, and one which is better acquired by obeying than by commanding. 'For the best, and also the shortest way of finding out what is good and what is bad is to consider what you would or would not have wished to have happen if another than you had been emperor.'

One consequence of this lack of coherence is to make royal government inconstant, for since it follows now one plan and now another, depending on the character of the prince who is reigning, or of the people who are reigning in his stead, it cannot long have a fixed objective or a consistent line of policy; this variability keeps the state continually wavering from principle to principle and from project to project, and is to be found in none of the other forms of government, where the prince is always the same. Thus, in general, it can be seen that, though there may be more wiliness in courts, there is more wisdom in a senate, and that republics proceed toward their objectives with more constant and coherent views; whereas in a monarchy each revolution in the ministry produces one in the state, the principle common to all ministers, and to nearly all kings, being to do in all respects the reverse of what their predecessor did.

This same incoherence also enables us to solve a sophistry very familiar to the theorists of monarchy; this sophistry consists not only in comparing civil government with domestic government, and the prince with the father of the family, an error we have already refuted, but also in endowing this magistrate liberally with all the virtues he would need, and in assuming always that the prince is what he ought to be; and if we make this assumption, royal government is obviously preferable to any other, because it is undeniably the strongest, and in order to be also the best it requires only a corporate will more in conformity with the general will.

But if, according to Plato, the king by nature is so rare a personage, how often will nature and fortune combine to give him a crown? And if the education of kings necessarily corrupts those who receive it, what hope can there be for a succession of men brought up to rule? It is wilful self-deception, therefore, to confuse royal government with the rule of a good king. To see what this form of government is like in itself, we must consider what it is like under stupid or wicked princes; for they will either be stupid or wicked when they come to the throne, or else the throne will make them so.

Our authors have not failed to notice these difficulties, but they are not troubled by them. The remedy, they say, is to obey without a murmur; God sends bad kings in His wrath, and they must be borne as heavenly chastisements. Such talk is no doubt edifying; but I am not sure that it would not be more suitable in a pulpit than in a book on politics. What would you say of a physician who promises miracles, and whose only skill consists in exhorting his invalid to be patient? We are well aware that we must suffer a bad government when we have one; the question would be to find a good one.

Chapter VII

MIXED GOVERNMENTS

STRICTLY speaking, there is no such thing as a simple government. A single ruler must have subordinate magistrates; a popular government must have a head of state. In the distribution of executive power, therefore, there is always a gradation from the greater to the lesser number, the difference being that sometimes the greater number depends on the lesser, and sometimes the lesser on the greater.

Sometimes there is an equal distribution; this may occur either when the constituent parts are in a condition of mutual dependence, as in the government of England, or when the authority of each part is independent but imperfect, as in Poland. This last form is bad, since there is no sort of unity in the government, and the state lacks bonds of union.

Which is better, a simple or a mixed government? This is a question much debated by political theorists, and requires the same answer that I have already given with regard to all forms of government.

Simple government is the best in itself, for the very reason that it is simple. But when the executive power is not sufficiently dependent on the legislative, in other words when the ratio of prince to sovereign is greater than the ratio of people to prince, this disproportion must be remedied by dividing the government; for then its several parts have no less authority over the subjects, and their division reduces their total power as against the sovereign.

The same difficulty is also forestalled by setting up intermediary magistrates who leave the government intact, and serve merely to balance the two powers and maintain their respective rights. Then the government is not mixed, but tempered.

The opposite difficulty can be remedied by similar means, and when the government is too weak, committees may be created to give it greater concentration. This is the practice of all democracies. In the first case the government is divided in order to weaken it, and in the second case in order to strengthen it. For it is among simple forms that the strongest and the weakest governments alike are to be found; whereas the mixed forms result in moderate strength.

Chapter VIII

THAT NO FORM OF GOVERNMENT IS SUITABLE TO ALL COUNTRIES

Since liberty is not the fruit of all climates, it does not lie within the reach of all peoples. The more one meditates on this principle of Montesquieu's, the more its truth is felt; the more it is disputed, the more occasions does one have to confirm it with new proofs.

In all the governments of the world, the public person consumes without producing. Where does it get the substance it consumes? From the labour of its members. The necessaries of the public are a product of the superfluities of private individuals. From this it follows that the civil state can subsist only in so far as the product of men's labour is greater than their needs.

This surplus is not the same, however, in all the countries of the world. In some it is considerable, in others small, in others nil, in others negative. This ratio of product to need depends on the fertility of the climate, the type of labour the land requires, the nature of its products, the strength of its inhabitants, their greater or lesser consumption needs, and a number of other such factors which go to make up the ratio.

On the other hand, all governments are not of the same nature; some are more, some less voracious; and these differences result from the operation of another general principle, which is that public contributions are burdensome in proportion to the distance from their source. This burden is to be measured not by the quantity of the impositions, but by the distance they have to travel before returning to the hands from which they came. When this circulation is quick and regular, it makes no difference whether much or little is paid; the people continues to be rich, and the public finances to flourish. On the other hand, no matter how little the people gives, if it never gets that little back, it is soon exhausted; the state is never rich, and the people is always impoverished.

From this it follows that, the greater the distance between the people and the government, the more burdensome the taxes become. Thus, in a democracy, the people is least burdened, in an aristocracy it is more so, and in a monarchy it bears the greatest weight of all. Monarchy is only suitable, therefore, to opulent nations, aristocracy to states which are moderate in wealth as well as in size, and democracy to states which are small and poor.

In fact, the more we reflect on the matter, the more clearly do we see that this is the essential difference between free states and monarchies. In the former everything is used for the common welfare; in the latter, public and private resources stand in inverse relation, the former increasing at the expense of the latter. Finally, instead of governing the subjects in order to make them happy, despotism makes them wretched in order to govern them.

In every region, therefore, there are natural causes which make it possible to determine the form of government necessitated by its climate, and even to say what sort of inhabitants it is bound to have.

Ungrateful and sterile places, where the product does not repay the labour, must remain uncultivated and deserted, or peopled only by savages. Places where the labour of men produces just the bare necessities of life must be inhabited by barbarous peoples; no form of polity would be possible there. Places where the surplus of product over labour is small are suitable for free peoples. Those whose abundant and fertile soil produces much with little labour need to be governed monarchically, in order that the luxury of the prince may consume the excessive surplus of the subjects; for it is better that this surplus should be absorbed by the government than that it should be dissipated by individual citizens. I know that there are exceptions; but these very exceptions confirm the rule, for sooner or later they lead to revolutions which restore things to the natural order.

Let us never fail to distinguish between general laws and the particular causes which may modify their effects. If the whole South were covered with republics, and the whole North with despotic states, this would not make it any the less true that, so far as climate is concerned, despotism is suitable to hot countries, barbarism to cold countries, and good polity to the intermediate regions. I can also see that, while granting the general principle, you may dispute its application in particular cases; you may say that there are cold countries which are very fertile, and tropical countries where the soil is very ungrateful. But this difficulty exists only for those who fail to examine all the factors involved. It is necessary, as I have already said, to include in the reckoning such things as labour, strength, and consumption.

Let us assume that there are two equal tracts of land, one of which produces five units and the other ten. If the inhabitants of the first consume four and those of the latter nine, the surplus in the first case will be one-fifth, and in the second one-tenth of the total. These two surpluses stand, therefore, in inverse ratio to the productivities of the two tracts, and the one which produces only five units will yield twice as great a surplus as the one which produces ten.

Actually there is no question of northern lands yielding a double product; and I do not believe that anyone would venture to estimate the general fertility of cold countries even as being equal to that of hot countries. Nevertheless, let us assume this equality; let us, if you wish, equate England with Sicily, and Poland with Egypt. Further south we have Africa and the East Indies; further north, there is nothing. But to achieve this equality of product, what a difference there is in methods of production! In Sicily you have merely to scratch the land; in England, what pains must be taken to till it! And in places where more hands are needed to yield the same product, the surplus must inevitably be less.

Consider, furthermore, that the same number of men consume much less in hot countries. The climate there requires them to be abstemious in order to be healthy; Europeans who try in such regions to live as they do at home all die of dysentery and digestive complaints. 'We are,' says Chardin, 'carnivorous animals, wolves, in comparison with the Asiatics. Some attribute the abstemiousness of the Persians to the fact that their country is less cultivated; but I, on the contrary, believe that their country is less abundant in foodstuffs because the inhabitants need less. If their frugality,' he continues, 'were a result of the poverty of the country, it would be the poor only who ate little, whereas everyone does so; and people would eat more or less from province to province, depending on the fertility of the region, whereas the same abstemiousness is found throughout the kingdom. They are very proud of their way of life, saying that it is necessary merely to look at their complexions to see how much better it is than that of the Christians. And the complexion of the Persians is, indeed, smooth and uniform, and their skin is handsome, fine and glossy; whereas the complexion of their Armenian subjects, who live in the European fashion, is rough and blotchy, and their bodies fat and heavy.'

The nearer you approach the equator, the more frugally do people live. They eat almost no meat; rice, maize, cuscus, millet and casava are their ordinary food. In the East Indies there are millions of people whose nourishment costs less than a cent a day. Even in Europe we see appreciable differences, in the matter of appetite, between northern and southern peoples. A Spaniard could live for a week on the dinner of a German. In countries where men are more voracious, luxury also turns to articles of consumption. In England it is shown by a table loaded down with meat; in Italy, you are regaled on sugar and flowers.

Luxury in clothes again shows similar differences. In climates where seasonal changes are rapid and violent, the clothing is better and simpler; in those where clothing is used only for ornament, showiness is more sought after than utility; clothes themselves are a luxury there. Every day in Naples you will see men promenading on the Posilipo, clad in gold-embroidered jackets, and wearing no breeches. With buildings it is the same story; magnificence is the only consideration, when you have nothing to fear from the weather. In Paris and London you want warm and comfortable lodgings; in Madrid you have superb drawing-rooms, but no windows that can be closed, and you go to bed in a wretched little rat-hole.

Foodstuffs are much more substantial and succulent in hot countries; this is a third difference that cannot fail to affect the second. Why are so many vegetables eaten in Italy? Because they are good, nourishing, and excellent in flavour. In France, where they are fertilised with water only, they are not at all nutritious, and count for little or nothing on the table; but even so they take up no less ground, and cost at least as much pains to cultivate. It has been found that the wheat of Barbary, though in other respects inferior to that of France, yields much more flour; and that French wheat, in turn, yields much more than that of the North. From which it may be inferred that a similar gradation is to be observed in general all the way from the equator to the pole. And is it not obviously disadvantageous to have less nourishment from an equal quantity of produce?

To all these different considerations I may add one more which follows from and reinforces the first; this is that hot countries need fewer inhabitants than cold ones, and are capable of feeding more; and this produces a double surplus, again to the advantage of despotism. The larger the space occupied by the same number of inhabitants, the more difficult does rebellion become; for it is impossible to take concerted action rapidly or in secret, and it is always easy for the government to get wind of plans and cut communications. But the closer together a numerous people lives, the less possible is it for the government to infringe on the sovereign; leaders deliberate as securely in their own homes as the prince in his council, and the mob assembles as quickly in public squares as troops in their quarters. In this respect, therefore, it is to the advantage of a tyrannical government to operate over great distances. By creating bases of operations to serve as a fulcrum, it increases its force, like the force of levers,[1] with distance. The force of the people, on the contrary, operates only when concentrated; it evaporates and disappears with extension, like gunpowder scattered on the ground, which ignites grain by grain only. Thus, the least populous countries are also the most suitable for tyranny; wild beasts reign only in desert places.

Chapter IX

THE SIGNS OF A GOOD GOVERNMENT

IF you ask, therefore, what is absolutely the best form of government, you are raising an indeterminate and thus an insoluble question; or if you prefer, the question is capable of as many correct solutions as there are possible combinations in the absolute and relative situations of peoples.

But if you were to ask what are the signs by which it is possible to know whether a given people is being well or ill governed, it would be a different matter, and the question of fact would be capable of solution.

People do not solve it, however, because each wants to solve it in his own way. Subjects boast of the public tranquillity, citizens of individual liberties; the former prefer security of possessions, the latter personal security; the former would have it that the best government is

[1] This does not contradict what I have already said (BOOK II, chap. 9) about the disadvantages of large states; for there it was a question of the authority of the government over its own members, and here a question of its power over the subjects. Its scattered members give it fulcra to exert distant pressure on the people; but it has no fulcrum to exert direct pressure on these same members. Thus in the one case the length of the lever is its weakness, and in the other its strength.

the harshest, the latter maintain that it is the mildest; the former want crimes to be punished, the latter want them to be prevented ; the former think it a good thing to be feared by one's neighbours, the latter prefer to be ignored by them; the former are content when money circulates, the latter demand that the people should have bread. Even if we were to reach agreement on these and other like points, would we be any nearer to a solution? Since moral quantities have no exact standard of measurement, even if we were agreed as to the sign of good government, how could we be sure that we were estimating any given government correctly?

For my own part, I am constantly astonished that people should fail to recognise, or that they should have the bad faith not to agree upon, a sign that is so simple. What is the purpose of political association? It is the preservation and prosperity of its members. And what is the most certain sign that they are living and prospering? It is the number and increase of the population. Look no further for this much disputed sign. Other things being equal, the government under which, without resort to naturalisation, colonisation and other external means, the citizens live and multiply the most is infallibly the best. That under which a people declines and wastes away is the worst. Statisticians, the business is now yours; count, measure and compare.[1]

---

[1] The same principle should be used to judge which centuries deserve to be called the most favourable to the prosperity of the human race. Too much admiration has been given to those in which the arts and letters were seen to flourish, without inquiring deeply into the hidden reasons for their cultivation, and without considering their fatal effects. ' Fools described as truly human that which was a part of their slavery.' Are we never going to realise that the precepts authors set down in their books are a gross expression of their own self-interest? No, whatever they may say, whenever a country, for all its surface brilliance, is losing population,

Chapter X

THE ABUSE OF GOVERNMENT AND ITS TENDENCY TO DEGENERATE

JUST as the particular will works unceasingly against the general will, so does the government make continuous efforts against the sovereign. The greater these efforts are, the more the constitution changes; and since in this case there is no other corporate will to resist the will of the prince by holding it in balance, the final result, sooner or later, must be for the prince to oppress the sovereign and break the social compact.

---

it is not true that all is going well; and just because a poet enjoys an income of 100,000 francs, it does not follow that his century is the best of centuries. Less attention should be paid to apparent peace and quiet, and to the tranquillity of rulers, than to the well-being of whole nations, particularly the most populous states. A hailstorm may ravage a few cantons, but it rarely causes a famine. Riots and civil wars frighten rulers greatly; but they do not constitute the true misfortune of peoples, who may even find some respite while men dispute as to who shall be tyrant. It is from their permanent condition that their real calamities and prosperities arise. It is when all remain crushed under the yoke that all waste away; it is then that the rulers, destroying them at their ease, ' call it peace when they make solitude.' When the vexations of the great agitated the kingdom of France, and the Bishop Coadjutor of Paris went to the Parlement with a dagger in his pocket, this did not prevent the French people from living happy and numerous in free and honest ease. Greece formerly flourished in the midst of the most cruel wars; blood flowed in streams, and the whole country was covered with men. It seems, says Machiavelli, that the Florentine Republic became all the more powerful for living in the midst of murders, proscriptions and civil wars; the virtue of its citizens, their manners and morals, and their independence had more power to strengthen it than all its dissensions had to weaken it. A little agitation gives vigour to souls; and what really makes the species prosper is not so much peace as liberty.

This is the inherent and inevitable defect which, from the birth of the body politic, tends without respite to destroy it, just as old age and death finally destroy the body of man.

There are, in general, two different ways in which a government degenerates: first, when the government itself contracts and, second, when the state is dissolved.

The government contracts when it passes from a larger to a smaller number; in other words, when it changes from democracy to aristocracy, and from aristocracy to monarchy. This is its natural inclination.[1] If it were to go back from a smaller to a larger number,

[1] The slow formation and evolution of the Republic of Venice in its lagoons is a noteworthy example of this progression; and it is most astonishing that, after more than twelve hundred years, the Venetians do not seem as yet to have proceeded beyond the second stage, which began with the *Serrar di Consiglio* of 1198. As for the ancient dukes who are held against them, it has been proved, whatever the *Squitinio della libertà veneta* may say, that they were not their sovereigns.

People will not fail to cite against me the Roman Republic, which, it will be said, followed an exactly contrary course, passing from monarchy to aristocracy, and from aristocracy to democracy. I am very far from sharing this opinion.

The constitution first established by Romulus was a mixed government, which promptly degenerated into despotism. For special reasons the state perished before its time, just as an infant sometimes dies before reaching the age of manhood. The expulsion of the Tarquins marks the real date of the birth of the Republic. But at first it did not assume a stable form, since the failure to abolish the patriciate meant that the work was only half done. For in view of the fact that hereditary aristocracy, the worst of all legitimate administrations, remained in conflict with democracy, the form of government continued uncertain and wavering, and was not stabilised, as Machiavelli has proved, until the establishment of the tribunes; then only was there a real government and a true democracy. At that time, indeed, the people was not only sovereign, but was also magistrate and judge; the senate was no more than a secondary body designed to temper and concentrate

it could be said to expand; but this reverse movement is impossible.

In fact, the government never changes its form until its mainspring has been so worn out that it is too weak to preserve the original form. If the government were to weaken itself by increasing its numbers, its force would become entirely null, and it would become even less capable of survival. Thus as the mainspring weakens, it must be repaired and tightened; otherwise the state it maintains would fall in ruins.

The dissolution of the state may occur in two different ways.

First, it takes place when the prince no longer administers the state according to law, and usurps the sovereign power. At this point a remarkable change takes place; it is not the government, but the state that contracts; by which I mean that the state as a whole is dissolved, and within it is formed another composed exclusively of members of the government;

---

the government; and the consuls themselves, though patricians, chief magistrates and absolute commanders in war, were in Rome itself no more than presiding officers of the people.

From that moment the government was also seen to assume its natural inclination, and to tend strongly in the direction of aristocracy. The patriciate having abolished itself more or less voluntarily, the aristocracy no longer resided in the body of patricians, as in Venice and Genoa, but in the body of the senate, which was composed of patricians and plebeians, and even in the body of tribunes, when the latter began to usurp active power. For words have nothing to do with things; and when a people has rulers who rule on its behalf, it is still an aristocracy no matter what those rulers are called.

The abuse of aristocracy gave rise to the civil wars and the Triumvirate. Sulla, Julius Caesar and Augustus became true monarchs in fact; and finally, under the despotism of Tiberius, the state was dissolved. Thus Roman history does not in the least contradict my principle; it confirms it.

and this new state, in relation to the rest of the people, is no longer anything more than a master and a tyrant. Thus at the moment when the government usurps sovereignty, the social compact is broken; and the ordinary citizens, having rightfully recovered their natural liberty, are all forced, but not obliged, to obey.

The same situation also arises when the members of the government severally usurp the powers they ought only to exercise as a body; this is no less serious an infraction of the laws, and produces still worse disorder. Then there are, in a manner of speaking, as many princes as there are magistrates; and the state, no less divided than the government, either perishes or changes its form.

When the state is dissolved the resulting abuse of government is known in general as *anarchy*. When the various forms of government are distinguished, the degeneration of democracy is called *ochlocracy*, and that of aristocracy *oligarchy*. I might also add that the degeneration of monarchy is known as *tyranny;* but this last word is ambiguous, and requires explanation.

In the popular sense of the word, a tyrant is a king who governs violently and without regard for law and justice. Precisely speaking, a tyrant is a private individual who arrogates the royal authority to himself without having any right thereto. That is how the Greeks understood the word *tyrant*, and they applied it indiscriminately to good or bad princes whose authority was not legitimate.[1] Thus the words *tyrant* and *usurper* are completely synonymous.

[1] 'For all those are called and considered tyrants who exercise perpetual power in a city accustomed to liberty' (Cornelius Nepos, *Life of Miltiades*, chap. 8). It is true that Aristotle (*Nicomachean Ethics*, BOOK VIII, chap. 10) distinguishes between the tyrant and the king by saying that the former governs for his own

To distinguish different things by different names, I call the usurper of royal authority a *tyrant*, and the usurper of sovereign power a *despot*. The tyrant is one who presumes, in defiance of law, to rule in accordance with law; the despot is one who places himself above the law itself. Thus a tyrant need not be a despot, but a despot is always a tyrant.

CHAPTER XI

THE DEATH OF THE BODY POLITIC

SUCH is the natural and inevitable inclination of the best constituted governments. If Sparta and Rome have perished, what state can hope to live for ever? If we want, therefore, to create a durable system of legislation, we must not think of making it eternal. If we are to succeed, we must not attempt the impossible, nor flatter ourselves that we can give the works of man a stability of which human things are incapable.

The body politic, no less than the body of man, begins dying from the moment of birth, and bears within itself the seeds of its destruction. But both may have a constitution which is either more or less robust, and likely to preserve it for a longer or shorter time. The constitution of man is a work of nature, that of the state a work of art. It is not within the power of men to

advantage, and the latter solely for the advantage of his subjects; but apart from the fact that all the Greek authors generally used the word *tyrant* in a different sense, as appears above all in the *Hiero* of Xenophon, it would follow from Aristotle's distinction that from the beginning of time there would never yet have been a single king.

prolong their lives; but it is within their power to prolong the life of the state as far as possible, by giving it the best constitution it is capable of having. The best constituted state will come to an end; but it will end later than another, unless some unforeseen accident destroys it before its time.

The vital force of political life lies in the sovereign authority. The legislative power is the heart of the state and the executive power is the brain, which gives movement to all the members. The brain may become paralysed and the individual still lives. A man goes on living as an imbecile; but as soon as the heart stops functioning, the animal is dead.

It is not by laws that the state subsists, but by the legislative power. Yesterday's law has no binding force today; but tacit consent is presumed from silence, and the sovereign is supposed to be continuously confirming those laws which it could, but does not, abrogate. Whatever it once has said it wills, it continues to will, unless it revokes it.

Why then do people pay so much respect to ancient laws? Precisely because they are ancient. We can only believe that it was the excellence of these ancient decisions that made it possible for them to last so long, for if the sovereign had not constantly found them salutary, it would have had innumerable opportunities to revoke them. That is why, far from growing weaker, laws acquire ever new strength in any well-constituted state; ancient precedent makes them every day more venerable; and wherever, on the contrary, laws grow weaker with age, it is a proof there is no longer any legislative power, and that the state has ceased to exist.

Chapter XII

HOW THE SOVEREIGN AUTHORITY IS MAINTAINED

The sovereign, having no other force than the legislative power, acts only through laws; and since the laws are nothing but authentic acts of the general will, the sovereign can only act when the people is assembled. A people assembled, you will say, what a chimera! It is a chimera nowadays, but two thousand years ago it was not. Has human nature changed?

The limits of the possible, in moral matters, are less narrow than we think; it is our weaknesses, our vices, our prejudices that restrict them. Base souls do not believe in great men; vile slaves smile contemptuously at the word *liberty*.

On the basis of what has been done, let us consider what it is possible to do. I shall not speak of the republics of ancient Greece; but the Roman Republic was, I think, a large state, and the city of Rome a large city. The last republican census gave Rome as having four hundred thousand citizens capable of bearing arms; and the last imperial census showed more than four million citizens, exclusive of subjects, foreigners, women, children and slaves.

What a problem it would seem to be to call into frequent assembly the immense populace of this capital and its environs! And yet few weeks passed when the Roman people was not assembled, and even several times. Not only did it exercise the rights of sovereignty, but also some of the rights of government. It negotiated certain pieces of business, it judged certain lawsuits, and when the whole of this people was in the public forum, it was almost as often in the capacity of magistrates as in that of citizens.

If we were to go back to the earliest history of nations, we should find that most ancient governments, even those which, like the Macedonian or the Frankish, were monarchies, had similar councils. In any case, the example of Rome alone is sufficient to settle the question; if we can show that a thing has existed, I think we are justified in concluding that it is possible.

CHAPTER XIII

THE SAME CONTINUED

It is not enough for the people in a single assembly to have determined the constitution of the state, by sanctioning a body of law; it is not enough for it to set up a permanent government, or provide once and for all for the election of magistrates. Apart from extraordinary assemblies, which unforeseen circumstances may require, there must also be fixed and periodic ones which can in no wise be abolished or prorogued, so that on a designated day the people will be legitimately convened by the law itself, without requiring any other formal convocation.

But with the exception of these assemblies, authorised by their date alone, any assembly of the people which has not been convened by the magistrates designated for that purpose, and in accordance with the prescribed forms, must be held illegal, and all its actions null and void; for the order to assemble should itself emanate from the law.

The question as to how frequent these lawful assemblies ought to be depends on so many considerations that no precise rules can be laid down in the matter. It is only possible to say in general that, the stronger the government, the more frequently the sovereign ought to show itself.

This, you will say, may be good for a single city; but what is to be done when the state includes several? Is the sovereign power to be parcelled out? Or should we concentrate it in a single city, and place all the rest under subjection?

My answer is that we should do neither. In the first place, the sovereign authority is a simple unity, and it cannot be divided without being destroyed. In the second place, a city cannot, any more than a nation, be legitimately subjected to another; for the essence of the body politic lies in the concurrence of obedience and liberty, and the words *subject* and *sovereign* are identical correlatives whose meaning is conjoined in the single word *citizen*.

I answer further that it is always bad to unite several cities in a single republic; and that if you try to create such a union, you must not flatter yourself that you will avoid its natural disadvantages. This is one of the abuses of large states, and should not be raised as an objection to the ideas of one who wants all states to be small. But how can small states be made strong enough to resist large ones? The answer is to do as the Greek cities once did in resisting the Great King, and as Holland and Switzerland more recently have done in resisting the House of Austria.

If the state cannot be reduced to its proper limits, however, there is still one resource left; this is to allow it to have no capital city, to have the government sit in all the cities successively, and likewise to convene the national assembly in each by turn.

Populate the whole territory equally, extend everywhere the same rights, bring prosperity and life to every region; in that way the state will become both as strong and as well governed as it is capable of being. Remember that the walls of cities are only built from the wreckage of farm houses. Every time I see a palace being erected in the capital, I have visions of a whole countryside being reduced to living in hovels.

Chapter XIV

THE SAME CONTINUED

THE moment the people is lawfully assembled as a sovereign body, the whole jurisdiction of the government ceases, the executive power is suspended, and the person of the meanest citizen is as sacred and inviolable as that of the chief magistrate; for in the presence of the person represented, the representative no longer exists. Most of the tumults which arose in the assemblies of Rome came from having neglected, or from having been ignorant of, this rule. In the assemblies the consuls were but presiding officers of the people, the tribunes but speakers; [1] and the senate was nothing at all.

These intervals of suspension, during which the prince does or should recognise a present superior, have always been redoubtable to it; and these assemblies of the people, which are the aegis of the body politic and the restraint of governments, have at all times been the horror of rulers; thus the latter regularly spare no efforts, objections, obstructions or promises

[1] In much the same sense in which the word is used in the English Parliament. The similarity of their functions would have brought the consuls and the tribunes into conflict even if all jurisdiction had been suspended.

to discourage the citizens from holding them. When the citizens are greedy, lazy, pusillanimous, and more enamoured of repose than of liberty, they do not long hold out against the redoubled efforts of the government. That is how, as the force of resistance constantly increases, the sovereign authority finally vanishes, and most states fall and perish before their time.

But between sovereign authority and arbitrary government there is sometimes introduced an intermediate power of which we now must speak.

CHAPTER XV

DEPUTIES OR REPRESENTATIVES

As soon as public service ceases to be the main business of citizens, and they prefer to serve with their purses rather than with their persons, the state is already on the brink of ruin. Is it necessary to go forth to war? They hire troops and remain at home. Is it necessary to take counsel? They appoint deputies and remain at home. By dint of laziness and money, they end by having mercenaries to enslave their country, and representatives to sell it.

Preoccupation with commerce and the arts, greedy interest in profits, effeminacy and love of comfort, these are the motives that convert personal services into money payments. People give up a part of their profits in order that they may have leisure to increase them. Give money, and you will soon have chains. *Public finance* is a slavish word unknown to republics. In a truly free country, the citizens do everything with their own hands, nothing with money; far from paying to be exempted from their duties, they would pay for the privilege of performing them in person. I am far from taking the common view; I consider corvées to be less inconsistent with liberty than taxes.

The better the state is constituted, the more does public rather than private business preoccupy the minds of citizens. The amount of private business will even be greatly reduced, for the aggregate of common happiness will constitute a larger fraction of the happiness of each individual, and he will therefore have less happiness to seek on his own account. In a well conducted republic, everyone rushes to the assemblies; under a bad government no one likes to move a step in that direction, because no one has any interest in what is done there, because it is foreseen that their proceedings will not be dominated by the general will, and finally because domestic interests are all-absorbing. Good laws cause better laws to be made, while bad ones lead to worse. As soon as any man says of the affairs of the state, ' What do I care ? ', the state should be accounted lost.

The cooling off of love of country, the activity of private interest, the immensity of states, conquests, and the abuse of government have suggested the device of sending deputies or representatives of the people to the assemblies of the nation. This is what, in some countries, has presumptuously been called the Third Estate, which means that the particular interest of two classes is placed in the first and second place, the public interest in the third only.

Sovereignty cannot be represented, for the same reason that it cannot be alienated. It consists essentially in the general will, and will cannot be represented; will either is, or is not, your own; there is no intermediate possibility. Thus deputies of the people are not, and cannot be, its representatives; they are merely its agents, and can make no final decisions. Any law which the people has not ratified in person is null and void; it is not a law. The English people thinks it is free; it is very much mistaken. It is free only when it is electing members of parliament; as soon as they are elected, it is enslaved and reduced to nothing. The use it makes of its liberty, during these brief moments, shows that it well deserves to lose it.

The idea of representatives is modern; it comes to us from the feudal system, that absurd and iniquitous government which degrades the human species, and dishonours the name of man. In the republics and even in the monarchies of antiquity, the people never had representatives; the very word was unknown. In Rome, where the tribunes were so sacrosanct, it is remarkable that no one ever so much as dreamed that they could usurp the functions of the people; and that in the midst of so great a multitude they never tried to pass a single plebiscite on their own authority. And yet the difficulties occasionally caused by such a crowd may be judged by what happened in the time of the Gracchi, when a part of the citizens cast their votes from the rooftops.

Where rights and liberties are everything, no difficulties are too great. Among this wise people, everything was given its proper value; it allowed its lictors to do what its tribunes would never have dared to do, for it had no fear that its lictors would try to represent it.

To explain, however, the way in which the tribunes sometimes did represent it, we need only think of the way in which the government represents the sovereign. Since law is only a declaration of the general will, it is clear that the people cannot be represented in the legislative power; but it can and must be represented in the executive power, which is merely the enforcement of law. This shows that, if the matter were properly examined, we should find that very few nations have laws. Be that as it may, it is certain that the tribunes, since they had no share in the executive power, were never able to represent the Roman people by virtue of their own office, but only by usurping the functions of the senate.

Among the Greeks, the people did for itself everything it had to do; it remained constantly assembled in the market-place. It lived in a mild climate; it was not greedy; slaves did its work; its primary business was its liberty. Lacking the same advantages, how can you preserve the same rights? Your harsher climates add to your needs;[1] for six months of the year the public square is uninhabitable; your muffled tongues cannot be heard in the open air; you are more interested in profit than in liberty; and you are much less afraid of slavery than of poverty.

What is this? Can liberty be maintained only on the basis of slavery? Perhaps. The two extremes meet. All artificial things have disadvantages, civil society most of all. There are some unfortunate situations where you can only preserve your own liberty at the expense of the liberty of others, and the citizen can only be perfectly free if the slave is extremely enslaved. Such was the case in Sparta. As for you, modern peoples, you have no slaves, but you are slaves yourselves; you have bought their freedom at the price of your own. It is in vain that you boast of this choice; I find in it more cowardice than humanity.

By all this I do not mean that it is necessary to have slaves, nor that the right of slavery is legitimate, since

[1] To adopt in a cold climate the luxury and effeminacy of orientals is to desire to assume their chains; it makes submission even more inevitable for us than it is for them.

I have proved the contrary. I am simply showing why modern peoples, which consider themselves free, have representatives; and why the peoples of antiquity did not. Be that as it may, as soon as a people gives itself representatives, it is no longer free, and no longer exists.

All things considered, I do not see how any future sovereign can preserve its rights among us unless the republic is very small. But if it is very small, will it be subjugated? No. I shall show hereafter [1] how it is possible to combine the external power of a large people with the simple administration and good order of a small state.

Chapter XVI

THAT THE ESTABLISHMENT OF GOVERNMENT IS NOT A CONTRACT

Once the legislative power has been properly established, it remains likewise to establish the executive power; for the latter, which operates only through particular acts, is essentially different from the former, and is therefore naturally separate from it. If it were possible for the sovereign, as such, to have the executive power, right and fact would be so confounded that it would no longer be possible to tell what was law and what was not; and the body politic, thus perverted, would soon fall prey to the violence against which it was instituted.

[1] This is what I had intended to do in the unwritten portion of this work when, in dealing with foreign relations, I came to confederations. The subject is wholly new, and its principles are yet to be established.

Since the citizens all are equal under the social contract, all may prescribe what all must do; but·no one has a right to require another to do anything he does not do himself. Yet this is the very right, indispensable to the giving of life and movement to the body politic, that the sovereign confers on the prince by instituting government.

Many have maintained that this act of establishing a government was a contract between the people and the rulers of its choosing, a contract whereby the two parties stipulated the conditions under which the one was obliged to command and the other to obey. You will agree, I am sure, that this is a strange way of making contracts. But let us see if this opinion is tenable.

In the first place, the supreme authority is no more capable of modification than of alienation; to limit it is to destroy it. It is absurd and contradictory for the sovereign to give itself a superior; to oblige yourself to obey a master is to return to absolute freedom.

Furthermore, it is obvious that this contract between the people and certain specific persons would be a particular act; from which it follows that it could be neither a law nor an act of sovereignty, and would therefore be illegitimate.

It can also be seen that the mutual relations of the contracting parties would be subject to the law of nature alone, and that there would be no sanction for their reciprocal engagements, all of which is in every respect repugnant to the civil state. Since he who has force at his command can always determine how the act will be executed, it would be like giving the name of a contract to the act of a man who said to another: ' I will give you all my property, on condition that you give me back as much of it as you like.'

There is only one contract in the state, the contract of association, and that in itself precludes all others. It is impossible to conceive of any public contract which would not be in violation of the first.

Chapter XVII

THE ESTABLISHMENT OF GOVERNMENT

In what terms then should we conceive of the act by which the government is instituted? I shall begin by remarking that this act is complex, being made up of two others, first the establishment of the law, and second its execution.

By the first, the sovereign decrees that some particular form of governmental body shall be set up; and it is clear that this act is a law.

By the second, the people appoints the rulers who are to be entrusted with the government thus established. Now this appointment, being a particular act, is not a second law, but simply a consequence of the first, and an act of government.

The difficulty is to see how an act of government can take place before the government exists; and how the people, which is sovereign or subject only, can become a prince or magistrate in certain circumstances.

Here once again the body politic reveals those astonishing properties whereby it reconciles apparently contradictory operations. For in this case the act is accomplished by a sudden transformation of sovereignty into democracy, with the result that, without any visible change and simply by means of a new relation of all to all, the citizens become magistrates and move from general acts to particular acts, from law to execution.

III. XVIII: MEANS OF FORESTALLING USURPATION

This change of relationship is by no means a speculative subtlety unexampled in practice, for it takes place every day in the Parliament of England, where the lower house, on certain occasions, turns itself into a committee of the whole for the better discussion of affairs, and thus becomes a mere agent of the sovereign body which it itself was a moment earlier; so that later it reports to itself, in its capacity as House of Commons, on what it has just decided in its capacity as committee of the whole, and again debates under one name what it has already resolved under another.

The peculiar advantage of democratic government is that it can be established in fact by a simple act of the general will. Thereafter this provisional government remains in possession, if democracy is the form adopted, or else sets up, in the name of the sovereign, the government prescribed by law; and everything is thus in order. It is impossible otherwise to set up the government in any way which is legitimate, and which does not violate the principles already established.

CHAPTER XVIII

MEANS OF FORESTALLING USURPATIONS OF GOVERNMENT

FROM these explanations it follows, in confirmation of Chapter 16, that the act which establishes the form of government is not a contract, but a law; that the depositaries of the executive power are not the masters of the people, but its officials; that the people can appoint and remove them at its pleasure; that there is no question for them of contracting, but of obeying; and that in assuming the functions the state puts upon them, they are doing no more than to fulfil their duty as citizens, and have no right whatever to argue over the conditions of their mandate.

Thus when the people decides to institute a hereditary government, whether it be a monarchy vested in a single family or an aristocracy vested in a particular class of citizens, it is in no sense assuming any obligations; the form it gives to the administration is provisional, and continues until the people is pleased to ordain otherwise.

It is true that such changes are always dangerous, and that an established government must never be touched until it becomes incompatible with the public welfare. But this circumspection is a precept of political prudence, not a rule of right; and the state is no more bound to leave civil authority with its rulers than to leave military authority with its generals.

It is also true that, in such cases, every possible attention must be paid to all those formalities which are required to distinguish a regular and legitimate act from a seditious tumult, and the will of a whole people from the clamour of a faction. It is in such cases, above all, that we are obliged to construe the law as strictly as possible. And it is also from this obligation that the prince derives a great advantage for the conservation of his power in defiance of the people, without it being possible to say that he has usurped it. For while appearing to do no more than exercise his rights, he finds it very easy to extend them, and to prevent, under pretext of the public peace, assemblies designed to re-establish good order; with the result that he makes use of the silence which he prevents from being broken, and of the irregularities which he causes to be committed, to claim in his favour the tacit consent of those who are kept silent by fear, and to punish those who dare to speak. It is thus that the decemvirs, first elected for one year and then continued for another, tried to keep their power in perpetuity by no longer permitting the assemblies to meet; and it is by this simple means that all the governments of the world, once the public force is in their hands, sooner or later usurp the sovereign authority.

The periodic assemblies of which I have already spoken are calculated to forestall or postpone this misfortune, above all when they require no formal convocation; for then the prince could not prevent them without openly declaring himself a lawbreaker, and an enemy of the state.

The opening of these assemblies, whose sole purpose is the maintenance of the social contract, should always be marked by two motions which can never be quashed, and are separately voted.

The first is: ' Does it please the sovereign to continue the present form of government? '

The second is: ' Does it please the people to leave the administration of that government in the hands of those who are presently entrusted with it? '

All this rests on the assumption, which I think I have already proved, that there is no fundamental law in the state which cannot be revoked, not even the social compact. For if all the citizens came together to break this compact by common accord, there would be no doubt that it was very legitimately broken. Grotius even believes that each individual can renounce the state of which he is a member, and recover his natural liberty and his goods by leaving the country.[1] And it would be absurd for all the citizens together to be unable to do what each one of them could do separately.

---

[1] Provided, of course, that we are not leaving to evade our duties, and to exempt ourselves from serving our country at the moment when she needs us. Flight then would be criminal and punishable; it would no longer be withdrawal, but desertion.

BOOK IV

CHAPTER I

THAT THE GENERAL WILL IS INDESTRUCTIBLE

IN so far as several men conjoined consider themselves as a single body, they have but a single will, which refers to their common conservation and to the general welfare.   Then all the motive forces of the state are vigorous and simple, its principles are clear and luminous ; it has no quarrelling and contradictory interests; the common good is everywhere clearly evident, and requires no more than common sense to be perceived. Peace, unity and equality are the enemies of political subtlety.   Upright and simple men are hard to deceive because of their simplicity; they are in no way imposed upon by wiles and subtle pleadings; they are not even clever enough to be dupes.   When, among the happiest people on earth, you see crowds of peasants deciding affairs of state under an oak-tree, and behaving with uniform wisdom, how can you help despising the subtleties of other nations, which devote so much skill and mystification to making themselves famous and wretched?

A state thus governed has need of very few laws; and as soon as it becomes necessary to promulgate new ones, this necessity is universally recognised.   The first to propose them does no more than to say what all have already felt; and it requires neither intrigue nor eloquence to secure the enactment of that which each has already decided to do, as soon as he is sure that the others will do likewise.

What deceives the theorists is the fact that, seeing nothing but states badly constituted from the beginning, they are impressed with the impossibility of maintaining such a polity among them. They laugh at the thought of all the stupidities that an adroit rascal, an insinuating talker, could persuade the people of Paris or London to commit. They fail to realise that Cromwell would have been drummed out of town by the people of Berne, and the Duc de Beaufort given the cat-o'-nine-tails by the Genevans.

But when the social bond begins to loosen and the state to grow weak, when particular interests begin to make themselves felt and lesser associations to influence the whole, then the common interest deteriorates and encounters opposition; unanimity no longer prevails in voting; the general will ceases to be the will of all; contradictions and debates arise; and the best opinion does not go by any means undisputed.

Finally, when the state, on the brink of ruin, maintains no more than a vain and illusory existence, when the social bond is broken in every heart, when the basest interest brazenly flaunts the sacred name of public good, then the general will falls silent; guided by secret motives, no one thinks as a citizen any more than as if the state had never existed; and under the guise of laws are enacted iniquitous decrees whose only purpose is to further private interests.

Does this mean that the general will is annihilated or corrupted? No, it is always constant, unalterable and pure; but it is subordinated to other interests which prevail over it. Each individual, when he detaches his interest from that of the community, is clearly aware that the two are not entirely separable; but his share of the common misfortune is as nothing to him in comparison with the exclusive benefit he hopes to appropriate to himself. Apart from this particular benefit, he seeks the general benefit, in his own interest, as vigorously as anyone else. Even when he sells his vote for money, he does not extinguish, but eludes, the general will within him. His fault lies in changing the terms of the question, and in answering one different from the one he has been asked; with the result that, instead of saying with his vote, ' It is advantageous to the state,' he says, ' It is advantageous to a certain individual or to a certain party that a certain proposal should be enacted.' Thus the maintenance of public order in assemblies depends not so much on maintaining the general will as on ensuring that it will always be interrogated, and that it will always answer.

There are many reflexions which I might make at this point on the mere right to vote in any act of sovereignty, a right of which the citizens can in no circumstances be deprived; and on the right to express an opinion, to initiate, to separate and to discuss, which government is always at great pains to confine to its own members. But this important subject would need a treatise in itself; I cannot deal with everything here.

Chapter II

VOTING PROCEDURES

From the preceding chapter it can be seen that the way in which general matters are handled is capable of giving us a fairly accurate indication of the current state of manners and morals and the health of the body politic. The more agreement there is in assemblies, that is to say, the more nearly unanimous their opinions are, the more also does the general will prevail; but long debates, dissensions and tumult announce the ascendancy of private and particular interests and the decline of the state.

This seems less obvious when two or more distinct classes enter into the composition of the state, as was the case in Rome with the plebeians and the patricians, whose quarrels even in the heyday of the Republic often disturbed her assemblies. But this exception is more apparent than real; for then, because of the defect inherent in the body politic, there were, in a manner of speaking, two states in one, and what is not true of the two together is severally true of each. And after all, even in the most troubled times, the plebiscites of the people, when the senate did not intervene, were always passed quietly and by a large majority; for the citizens had a single interest only, the people but a single will.

At the end of the cycle, unanimity again is found; this takes place when the citizens, reduced to servitude, no longer have either liberty or will. Then fear and flattery change voting into acclamation; people no longer deliberate; they either curse or adore. Such was the base way in which the senate expressed its opinion under the emperors. Sometimes it took absurd precautions while doing so. Tacitus observes that, under the Emperor Otho, the senators heaped execrations on Vitellius, and at the same time were careful to make such a frightful din that, if perchance the latter should become master, he would not be able to know what each of them had said.

From these various considerations arise the general principles by which one ought to regulate the method of counting votes and comparing opinions, depending on whether the general will is more or less easy to recognise, and the state more or less decadent.

There is only one law which, by its very nature, requires unanimous consent; this is the social compact. For civil association is the most voluntary act in the world; since every individual is born free and his own master, no one is able, on any pretext whatsoever, to subject him without his consent. To decide that the son of a slave is born a slave is to decide that he is not born a man.

If, therefore, at the time of the social compact there are opponents to it, their opposition does not invalidate the contract, but simply prevents them from being included in it; they are foreigners dwelling among citizens. When the state is instituted, residence is consent; to dwell in a territory is to submit to its sovereign.[1]

Except for the original contract, the majority always binds the minority; this is a consequence of the contract itself. But it may be asked how a man can be free, and yet compelled to comply with wills which are not his own. How can the opposition be free, and at the same time subject to laws to which it has not consented?

My answer is that the question is badly framed. The citizen consents to all the laws, even to those which have been passed over his opposition, and even to those which punish him for any violation. The constant will of all the members of the state is the general will; that is what makes them citizens and free.[2] When a law is

[1] This should always be understood as applying to free states only. For elsewhere family, property, compulsion, violence and lack of asylum may always hold an inhabitant unwillingly in the country; and then his mere residence no longer presupposes his consent to the contract, or to the violation of the contract.

[2] In Genoa, the word *libertas* is inscribed on the front of prisons and on the fetters of galley-slaves. This use of the motto is splendid

proposed in the assembly of the people, what the voters are being asked is not precisely whether they do or do not approve of the proposal, but whether or not it is in conformity with the general will, which is their own. Each, when casting his vote, gives his opinion on this question; and the declaration of the general will is found by counting the ballots. Thus when an opinion contrary to my own prevails, this proves nothing more than that I was mistaken, and that what I thought to be the general will was not. If my private opinion had prevailed against it, I should have done something I did not intend; and it is then that I would not have been free.

This assumes, to be sure, that all the characteristics of the general will continue to be found in the majority. When this ceases to be true, whatever action is taken there is no more liberty.

In my earlier discussion of the ways in which particular wills supplant the general will in public deliberations, I have sufficiently indicated the practicable ways of forestalling that abuse; I shall have more to say on the subject later on. With regard to the fraction of the total vote needed to declare this will, I have also given the general principles by which to decide the question. A single vote makes the difference between a majority and a minority; a single opponent destroys unanimity. But between unanimity and a bare majority, there are many qualified majorities, each of which may be used as the population of the state and the needs of the body politic may require.

Two general principles may serve to determine these

and just. Actually it is the malefactors in all walks of life who alone prevent the citizen from being free. In a country where all of their sort were in the galleys, the most perfect liberty would be enjoyed.

proportions; the first is that the more important and crucial the decision is, the more nearly unanimous should be the opinion which prevails; the second is that, the more speedy the decision required by the matter in hand, the smaller should be the required margin of agreement; on questions which have to be decided immediately, a majority of one must suffice. The first of these principles seems the more suited to the enactment of laws, the latter to the handling of specific business. In any case, it is by combining these two principles that we can determine the size of the majority needed to pronounce on any given question.

CHAPTER III

ELECTIONS

WITH regard to the selection of the prince and of the magistrates, which are, as I have said, complex acts, there are two possible modes of procedure, namely, election and sortition. Both have been used in various republics, and a very complicated mixture of the two procedures is still found at the present time in the election of the doge of Venice.

'Selection by lot,' says Montesquieu, 'is natural to democracy.' I agree, but why so? 'The lot,' he continues, 'is a method of selection which affronts no one; it gives each citizen a reasonable hope of serving his country.' These are not reasons.

If we pay due attention to the fact that the selection of rulers is a function of government, and not of sovereignty, we shall see why the method of sortition is more natural to democracy, where the best administration is the one which is least active.

In any true democracy, public office is not an

advantage but a heavy responsibility, which cannot justly be imposed on one rather than on another. The law alone can impose this burden on anyone whom the lot designates. For then, since the conditions are equal for all, and the choice depends on no human will, there is no specific application to impair the universality of the law.

In an aristocracy the prince chooses the prince; the government preserves itself by its own efforts; and it is there that elections lead to good results.

The example of the election of the doge of Venice, far from refuting this distinction, confirms it; this mixed form is suitable to a mixed government. For it is a mistake to take the government of Venice as a true aristocracy. Although the common people there have no part in the government, the Venetian nobility itself is a people. It includes a multitude of poor Barnabites [1] who never came within striking distance of any magistracy, and whose nobility gives them nothing but the empty title of *Excellency*, and the right to attend the grand council. Since this grand council is as large as our general council at Geneva, its illustrious members are no more privileged than our simple citizens. It is obvious that, if we discount the extreme disparity of the two republics, the burghers of Geneva are exactly comparable to the patricians of Venice, our natives and inhabitants to the citizens and people of Venice, our peasants to its mainland subjects; and so, apart from the question of size, this republic, no matter how we look at it, is after all no more aristocratic than our own. The only difference is that we, having no ruler for life, do not have the same need for sortition.

Selection by lot would have few disadvantages in a true

[1] [The lesser nobles, resident in the St Barnabas district.—Tr.]

democracy, where the fact that all are equal in manners, morals and talents, as well as in political beliefs and fortune, means that it would make little difference who was chosen. But I have already said that there is no such thing as a true democracy.

When election and sortition are combined, the former should fill those positions which demand particular talents, such as military offices. The latter is appropriate for those where common sense, justice, and integrity are sufficient, as is the case with judicial offices; for in a well constituted state, these qualities are common to all citizens.

Neither sortition nor election has any place in monarchical government. Since the monarch is by right the sole prince and magistrate, the choice of his lieutenants belongs to him only. When the Abbé de Saint-Pierre proposed to multiply the councils of the King of France, and to elect their members by ballot, he did not realise that he was proposing to change the form of government.

I might go on to speak of the methods of casting and counting votes in the assembly of the people. But perhaps, in this respect, the history of the Roman polity will explain the matter more graphically than all the general precepts I could establish. A judicious reader will not find it beneath his dignity to see in some detail how public and private business was conducted in a council of two hundred thousand men.

CHAPTER IV

THE ROMAN ASSEMBLIES

WE have no very certain records of the earliest days of Rome. It even seems very probable that most of the stories told about those days are fables; [1] and it is generally true that the most instructive part of the annals of peoples, namely the history of their foundation, is the one most lacking to us. Experience daily teaches us the causes of revolutions in empires; but since peoples are no longer being created, we have little more than conjecture to go on in explaining how they were formed.

The usages that we find already in existence prove, at least, that they originated somehow. Of the traditions which go back to the earliest period, those which are supported by the best authorities, and in themselves are the most reasonable, should be accepted as the most certain. These are the principles I have tried to follow in investigating how the freest and most powerful people on earth exercised its supreme power.

After the foundation of Rome, since the new Republic, that is to say, the army of the founder, was composed of Albans, Sabines and foreigners, it was divided into three classes which were consequently known as *tribes*. Each of these tribes was subdivided into ten curias, and each curia into decuries, at the head of which were rulers known as *curions* and *decurions*.

In addition, there was drawn from each tribe a body of one hundred knights, or cavalrymen, known as a *century;* from which it can be seen that these divisions, hardly necessary in the city itself, were at first purely military. But it seems that an instinct of greatness led the little town of Rome to give itself in advance a polity suitable to the capital of the world.

From this first division a difficulty soon arose; this came from the fact that the tribes of the Albans and

[1] The name *Rome*, which is supposed to be derived from *Romulus*, is Greek, and means *force:* the name *Numa* is also Greek, and means *law*. How likely is it that the first two kings of this city were called in advance by names so appropriate to their accomplishments?

the Sabines remained constant, while that of the foreigners grew continuously as more and more foreigners came in, with the result that it soon became larger than both the others. The remedy Servius found for this dangerous abuse was to change the division; and in the place of the distinction by races, which he abolished, to substitute another based on the section of the city occupied by each of the tribes. Instead of three tribes he created four, each of which occupied one of the hills of Rome, and bore its name. Thus, while remedying the existing inequality, he prevented others from arising in the future; and in order that this division might not be merely a division of places, but also of men, he forbade the inhabitants of one quarter to move to another, which prevented the races from losing their identity.

He also doubled the three old centuries of knights, and added to them twelve others, but still kept the old names, a simple and judicious measure by which he succeeded in distinguishing the body of knights from that of the common people, without causing the latter to grumble.

To these four urban tribes Servius added fifteen others, called *rustic tribes*, because they were made up of the inhabitants of the countryside, divided into as many cantons. Subsequently fifteen more new ones were created; and in the end the Roman people found itself divided into thirty-five tribes, a number which remained unchanged down to the end of the Republic.

From this distinction between urban and rustic tribes there followed a consequence which is worthy of remark, since it is unexampled, and since Rome owed to it both the preservation of her manners and morals and the increase of her empire. You would think that the urban tribes would soon have arrogated power and honours to themselves, and would not have been slow to degrade the rustic tribes; but the contrary happened. The taste of the early Romans for country life is well known. This taste they owed to the wise legislator who united rustic and military labour with liberty, and who may be said to have relegated to the city the arts and crafts, the professions, intrigue, wealth and slavery.

Since, therefore, the most illustrious men of Rome all lived in the country and tilled the soil, people grew used to looking there only for mainstays of the Republic. The farmer's calling being that of the worthiest patricians, it was universally honoured; the simple and industrious life of the villagers was preferred to the loose and idle life of the Roman burghers; and a man who in the city would have been nothing but a wretched proletarian became a respected citizen when he tilled the soil. It is not without reason, Varro said, that our magnanimous ancestors made villages the nursery of those robust and valiant men who defended them in time of war and fed them in time of peace. Pliny states positively that the rustic tribes were honoured because of the men who composed them; while idlers were degraded by being transferred ignominiously to the urban tribes. When Appius Claudius the Sabine moved to Rome, he was loaded with honours, and enrolled in a rustic tribe, which thereafter took the name of his family. Finally, freedmen all joined the urban, never the rustic tribes; and throughout the Republic there is not a single example of one of these freedmen, citizen though he had become, being elected to any magistracy.

This principle was excellent; but it was pushed so far that it finally led to a change, and certainly to an abuse, in the polity.

First, the censors, having long since arrogated to themselves the right to transfer citizens arbitrarily from tribe to tribe, permitted most of them to enrol in the one of their choice, a privilege which certainly served no useful purpose, and deprived the censorship of one of its great springs of action. Furthermore, since the great and powerful all had themselves enrolled in the rustic tribes, and the freedman upon acquiring citizenship remained in the urban tribes along with the common people, the tribes generally lost their local and territorial character, but were all so intermingled that it was no longer possible to identify the members of each without consulting the rolls; with the result that the meaning of the word *tribe* shifted from the real to the personal, or rather it became little more than a fiction.

It also happened that the urban tribes, being nearer to hand, often found themselves predominant in the assemblies, and sold the state to those who deigned to buy the votes of the rabble who composed them.

With regard to the curias, since the founder had set up ten in each tribe, the whole Roman people, which at that time lived within the walls of the city, was composed of thirty curias, each with its own temples, gods, officers and priests, and with its own festivals, known as *compitalia*, which were like the *paganalia* subsequently held by the rustic tribes.

When Servius made his new division, this number of thirty could not be divided equally between his four tribes, and he did not wish to change it; thus the curias, independent of the tribes, became another division of the inhabitants of Rome. But among the rustic tribes and tribesmen, there was no question of curias; for now that the tribes were a purely civil institution, and another system had been introduced for the levying of troops, the military divisions of Romulus had become superfluous. Thus, although

125

every citizen was enrolled in a tribe, there were a great
many who were not enrolled in a curia.

Servius also made a third division, which had no
connexion with the two preceding, and became in its
effects the most important of all He distributed the
whole Roman people into six classes, which he distinguished neither on an individual nor on a geographical basis, but by wealth, filling the first two
classes with the rich, the last two with the poor, and the
middle two with men of moderate means. These six
classes were subdivided into one hundred and ninety-
three other bodies, called *centuries;* and these bodies
were so distributed that the first class alone comprised
more than half, and the last a single one only. Thus it
came about that the class with the smallest number of
men had the largest number of centuries, and that the
last class counted only as a single subdivision, though it
alone contained more than half the inhabitants of
Rome.

In order that the people might less clearly see the
consequences of this last arrangement, Servius pretended
to give it a military character; he included in the
second class two centuries of armourers, and two of
weapon-makers in the fourth. In each class, except
the last, he distinguished between the young and the
old, that is to say, between those obliged to bear arms
and those legally exempt on grounds of age; and this
distinction, even more than the property qualification,
made it necessary to carry out a census or enumeration
at frequent intervals. Finally, he prescribed that the
assembly should be held on the Campus Martius, and
that those of military age should come bearing arms.

The reason why he did not follow this same division
of old and young in the last class is that the populace,
of which it was composed, were not accorded the honour

of bearing arms for their country; only the owners of hearths had the right to defend them. And of all the countless hordes of beggars who today are the glory of royal armies, there is perhaps not a single man who would not have been expelled with disdain from a Roman cohort, in the days when soldiers were the defenders of liberty.

Within the last class, nevertheless, a distinction was also made between the *proletarians* and those who were called *capite censi*. The former, not wholly reduced to nothingness, at least gave citizens to the state, and sometimes even soldiers in time of pressing need. As for those who had nothing at all and could only be counted by heads, they were regarded as absolutely nil, and Marius was the first to deign to enrol them.

Without deciding here whether this third classification was good or bad in itself, I believe it possible to affirm that it would never have been practicable if it had not been for the simple manners and morals of the early Romans, their unselfishness, their taste for agriculture, and their contempt for trade and the profit motive. Where can you find a modern people among whom devouring avidity, restlessness, intrigue, continuous changes of residence, and perpetual reversals of fortune would have allowed such a system to continue for twenty years without upsetting the whole state? It should also be observed that even in Rome it was the manners and morals of the people and the institution of the censorship which, by proving stronger than the system itself, corrected its defects, and that any rich individual found himself relegated to the class of the poor if he made too much show of his wealth.

From all this it is easy to see why there is almost never any mention of more than five classes, although there were really six. The sixth, which provided neither soldiers for the army nor voters for the Campus Martius,[1] and which had almost no use in the Republic, was rarely taken into account.

Such were the different divisions of the Roman people. Let us now see what effect they had in the assemblies. These assemblies, when legitimately convened, were called *comitia;* they were ordinarily held in the Roman forum or in the Campus Martius, and were distinguished as *curiate, centuriate* or *tribal* assemblies, depending on which of the three divisions was being used. The curiate assembly was derived from the system of Romulus, the centuriate from that of Servius, and the tribal from that established by the tribunes of the people. No law was sanctioned and no magistrate elected except in the assemblies; and since there was no citizen who was not enrolled either in a curia, a century or a tribe, it follows that no citizen was excluded from the right of suffrage, and that the Roman people was truly sovereign *de facto* and *de jure.*

For the assemblies to be legitimately assembled, and for their proceedings to have the force of law, three conditions had to be fulfilled: first, the magistrate or body which convened them had to be vested with the authority to do so; second, the assembly had to take place on one of the days allowed by law; third, the auguries had to be favourable.

The reason for the first rule requires no explanation. The second was a matter of policy; thus the holding of assemblies was not permitted on holidays and market days, when the country people, having come to Rome on business, did not have time to spend the day in the

---

[1] I say 'for the Campus Martius' because that was where the centuriate assemblies met. In the two other forms of assembly, the people met in the forum or elsewhere, and then the *capite censi* had as much influence and authority as the leading citizens.

forum. By the third rule the senate held in check a proud and restless people, and properly restrained the ardour of seditious tribunes; but the latter found more than one means of escaping this constraint.

Laws and the election of rulers were not the only questions submitted to the judgment of the assemblies. Since the Roman people had usurped the most important functions of the government, it may be said that the fate of Europe was determined in these gatherings. This variety of objects gave rise to the various forms assumed by these assemblies, depending on the questions to be decided.

To judge these various forms, it is sufficient to compare them. Romulus, in founding the curias, had it in mind to use the people to restrain the senate and the senate to restrain the people, while dominating both alike. In this form of assembly, therefore, he gave the people the full authority of numbers to balance the authority of power and wealth, which he left to the patricians. But, in accordance with the spirit of monarchy, he nevertheless left the advantage with the patricians, because of the influence their clients had in determining popular majorities. This admirable institution of patrons and clients was a masterpiece of politics and humanity, without which the patriciate, so contrary to the spirit of the Republic, would have been unable to survive. Rome alone has had the honour of setting the world this splendid example, which never led to abuses, and yet has never been followed.

Since this curiate form of assembly continued under the kings down to Servius, and since the reign of the last Tarquin was not accounted legitimate, the laws of the royal period were generally distinguished by the name of *leges curiatae*.

Under the Republic the curias, still limited to the

four urban tribes, and no longer containing anything but the population of Rome itself, were necessarily displeasing both to the senate, which led the patricians, and to the tribunes, who, though plebeians, were leaders of the well-to-do citizens. They accordingly fell into discredit; their degradation was such that their thirty lictors met in their name and did the things the curiate assemblies ought to have done.

The division by centuries was so favourable to the aristocracy that it is not at first easy to see why the senate did not always have its way in the assemblies which bore this name, and by which the consuls, censors and other curule magistrates were elected. Actually, of the one hundred and ninety-three centuries which constituted the six classes of the entire Roman people, the first comprised ninety-eight, and since the votes were counted by centuries only, this first class alone had more votes than all the rest together. When all these centuries were in agreement, the rest of the votes were not even taken; what the least numerous class had decided was taken as a decision of the multitude; and it may be said that, in the centuriate assemblies, matters were determined by majorities of wealth rather than of votes.

But this extreme authority was tempered in two ways. First, since the tribunes ordinarily, and a large number of plebeians always, were members of the wealthy group, they counterbalanced the influence of the patricians in this first class.

The second way was this, that instead of having the centuries vote in order, which would always have meant beginning with the first, one was drawn by lot, and that alone [1] proceeded to elect; after which, on

[1] The century thus drawn by lot was called *praerogativa*, because it was the first required to vote; and that is the origin of the word *prerogative*.

another day, all the centuries having been summoned in order of rank, they repeated the same election, and generally confirmed it. Thus the authority of example was taken away from rank and given to the lot, according to the democratic principle.

This custom had still another advantage, which was to give citizens from the country time, between the two elections, to inform themselves as to the merit of the candidate provisionally appointed, and thus to cast their ballots only when well-informed. But under the pretext of celerity, a successful attempt was finally made to abolish this custom, and both elections were held the same day.

The tribal assemblies were strictly the council of the Roman people. They were convened by the tribunes only; they elected the tribunes and passed their plebiscites. Not only did the senate have no standing in them, it did not even have the right to be present; and since the senators were forced to obey laws on which they had not been able to vote, they were in this respect less free than the lowliest of citizens. This injustice was a great mistake, and in itself was enough to invalidate the decrees of a body to which all its members were not admitted. If all the patricians had attended these assemblies in accordance with their rights as citizens, they would hardly have been able, now that they had become no more than mere private individuals, to influence a form of voting which was counted by heads, and in which the lowliest proletarian counted for as much as the prince of the senate.

Thus it can be seen that these divisions were not just convenient and mutually interchangeable ways of collecting the votes of so numerous a people, but that each had effects relative to the purposes of those who gave it the preference.

Without going into the matter in further detail, it follows from the explanations already given that the tribal assemblies were the most favourable to popular government, and the centuriate assemblies the most favourable to aristocracy. With regard to the curiate assemblies, in which the populace of the city of Rome itself formed the majority, since they were suitable only to the favouring of tyranny and evil designs, they necessarily fell into discredit, and even the seditious abstained from using a means which too clearly exposed the nature of their plans. It is clear that the whole majesty of the Roman people resided in the centuriate assemblies only; for the rustic tribes were lacking in the curiate assemblies, and the senate and patricians were lacking in the tribal assemblies.

As for voting methods, among the early Romans they were as simple as their manners and morals, though not so simple as in Sparta. Each man gave his vote orally, and a clerk recorded it; a majority of votes in each tribe determined the vote of that tribe, and a majority of tribes determined the vote of the people; and the same was true of curias and centuries. This practice was good as long as honesty reigned among the citizens, and each was ashamed to vote publicly for an unjust proposal or an unworthy candidate. But when the people grew corrupt and votes were bought, it became proper for them to be cast secretly, in order that the purchasers might be held back by distrust, and rascals given the opportunity not to be traitors.

I know that Cicero disapproves of this change, and considers it partly responsible for the ruin of the Republic. But conscious as I am of the weight which must be given to Cicero's authority in the matter, I am not of his opinion; on the contrary, I believe that the ruin of the state was accelerated by the failure to make enough changes of this sort. Just as the regimen of healthy people is not suitable for invalids, we should not try to govern a corrupt people by the same laws as are suitable to a good people. Nothing does more to prove the truth of this principle than the longevity of the Venetian Republic, which still retains a simulacrum of existence for the sole reason that its laws are suited to wicked men only.

Thus, the citizens were given ballots which enabled each to vote without revealing his opinion. New procedures were also established to govern the collection of ballots, the counting of votes, the comparison of their number, etc., all of which did not prevent the honesty of the officers entrusted with these functions from being frequently suspect. And finally, to prevent intrigue and the buying and selling of votes, edicts were passed the very number of which is proof of their ineffectiveness.

Toward the end of the Republic, it often became necessary to resort to extraordinary expedients to supplement the inadequacies of the law. Prodigies were sometimes invented, but this method, though it might deceive the people, did not deceive their rulers; sometimes an assembly was convened suddenly, before the candidates had time to carry out their intrigues; sometimes a whole session was taken up with idle talk, when it was seen that the people had been won over, and was about to make a bad decision. But ambition in the end overcame all obstacles; and the incredible thing is that so numerous a people, in the midst of so many abuses, still continued, by virtue of its ancient regulations, to elect the magistrates, to enact the laws, to judge lawsuits, and to expedite private and public business, and this with almost as much facility as the senate itself could have shown.

Chapter V

THE TRIBUNATE

WHEN it is impossible to establish an exact proportion between the constituent parts of the state, or when inevitable causes constantly worsen their relationships, then a particular magistracy is established, one which stands apart from the others, restores the proper balance between them, and constitutes a link or middle term between the prince and the people, or between the prince and the sovereign, or if necessary between all three.

This body, which I shall call the *tribunate*, is the preserver of the laws and of the legislative power. Sometimes it serves to protect the sovereign against the government, as the tribunes of the people did in Rome; sometimes to support the government against the people, as the Council of Ten now does in Venice; and sometimes to maintain the balance in both directions, as the ephors did in Sparta.

The tribunate is in no sense a constituent part of the republic, and should have no share in the executive or legislative power. But its own power is for that reason all the greater; for although it can do nothing, it can prevent anything from being done. As the defender of the laws it is more sacred and revered than the prince who executes them, and the sovereign who gives them. This was clearly seen in Rome, where the haughty patricians, who always held the people as a whole in contempt, were forced to bow before a mere officer of the people, who had neither auspices nor jurisdiction.

The tribunate, wisely tempered, is the strongest support of a good constitution; but if its force is in the least excessive, it upsets everything. As for its being too weak, that is not in the nature of the institution; and if it is anything at all, it is never less than it ought to be.

It degenerates into tyranny when it usurps the executive power, which it ought only to moderate, and when it tries to dispense with the laws, which it ought only to protect. The immense power of the ephors, which was not dangerous as long as Sparta preserved her manners and morals, accelerated her decline as soon as she began to grow corrupt. The blood of Agis, murdered by these tyrants, was avenged by his successor; both the crime and the punishment alike hastened the fall of the Republic; and after Cleomenes Sparta was no longer anything. Rome also perished in the same way; and the excessive power of the tribunes, gradually usurped, served in the end, with the aid of laws made in the interests of liberty, to protect the emperors who destroyed liberty. As for the Council of Ten in Venice, it is a bloody tribunal, horrible alike to the patricians and to the people; and one which, far from giving high protection to the laws, does nothing more, now that the laws have been debased, than strike, under cover of darkness, blows which no one dares to notice.

The tribunate, like the government, becomes weaker as its numbers increase. When the tribunes of the Roman people, first two, then five in number, wanted to double this latter number, the senate allowed them to do so, being very sure of its ability to use some to check the rest; and this did not fail to happen.

The best means of forestalling the usurpations of so redoubtable a body, a means of which no government has as yet bethought itself, would be to make it impermanent, and to provide fixed intervals during which it would lie in abeyance. These intervals, which should not be long enough to allow the abuses of time to become inveterate, may be so fixed by law that they can easily be shortened when necessary by extraordinary commissions.

This method seems to me to offer no disadvantages, since the tribunate, as I have said, is no part of the constitution, and thus can be eliminated without causing it to suffer; and it seems efficacious, since a newly reestablished magistrate does not start from the position of power occupied by his predecessor, but from that which the law gives him.

CHAPTER VI

DICTATORSHIP

THE inflexibility of the laws, which prevents them from adapting themselves to the course of events, may render them pernicious in certain cases and make them the ruin of the state in time of crisis. Orderly and leisurely procedures require a period of time which circumstances do not always permit. Innumerable cases may arise which the legislator has by no means foreseen; and to realise that you cannot foresee everything is a very necessary form of foresight.

You must not try, therefore, to strengthen political institutions to the point of depriving yourselves of the power to suspend their operation. Sparta herself allowed her laws to slumber.

But only the greatest dangers are great enough to equal the danger of changing the public order; and the sacred power of the laws must never be suspended unless it is a question of saving the country. In these rare and apparent cases, the public security is provided for by a particular act which entrusts it to him who is most worthy. This commission may be given in two different ways, depending on the nature of the danger.

If, in order to counteract it, it is sufficient to increase the activity of the government, its powers are concentrated in one or two of its members; in this case it is not the authority of the laws that is changed, but simply the form in which they are administered. But if the peril is such that the apparatus of law itself is an obstacle to security, then you must appoint a supreme ruler who will silence all the laws and suspend the sovereign authority for the time being. In such cases, there is no doubt as to the general will, and it is evident that the primary intention of the people is that the state should not perish. Thus the suspension of the legislative authority does not in the least abolish it. The magistrate who causes it to be silent cannot make it speak; he dominates it without being able to represent it. He can do everything, except make laws.

The first means was used by the Roman senate when, by a hallowed formula, it charged the consuls to provide for the safety of the Republic. The second took place when one of the two consuls appointed a dictator,[1] a custom which Rome had borrowed from Alba.

In the early days of the Republic, recourse was very often had to dictatorship, because the state was not as yet firmly enough established to be able to maintain itself merely by the force of its constitution.

Since manners and morals at that time rendered superfluous many of the precautions which would have been necessary in another period, there was no fear either that a dictator would abuse his authority, or that

[1] This appointment was made secretly, and by night, as if it were shameful to place a man above the laws.

he would try to keep it beyond its proper term. It seemed, on the contrary, as if so great a power were a burden to those entrusted with it, so great was their hurry to divest themselves of it; it was as if replacing the laws had been a post too painful and perilous to be long endured.

Thus my complaint against the imprudent use of this supreme magistracy in the early days is not that it was in danger of being abused, but that it was in danger of being cheapened. For by wasting it on elections, dedications and purely formal acts, it was to be feared that it would become less terrible in time of need, and that people would come to regard as an empty title one which was used only in empty ceremonies.

Toward the end of the Republic the Romans, now grown more circumspect, were as unreasonably sparing in their use of dictatorship as they had formerly been prodigal. It was easy to see that their fears were ill-founded; that the weakness of the capital was now its insurance against the magistrates in its midst; that a dictator could defend the public liberty in certain cases without ever being able to make attempts upon it; that the chains of Rome would not be forged in Rome herself, but in her armies. The feeble resistance put up by Marius against Sulla, and by Pompey against Caesar, showed clearly how little internal authority could be expected to accomplish against external force.

This error caused the Romans to commit serious mistakes, such as, for example, their failure to appoint a dictator in the Catiline affair. For considering that this involved nothing more than the city itself, or at most a few Italian provinces, a dictator would easily have been able, with the unlimited authority legally at his disposal, to break up the conspiracy, whereas it was actually suppressed only by a series of lucky accidents on which human prudence ought never to have relied.

Instead of appointing a dictator, the senate contented itself with transferring all its powers to the consuls. This made it necessary for Cicero, in the interests of effective action, to exceed his powers in one important respect; and although the first transports of joy made people approve of his conduct, it was with justice that they subsequently called him to account for illegally shedding the blood of citizens, a reproach which could not have been levelled against a dictator. But the eloquence of the consul bore all before it; and he himself, though a Roman, set personal glory ahead of country, and was less interested in trying to find the safest and most lawful means of saving the state, than in gaining the whole credit for himself.[1] Thus he was justly honoured as the liberator of Rome, and justly punished as a lawbreaker. However creditable his recall from exile may have been, there can be no doubt that it was an act of pardon.

It should be observed, in conclusion, that no matter how this important commission is conferred, it is important that it should be granted for a very short period which should never be capable of extension. In the crises which require its establishment, the state is soon lost or saved; and as soon as the pressing need is past, dictatorship becomes either tyrannical or useless. In Rome, where the dictators held office for six months only, most of them abdicated before the end of their term. If the term had been longer, they might have been tempted to prolong it still further, as did the decemvirs, whose term was for a year. The dictator

---

[1] He could not have been sure of this if he had suggested the appointment of a dictator, for he did not dare appoint himself, and he could not be certain that his colleague would appoint him.

had only time enough to provide against the need which had caused him to be elected; he did not have enough to contemplate other plans.

Chapter VII

THE CENSORSHIP

Just as the law is the means whereby the general will declares itself, the censorship is the means of declaring the judgment of the people. Public opinion is a species of law which the censor administers, and which he, like the prince, merely applies in specific cases.

Thus the censorial body, far from being the arbiter of the opinion of the people, is merely its enunciator; and as soon as it departs from that opinion, its decisions are null and void.

It is useless to distinguish the manners and morals of a nation from the objects of its esteem; for both come from the same principles, and are necessarily intermingled. Among all the peoples on earth, it is not nature, but opinion, which determines the choice of their pleasures. Reform the opinions of men, and their manners and morals will automatically be purified. People always love the beautiful, or that which they think to be so; but it is on this latter judgment that they deceive themselves, and this judgment is, therefore, the thing to be regulated. Whoever judges manners and morals judges honour; and he who judges honour takes opinion as his law.

The opinions of a people arise from its constitution. Although the law does not regulate manners and morals, it is legislation that causes them to arise; when legislation weakens, manners and morals degenerate.

But then the judgment of the censors will not accomplish what the force of the laws has not.

From this it follows that the censorship may be useful in preserving manners and morals, but never in restoring them. Establish censors while the laws are still vigourous; as soon as their vigour is lost, there is no hope; nothing legitimate continues to have force when the laws no longer do.

The censorship preserves manners and morals by preventing opinions from growing corrupt, by preserving their rectitude through wise applications, sometimes even by making them definite when they are still uncertain. The use of seconds in duels, which had been carried to an insane point in the Kingdom of France, was abolished merely by the words of a royal edict entitled: ' Concerning those who are so cowardly as to call upon seconds.' This judgment, by anticipating that of the public, decided the question immediately. But when royal edicts tried to pronounce that it was also cowardly to fight a duel, which is very true but contrary to the common opinion, the public laughed at this decision, on which it had already made up its own mind.

I have said elsewhere [1] that, since public opinion is not subject to constraint, there should be no trace of coercion in the body set up to represent it. We cannot too much admire the skill with which this motive force, entirely lost among the moderns, was set in operation among the Romans, and still better among the Lacedaemonians.

When a man of bad moral character made a good proposal in the Spartan assembly, the ephors, without paying any attention to him, had a virtuous citizen make the same proposal. What an honour for the one,

[1] In this chapter I am merely outlining things discussed at greater length in my *Letter to M. d'Alembert.*

what a rebuke to the other, even though neither of them had been blamed or praised! Certain drunkards from Samos [1] polluted the tribunal of the ephors; the next day, by public edict, Samians were given permission to be vile. A real punishment would have been less severe than such an act of impunity. When Sparta pronounced on questions of good conduct, Greece did not appeal against her judgments.

Chapter VIII

CIVIL RELIGION

In the beginning, men had no other kings than the gods, and no other government than theocracy. They reasoned like Caligula, and in this case they were right. It takes a long time for ideas and sentiments to change to the point where men can bring themselves to take other men as masters, and to flatter themselves that this will be to their advantage.

For the very reason that God was placed at the head of each political society, it followed that there were as many gods as peoples. Two peoples who were foreign to one another, and almost always enemies, could not long recognise a single master, for two armies engaged in battle could hardly obey a single commander. Thus national divisions resulted in polytheism, and hence in that theological and civil intolerance with which it is naturally identified, as we shall see hereafter.

The fantastic notion of the Greeks that they were always rediscovering their own gods among the barbarians came from their equally fantastic notion that

[1] They actually came from another island [Chios.—Tr.], which the delicacy of our language here prevents us from calling by name.

they were the natural sovereigns of those same peoples. But in our own times it is ridiculous pedantry to keep speculating on the identity of the gods of various nations; as if Moloch, Saturn and Chronos could be the same god; as if the Baal of the Phoenicians, the Zeus of the Greeks and the Jupiter of the Latins could be the same; as if there could be anything in common between imaginary beings bearing different names!

If you ask how it happened that in a pagan world where each state worshipped its own gods, there were no wars of religion, my answer is that this was due to the very fact that each state, having its own cult just as it had its own government, made no distinction between its gods and its laws. Political warfare was also theological; the sphere of gods was determined, so to speak, by the boundaries of nations. The god of one people had no rights over other peoples. The gods of the pagans were in no sense jealous gods; they divided the governance of the world between them. Even Moses and the Hebrew people sometimes lent themselves to this idea by speaking of the God of Israel. It is true that they denied the existence of the gods of the Canaanites, a proscribed people which was destined for destruction, and whose place they were to occupy. But see how they spoke of the gods of neighbouring peoples whom they were forbidden to attack: ' Is not the possession of what belongs to your god Chamos lawfully your due? ' said Jephthah to the Ammonites. ' We have the same title to the lands our conquering God has made his own.' [1] This was, in my opinion, a full

---

[1] *Nonne ea quae possidet Chamos deus tuus, tibi jure debentur?* (Judges, xi. 24). Such is the text of the Vulgate. Father de Carrières has translated it as follows: ' Do you not think you have the right to possess that which belongs to your god Chamos? ' I do not know the implications of the Hebrew text, but I can see that, in the

recognition of parity of right as between Chamos and the God of Israel.

But when the Jews, as subjects of the kings of Babylon and clients of the kings of Syria, stubbornly tried to refuse to recognise any god beside their own, this refusal was regarded as rebellion against the conqueror, and thus brought upon them those persecutions of which we read in their history, and of which there was no other example before the advent of Christianity.[1]

Thus each religion was exclusively attached to the laws of the state which prescribed it, and the only way to convert a people was to place it under subjection, the only missionaries were conquerors; and since the obligation to change cults was the law of the vanquished, it was necessary to begin by conquering before speaking of such a change. So far were men from fighting for the gods, that it was the gods, as in Homer, who fought for men; everyone asked for victories from his own deity, and paid for them with altars. The Romans, before storming a fortress, called upon its gods to abandon it; and when they let the Tarentines keep their angry gods, it was in the belief that those gods were by then subject to their own, and forced to do them homage. They let the vanquished keep their own gods just as they let them keep their own laws. A crown dedicated to the Jupiter of the Capitol was often the only tribute they levied.

When the Romans finally had extended their cult and their gods along with their empire, and when they

---

Vulgate, Jephthah positively recognises the rights of the god Chamos, and that the French translator weakens this recognition with an ' according to you ' which is not in the Latin.

[1] According to the latest evidence, the Phocian war, known as the *Sacred War*, was not a war of religion. Its purpose was to punish sacrilege, and not to bring miscreants under subjection.

themselves had often adopted those of the vanquished by granting the vanquished and their gods alike the rights of citizenship, the peoples of this vast empire gradually found themselves with multitudes of gods and cults which everywhere were more or less the same; and that is how paganism, within the known world, became in the end one and the same religion.

These were the circumstances under which Jesus came to establish a spiritual kingdom on earth, a kingdom which, by separating the theological system from the political system, deprived the state of its unity, and gave rise to those intestine divisions which have never ceased to agitate Christian peoples. Now in view of the fact that this new idea of a heavenly kingdom had never entered the head of the pagans, they always regarded the Christians as mere rebels who, under a hypocritical mask of submission, were simply awaiting the opportunity to make themselves independent and dominant, and adroitly to usurp the authority which, in their weakness, they pretended to respect. That was the cause of the persecutions.

The thing the pagans feared came to pass. The face of things immediately changed; the humble Christians began to sing a different tune; and the so-called heavenly kingdom soon revealed itself, under a visible ruler, as the most violent of worldly despotisms.

But since, nevertheless, there is always a prince and civil laws, this double power has resulted in an unending jurisdictional conflict which has made any sort of good polity impossible in Christian states; and it has never been possible to decide, once and for all, whether it is the ruler or the priest who ought to be obeyed.

Nevertheless many people, even in Europe or its environs, have tried to preserve or re-establish the ancient system, but without success. The spirit of

Christianity has swept all before it. The religious cult has always retained, or recovered, its independence of the sovereign, and has remained without any necessary connexion with the body of the state. Mohammed had very sound ideas; he kept his political system well unified; and as long as his form of government continued under the caliphs who succeeded him, that government remained strictly unitary, and therefore good. But the Arabs having become prosperous, literate, polished, soft and cowardly, they were conquered by barbarians; then the separation of the two powers began again. Although it is less apparent among the Mohammedans than among the Christians, it is there none the less, especially in the sect of Ali; and there are states, like Persia, where it has never ceased to be felt.

Among us, the kings of England have set themselves up as heads of the church; the same is true of the Czars. But in doing so, they have given themselves less mastery than the churchmen; they have acquired the right not so much to change the church as to preserve it; in it they are not legislators, but only princes. Wherever the clergy forms a body,[1] it is master and legislator in all that concerns it. Thus there are two powers, two sovereigns, in England and Russia just as everywhere else.

Of all the Christian authors, the philosopher Hobbes is the only one who clearly saw the evil and its remedy,

[1] It should be observed that it is not so much formal assemblies, like those of France, which bind the clergy into a body, as the communion of churches. Communion and excommunication are the social compact of the clergy, a compact which will always make them the master of peoples and kings. All priests who communicate together are fellow-citizens, even though they are at opposite ends of the earth. This invention is a political masterpiece. There was nothing like it among the pagan priests, and that is why they never constituted a body of clergy.

who dared to suggest reuniting the two heads of the eagle, and fully restoring that political unity without which no state or government will ever be well-constituted. But he should have seen that the prevailing spirit of Christianity was incompatible with his system, and that the interest of the priest would always be stronger than that of the state. It is not so much that which is false and horrible in his political theory, as that which is just and true, that has made him odious.[1]

I believe that, if the facts of history were investigated from this point of view, it would be easy to refute the opposing views of Bayle and Warburton, the former of whom asserts that no religion is useful to the body politic, while the latter maintains, on the contrary, that Christianity is its strongest support. To the former it could be demonstrated that no state was ever founded without having religion as its basis; and to the latter that the Christian law is fundamentally more harmful than useful to the vigorous constitution of the state. To make my meaning wholly clear, it is necessary merely to define rather more precisely this extremely vague word religion, so far as it relates to my subject.

Religion, considered with reference to society, which is either general or particular, may likewise be divided into two species, private and civic. The first, without temples, altars and rites, and limited to the purely interior cult of omnipotent God and the eternal duties of morality, is the pure and simple religion of the Gospels, true theism, and may be called divine natural law. The second, limited to a single country only,

[1] See, for example, what the learned Grotius, in his letter to his brother dated 11 April 1643, approves and disapproves in the *De cive*. It is true that, in an indulgent mood, he seems to forgive the author the bad for the sake of the good, but not everyone is so merciful.

147

gives that country its special patrons and tutelary deities. Its dogmas, its rites, and its external cult are prescribed by law; outside of the single nation which follows it, it regards everything as infidel, foreign and barbarous; it extends the rights and duties of man no farther than its altars. Such was the religion of all early peoples, and we may call it civil or positive divine law.

There is a third, more bizarre sort of religion which, by giving men two systems of legislation, two rulers and two countries, subjects them to contradictory duties, and prevents them from being devoted at once to god and to country. Such is the religion of the lamas, the Japanese, and the Roman Catholics. This may be called priestly religion. It results in a kind of mixed and unsociable law, for which there is no name.

When these three kinds of religion are considered from a political standpoint, each has its faults. The third is so obviously bad that it is a waste of time to go to the trouble of proving it. Anything which breaks the unity of society is worthless; all institutions which set man at odds with himself are worthless.

The second is good, in so far as it combines divine worship with love of the laws and, by making the country the object of the adoration of its citizens, teaches them that to serve the state is to serve its tutelary deity. It is a species of theocracy in which there should be no other pontiff than the prince, and no other priests than the magistrates. Then, to die for your country is to suffer martyrdom; to violate its laws is to be impious; and to deliver a criminal to public execration is to hand him over to the wrath of the gods: *Sacer esto*.

But it is bad in that, being founded on mistakes and lies, it deceives men, makes them credulous and super-stitious, and drowns the true cult of the Deity in empty ceremonial. It is also bad when, becoming exclusive and tyrannical, it makes a people bloodthirsty and intolerant; with the result that it lives only for murder and massacre, and thinks it is performing a holy action when it kills anyone who does not recognise its gods. The result is to place such a people in a natural state of war with all others, which is extremely harmful to its own security.

And so there remains the religion of man, or Christianity, not the Christianity of our own times but that of the Gospels, which is wholly different. By this holy, sublime and true religion, men, as children of the same God, recognise that they are all brothers; and the society which unites them is not even dissolved by death.

But this religion, since it has no specific relation to the body politic, leaves the laws with nothing more than their own intrinsic force, without adding another force to them; and thus one of the great bonds uniting particular societies remains without effect. Nay more, instead of binding the hearts of citizens to the state, Christianity detaches them from it, as from all worldly things. I know of nothing more contrary to the social spirit.

We are told that a people of true Christians would constitute the most perfect society imaginable. As I see it, this supposition has only one major difficulty, which is that a society of true Christians would not be a society of men.

I would even say that the society thus postulated would, for all its perfection, be neither the strongest nor the most enduring. By being perfect it would lack bonds of union; its very perfection would be its fatal defect.

Everyone would do his duty, and the people would be submissive to the laws; the rulers would be just and moderate, the magistrates honest and incorruptible; the soldiers would have no fear of death; there would be no vanity or luxury. All this is very well; but consider the matter further.

Christianity is a wholly spiritual religion, exclusively concerned with heavenly things; the home country of the Christian is not of this world. It is true that he does his duty; but he does so with profound indifference as to the good or ill success of his efforts. As long as he has no occasion for self-reproach, it matters little to him whether things on earth go well or ill. If the state is prosperous, he hardly dares to enjoy the public felicity; he is afraid that his country's glory will make him proud. If the state is declining, he blesses the hand of God which weighs down upon His people.

For such a society to be peaceful and harmony maintained, it would be necessary for all the citizens, without exception, to be equally good Christians. But if there were unfortunately a single self-seeking man, a single hypocrite, a single Catiline or Cromwell, for example, such a person would very certainly make short work of his pious compatriots. Christian charity does not lightly permit us to think ill of our neighbours. Once a man like this has discovered the trick of imposing on the rest and acquiring some share of public authority, he immediately becomes a man of established position, and God tells us to respect him. Soon he is a power, and God tells us to obey him. Does the depositary of this power use it abusively? It is the scourge of God punishing His children. To drive out the usurper would involve conscientious scruples; it would be necessary to disturb the public peace, use violence, shed blood. All that would hardly be compatible with Christian mildness; and after all, what does it matter, in this vale of tears, whether we are free or slave? The

essential problem is to go to Paradise; and resignation
is just one more way of attaining it.

Are we engaged in some foreign war? The citizens
march readily to battle; none thinks of fleeing; all do
their duty, but without any passionate desire for
victory; they know better how to die than to conquer.
What does it matter whether they are victors or vanquished? Does not Providence know better than they
what is good for them? How edifying their stoicism
will be to a proud, impetuous and impassioned enemy!
Imagine them locked in combat with a people consumed
with the love of glory and country; oppose your
Christian republic to Sparta or Rome. The pious
Christians will be beaten, crushed, destroyed, before
they know it, or they will owe their salvation only to
the contempt in which the enemy will hold them. As
for me, I admire the oath taken by the soldiers of
Fabius, when they swore not to conquer or die, but to
return victorious, and kept their word. Christians
would never have dared to do the like; they would
have been afraid of tempting God.

But I am mistaken in speaking of a Christian republic;
each of these words excludes the other. Christianity
preaches only servitude and dependence. Its spirit is
too favourable to tyranny for tyranny not to profit
always by it. True Christians were made to be slaves;
they know it, and do not really mind; this brief life
has too little value in their eyes.

Christian troops are excellent, we are told. I deny
it. Show me your Christian troops. I myself do not
know of any. You will cite the crusades. Without
questioning the valour of the crusaders, I shall point
out that, far from being Christians, they were the
soldiers of priests, and citizens of the Church. They
were fighting for their spiritual country, which the

Church had mysteriously transformed into a temporal kingdom. Properly speaking, this is a form of paganism. Since the Gospels do not set up a national religion, no religious war is possible among Christians.

Under the pagan emperors, Christian soldiers were brave; all the Christian authors say so, and I believe them; they were vying for honour with the pagan troops. As soon as the emperors became Christian, this emulation ceased; and when the cross had driven out the eagle, all Roman valour disappeared.

But leaving political considerations aside, let us return to the question of law and right, and settle the principles governing this important matter. The right which the social compact gives the sovereign over the subjects does not, as I have said, go beyond the bounds of public utility.[1] Thus citizens have no duty to account for their opinions to the sovereign except in so far as those opinions are important to the community. Now it is very important to the state that each citizen should have a religion which makes him love his duties; but the dogmas of that religion are important neither to the state nor to its members except in so far as they have a bearing on morals and on the duties that he who professes it is bound to fulfil toward others. Apart from this, each may hold any opinions he pleases, without it being the sovereign's function to take cognisance of them. For the sovereign's competence does not extend to the next world, and thus the fate of its subjects in the

[1] ' In the republic,' says the Marquis d'Argenson, ' everyone is perfectly free to do anything that does not harm others.' That is the invariable boundary-line; it cannot be more accurately defined. I have not been able to deny myself the pleasure of quoting occasionally from this manuscript, although it is not known to the public, that I might do honour to a worthy and illustrious man who, even as a cabinet minister, retained the heart of a true citizen, and held upright and sound views on the government of his country.

life to come is none of its business, provided that they are good citizens in the present one.

There is, therefore, a purely civil profession of faith whose articles the sovereign is competent to determine, not precisely as religious dogmas, but as sentiments of sociability, without which it is impossible to be either a good citizen or a faithful subject.[1] Without being able to oblige anyone to believe them, it can banish from the state anyone who does not; it can banish him not for impiety, but for unsociability, for being incapable of sincerely loving law and justice, and of sacrificing his life to his duty when necessary. And if anyone, after having publicly recognised these same dogmas, behaves as if he did not believe them, he should receive the death penalty; he has committed the gravest of crimes; he has lied in the presence of the law.

The dogmas of the civil religion ought to be simple, few, and precisely formulated, without explanations or commentaries. The existence of a powerful, intelligent, benevolent, foreseeing and providential God, the continuance of life after death, the happiness of the just, the punishment of the wicked, the sanctity of the social contract and the laws, these are the positive dogmas. As for the negative dogmas, I would limit them to one only, namely intolerance. It is a feature of the cults we have rejected.

Those who distinguish between civil and theological intolerance are, in my opinion, mistaken. These two forms of intolerance are inseparable. It is impossible

[1] Caesar, in his plea for Catiline, tried to establish the dogma of the mortality of the soul. Cato and Cicero, in refutation, did not take the trouble to philosophise; they contented themselves with showing that Caesar was speaking like a bad citizen, and advancing a doctrine pernicious to the state. That, after all, was the question to be decided by the Roman senate, not a point of theology.

153

to live at peace with people whom you consider damned;
to love them would be to hate the God who punishes
them; you are bound either to save or to torment them.
Wherever theological intolerance is allowed, it cannot
fail to have some civil consequences; [1] and as soon as
it does, the sovereign is no longer sovereign, even in
temporal matters. Henceforth the priests are the real
masters, and the kings are only their officers.

Now that there no longer is, nor can be, any exclusively
national religion, you should tolerate all those which
tolerate others, in so far as their dogmas contain nothing
contrary to the duties of the citizen. But anyone who
dares to say: ' There is no salvation outside the church ',
must be driven out of the state, unless the church is the
state and the prince the pontiff. Such a dogma is
good only in a theocratic government; in any other
it is pernicious. The grounds on which Henry IV is

[1] Since marriage, for example, is a civil contract, it has civil
consequences without which society could not even subsist. Let
us assume, therefore, that a clergy has succeeded in arrogating to
itself the exclusive right to pass on this act, a right which it is bound
to usurp under any intolerant religion. Is it not then clear that by
making the authority of the church prevail in the matter, it will
nullify that of the prince, who will thereafter have no other subjects
than those the priest is pleased to give him? If the clergy is free
to marry or not to marry people, depending on whether they do or
do not share a certain doctrine, whether they do or do not accept
a certain formula, or whether they are more or less pious, is it not
clear that if it acts prudently and holds firm, it alone will dispose
of inheritances, offices, citizens, even of the state itself, which could
hardly subsist if it were composed exclusively of bastards? But, you
will say, an appeal will be made against such abuses; there will
be summonses, decrees, and seizures of church property. What a
pity! If the clergy has, I will not say courage, but common
sense, it will pay no attention and go its way. It will let appeals,
summonses, decrees and seizures continue, and in the end will
remain the master. It is, in my opinion, no great sacrifice to
abandon the part, when you are sure of securing the whole.

said to have embraced the Roman Catholic religion should make every honest man abandon it, and above all every prince who is capable of reason.

Chapter IX

CONCLUSION

AFTER having established the true principles of political law, and having tried to establish the state on that basis, I should now go on to consider its foreign relations, which would include international law, commerce, the right of war and conquest, public law, leagues, negotiations, treaties, etc. But all this is a new subject too vast for my weak vision. I ought never in the first place to have set my sights so high.

CONSIDERATIONS
ON THE
GOVERNMENT OF POLAND
AND ON ITS PROPOSED
REFORMATION

Completed but not published
April 1772

Chapter I

THE NATURE OF THE PROBLEM

COUNT WIELHORSKI'S [1] description of the government of Poland, and the comments he has added to it, are instructive documents for anyone who wants to form a regular plan for the reconstruction of that government. I do not know of anyone better suited than he himself to work out such a plan, for along with the requisite general knowledge he possesses all that detailed familiarity with the local situation which cannot possibly be gained from reading, and which nevertheless is indispensable if institutions are to be adapted to the people for whom they are intended. Unless you are thoroughly familiar with the nation for which you are working, the labour done on its behalf, however excellent in theory, is bound to prove faulty in practice; especially when the nation in question is one which is already well-established, and whose tastes, customs, prejudices and vices are too deeply rooted to be readily crowded out by new plantings. Good institutions for Poland can only be the work of Poles, or of someone who has made a thorough first-hand study of the Polish nation and its neighbours. A foreigner can hardly do more than offer some general observations for the enlightenment, but not for the guidance, of the law-reformer. Even when my mind was at its best I would never have been able to comprehend the problem in all its ramifications. Now that I have nearly lost the capacity for consecutive thought, I must confine myself, if I am to obey Count Wielhorski and give evidence of my zeal for his country, to rendering him an account of the impressions made

[1] [See Editorial Note, above, p. xxxvi.—TR.]

THE GOVERNMENT OF POLAND

upon me, and of the comments suggested to me, by the perusal of his work.

While reading the history of the government of Poland, it is hard to understand how a state so strangely constituted has been able to survive so long. A large body made up of a large number of dead members, and of a small number of disunited members whose movements, being virtually independent of one another, are so far from being directed to a common end that they cancel each other out; a body which exerts itself greatly to accomplish nothing; which is capable of offering no sort of resistance to anyone who tries to encroach upon it; which falls into dissolution five or six times a century; which falls into paralysis whenever it tries to make any effort or to satisfy any need; and which, in spite of all this, lives and maintains its vigour: that, in my opinion, is one of the most singular spectacles ever to challenge the attention of a rational being. I see all the states of Europe rushing to their ruin. Monarchies, republics, all these nations for all their magnificent institutions, all these fine governments for all their prudent checks and balances, have grown decrepit and threaten soon to die; while Poland, a depopulated, devastated and oppressed region, defenceless against her aggressors and at the height of her misfortunes and anarchy, still shows all the fire of youth; she dares to ask for a government and for laws, as if she were newly born. She is in chains, and discusses the means of remaining free; she feels in herself the kind of force that the forces of tyranny cannot overcome. I seem to see Rome, under siege, tranquilly disposing of the land on which the enemy had just pitched camp. Worthy Poles, beware! Beware lest, in your eagerness to improve, you may worsen your condition. In thinking of what you wish to gain, do not forget what you may lose. Correct, if possible, the abuses of your constitution; but do not despise that constitution which has made you what you are.

You love liberty; you are worthy of it; you have defended it against a powerful and crafty aggressor who, under the pretence of offering you the bonds of friendship, was loading you down with the chains of servitude. Now, wearied by the troubles of your fatherland, you are sighing for tranquillity. That can, I think, be very easily won; but to preserve it along with liberty, that is what I find difficult. It is in the bosom of the very anarchy you hate that were formed those patriotic souls who have saved you from the yoke of slavery. They were falling into lethargic sleep; the tempest has reawakened them. Having broken the chains that were being prepared for them, they feel the heaviness of fatigue. They would like to combine the peace of despotism with the sweets of liberty. I fear that they may be seeking contradictory things. Repose and liberty seem to me to be incompatible; it is necessary to choose between them.

I do not say that things must be left in their present state; but I do say that they must be touched only with extreme circumspection. For the time being you are struck rather by their defects than by their advantages. The day will come, I fear, when you will have a better appreciation of hose advantages; and that, unfortunately, will be when they are already lost.

Although it is easy, if you wish, to make better laws, it is impossible to make them such that the passions of men will not abuse them as they abused the laws which preceded them. To foresee and weigh all future abuses is perhaps beyond the powers even of the most consummate statesman. The subjecting of man to law is a problem in politics which I liken to that of the squaring of the circle in geometry. Solve this problem well, and the government based on your solution will be good and free from abuses. But until then you may rest assured that, wherever you think you are establishing the rule of law, it is men who will do the ruling.

There will never be a good and solid constitution unless the law reigns over the hearts of the citizens; as long as the power of legislation is insufficient to accomplish this, laws will always be evaded. But how can hearts be reached? That is a question to which our law-reformers, who never look beyond coercion and punishments, pay hardly any attention; and it is a question to the solving of which material rewards would perhaps be equally ineffective. Even the most upright justice is insufficient; for justice, like health, is a good which is enjoyed without being felt, which inspires no enthusiasm, and the value of which is felt only after it has been lost.

How then is it possible to move the hearts of men, and to make them love the fatherland and its laws? Dare I say it? Through children's games; through institutions which seem idle and frivolous to superficial men, but which form cherished habits and invincible attachments. If I seem extravagant on this point, I am at least whole-hearted; for I admit that my folly appears to me under the guise of perfect reason.

Chapter II

THE SPIRIT OF THE INSTITUTIONS OF ANTIQUITY

WHEN reading ancient history, we seem transported to another world with another breed of men. What do Frenchmen, Englishmen or Russians have in common with the Romans and the Greeks? Almost nothing but their external appearance. The heroic souls of the ancients seem to us like the exaggerations of historians. How can we, who feel that we are so small, believe that there were ever men of such greatness? Such men did exist, however, and they were human beings like ourselves. What prevents us from being like them? Our prejudices, our base philosophy, and those passions of petty self-interest which, through inept institutions never dictated by genius, have been concentrated and combined with egoism in all our hearts.

I look at the nations of modern times. I see in them many lawmakers, but not one legislator. Among the ancients I see three outstanding men of the latter sort who deserve particular attention: Moses, Lycurgus and Numa. All three devoted their main efforts to objects which our own men of learning would consider laughable. All three achieved successes which would be thought impossible if they were not so well attested.

The first conceived and executed the astonishing project of creating a nation out of a swarm of wretched fugitives, without arts, arms, talents, virtues or courage, who were wandering as a horde of strangers over the face of the earth without a single inch of ground to call their own. Out of this wandering and servile horde Moses had the audacity to create a body politic, a free people; and while they were wandering in the desert without a stone on which to lay their heads, he gave them that durable set of institutions, proof against time, fortune and conquerors, which five thousand years have not been able to destroy or even to alter, and which even to-day still subsists in all its strength, although the national body has ceased to exist.

To prevent his people from melting away among foreign peoples, he gave them customs and usages incompatable with those of the other nations; he over-burdened them with peculiar rites and ceremonies; he inconvenienced them in a thousand ways in order to keep them constantly on the alert and to make them forever strangers among other men; and all the fraternal bonds with which he drew together the members of his republic were as many barriers keeping them separate from their neighbours and preventing them from mingling with them. That is how this peculiar nation, so often subjugated, so often dispersed and apparently destroyed, but always fanatical in devotion to its Law, has nevertheless maintained itself down to the present day, scattered among but never intermingled with the rest ; and that is why its customs, laws and rites subsist, and will endure to the end of time, in spite of the hatred and persecution of the rest of the human race.

Lycurgus undertook to give institutions to a people already degraded by slavery and by the vices which follow from it. He imposed on them an iron yoke, the like of which no other people ever bore; but he attached them to and, so to speak, identified them with this yoke by making it the object of their constant pre-occupation. He kept the fatherland constantly before their eyes in their laws, in their games, in their homes, in their loves, in their festivals; he never left them an instant for solitary relaxation. And out of this perpetual constraint, ennobled by its purpose, was born that ardent love of country which was always the strongest, or rather the sole, passion of the Spartans, and which turned them into beings above the level of humanity. It is true that Sparta was only a city: but by the mere strength of its institutions, this city gave laws to the whole of Greece, became its capital, and made the Persian Empire tremble. Sparta was the centre from which its legislation spread its influence in all directions.

Those who have seen in Numa only a creator of religious rites and ceremonies have sadly misjudged this great man. Numa was the true founder of Rome. If Romulus had done no more than to bring together a band of brigands who could have been scattered by a single set-back, his imperfect work would not have been able to withstand the ravages of time. It was Numa who made it solid and enduring by uniting these brigands into an indissoluble body, by transforming them into citizens, doing this less by means of laws, for which in their state of rustic poverty they still had little need, than by means of attractive institutions which attached them to one another, and to their common soil; he did this, in short, by sanctifying their city with those rites, frivolous and superstitious in appearance, the force and effect of which is so rarely appreciated, and the first foundations of which were nevertheless laid by Romulus, fierce Romulus himself.

It was the same spirit that guided all the ancient legislators in their work of creating institutions. They all sought bonds that might attach citizens to the fatherland and to one another; and they found them in peculiar usages, in religious ceremonies which by their very nature were always national and exclusive; in games which kept citizens frequently assembled; in exercises which increased not only their vigour and strength but also their pride and self-esteem; in spectacles which, by reminding them of the history of their ancestors, their misfortunes, their virtues, their victories, touched their hearts, inflamed them with a lively spirit of emulation, and attached them strongly to that fatherland with which they were meant to be incessantly preoccupied. It was the poems of Homer recited before the Greeks in solemn assembly, not on stages in darkened theatres for ticket-holders only, but in the open air and in the presence of the whole body of the nation; it was the tragedies of Aeschylus, Sophocles and Euripides, which were often performed before them; it was the prizes with which, to the acclamations of all Greece, they crowned the victors in their games; all this, by continually surrounding them with an atmosphere of emulation and glory, raised their courage and their virtues to that degree of energy for which there is no modern parallel, and in which we moderns are not even capable of believing. If we have laws, it is solely for the purpose of teaching us to obey our masters well, to keep our hands out of other people's pockets, and to give a great deal of money to public scoundrels. If we have social usages, it is in order that we may know how to amuse the idleness of light women, and to display our own with grace. If we assemble, it is in the temples of a cult which is in no sense national, and which does nothing to remind us of the fatherland; it is in tightly closed halls, and for money, to see play-actors declaim and prostitutes simper on effeminate and dissolute stages where love is the only theme, and where we go to learn those lessons in corruption which, of all the lessons they pretend to teach, are the only ones from which we profit; it is in festivals where the common people, for ever scorned, are always without influence, where public blame and approbation are inconsequential; it is in licentious throngs, where we go to form secret liaisons and to seek those pleasures which do most to separate, to isolate men, and to corrupt their hearts. Are these stimulants to patriotism? Is it surprising that ways of life so different should be so unlike in their effects, and that we moderns can no longer find in ourselves anything of that spiritual vigour which was inspired in the ancients by everything they did? Pray forgive these digressions from one whose dying embers you yourself have rekindled. I shall return with pleasure to a consideration of that people which, of all those now living, least separates me from those ancients of whom I have just been speaking.

CHAPTER III

APPLICATION

POLAND is a large state surrounded by even more considerable states which, by reason of their despotism and military discipline, have great offensive power. Herself weakened by anarchy, she is, in spite of Polish valour, exposed to all their insults. She has no strongholds to stop their incursions. Her depopulation makes her almost entirely defenceless. No economic organisation; few or no troops; no military discipline, no order, no subordination; ever divided within, ever menaced from without, she has no intrinsic stability, and depends on the caprice of her neighbours. In the present state of affairs, I can see only one way to give her the stability she lacks: it is to infuse, so to speak, the spirit of the Confederation[1] throughout the nation; it is to establish the Republic so firmly in the hearts of the Poles that she will maintain her existence there in spite of all the efforts of her oppressors. There, it seems to me, is the only sanctuary where force can neither reach nor destroy her. An ever-memorable proof of this has just been given; Poland was in the bonds of Russia, but the Poles have remained free. A

[1] [i.e. the Confederation of Bar. See Editorial Note, above, p. xxxvi.—TR.]

great example, which shows you how to set at defiance the power and ambition of your neighbours. You may not prevent them from swallowing you up; see to it at least that they will not be able to digest you. No matter what is done, before Poland has been placed in a position to resist her enemies, she will be overwhelmed by them a hundred times. The virtue of her citizens, their patriotic zeal, the particular way in which national institutions may be able to form their souls, this is the only rampart which will always stand ready to defend her, and which no army will ever be able to breach. If you see to it that no Pole can ever become a Russian, I guarantee that Russia will not subjugate Poland.

It is national institutions which shape the genius, the character, the tastes and the manners of a people; which give it an individuality of its own; which inspire it with that ardent love of country, based on ineradicable habits, which make its members, while living among other peoples, die of boredom, though surrounded by delights denied them in their own land. Remember the Spartan who, gorged with the pleasures of the Great King's court, was reproached for missing his black broth. 'Ah,' he said to the satrap with a sigh, 'I know your pleasures, but you do not know ours!'

Today, no matter what people may say, there are no longer any Frenchmen, Germans, Spaniards, or even Englishmen; there are only Europeans. All have the same tastes, the same passions, the same manners, for no one has been shaped along national lines by peculiar institutions. All, in the same circumstances, will do the same things; all will call themselves unselfish, and be rascals; all will talk of the public welfare, and think only of themselves; all will praise moderation, and wish to be as rich as Croesus. They have no ambition but for luxury, they have no passion but for gold; sure that money will buy them all their hearts desire, they all are ready to sell themselves to the first bidder. What do they care what master they obey, under the laws of what state they live? Provided they can find money to steal and women to corrupt, they feel at home in any country.

Incline the passions of the Poles in a different direction, and you will give their souls a national physiognomy which will distinguish them from other peoples, which will prevent them from mixing, from feeling at ease with those peoples, from allying themselves with them; you will give them a vigour which will supplant the abusive operation of vain precepts, and which will make them do through preference and passion that which is never done sufficiently well when done only for duty or interest. These are the souls on which appropriate legislation will take hold. They will obey the laws without evasion because those laws suit them and rest on the inward assent of their will. Loving the fatherland, they will serve it zealously and with all their hearts. Given this sentiment alone, legislation, even if it were bad, would make good citizens; and it is always good citizens alone that constitute the power and prosperity of the state.

I shall expound hereafter the system of government which, with little fundamental change in your laws, seems to me to be capable of bringing patriotism and its attendant virtues to the highest possible degree of intensity. But whether or not you adopt this system, begin in any case by giving the Poles a great opinion of themselves and of their fatherland: given the qualities they have just been displaying, this opinion will not be false. The circumstances of the present moment must be used to elevate souls to the level of the souls of the ancients. It is certain that the Confederation of Bar has saved the dying fatherland. This great epoch must be engraved in sacred letters on every Polish heart. I should like to see a monument erected in its memory; let there be placed upon it the names of all the confederates, even of those who may thereafter have betrayed the common cause. So great an action ought to wipe out the faults of a whole lifetime. Let a decennial solemnity be instituted to celebrate it with a pomp not brilliant and frivolous, but simple, proud and republican; there let eulogy be given, worthily but without exaggeration, to those virtuous citizens who have had the honour to suffer for the fatherland in the chains of the enemy; let their families even be granted some honorific privilege which will constantly recall this great memory before the eyes of the public. I should not wish, however, that any invectives against the Russians, or even any mention of them, be permitted at these solemnities; it would be doing them too much honour. This silence, the memory of their barbarity, and the eulogy of those who resisted them, will say all that needs to be said about them: you must despise them too much to hate them.

I should wish that, by honours and public rewards, all the patriotic virtues should be glorified, that citizens should constantly be kept occupied with the fatherland, that it should be made their principal business, that it should be kept continuously before their eyes. In this way, I confess, they would have less time and opportunity to grow rich; but they would also have less desire and need to do so. Their hearts would learn to know other pleasures than those of wealth. This is the art of ennobling souls and of turning them into an instrument more powerful than gold.

The brief description of Polish manners so kindly forwarded to me by M. de Wielhorski does not suffice to familiarise me with their civil and domestic usages. But a great nation which has never mingled too much with its neighbours must have many such which are peculiar to itself, and which perhaps are daily being bastardised by the general European tendency to adopt the tastes and manners of the French. It is necessary to maintain, to re-establish these ancient usages, and to introduce other appropriate ones which will be peculiar to the Poles. These usages, even though they may be indifferent or even in some respects bad, provided that the vice be not radical, will always have the advantage of making Poles love their country, and of giving them a natural repugnance to mingling with foreigners. I consider it fortunate that they have a peculiar mode of dress. Preserve this advantage carefully: do exactly the opposite of what was done by that highly-touted Czar.[1] Let neither the king nor the senators nor any public figure wear anything but the national costume, and let no Pole venture to appear at court dressed in the French fashion.

Have many public games, where the good mother country is pleased to see her children at play! Let her pay frequent attention to them, that they may pay constant attention to her. In order to set a good example, it is necessary to abolish, even at court, the ordinary amusements of courts, gambling, drama, comedy, opera; all that makes men effeminate; all that distracts them, isolates them, makes them forget their fatherland and their duty; all that makes it possible for them to be happy anywhere as long as they are entertained. You must invent games, festivals and solemnities so peculiar to this particular court that they will be encountered in no other. People in Poland must be entertained even more than in other countries,

[1] [Peter the Great.—Tr.]

but not in the same manner. In a word, the execrable proverb must be reversed, and every Pole made to say from the bottom of his heart: *Ubi patria, ibi bene.*

Nothing, if possible, exclusively for the rich and powerful! Have many open-air spectacles, where the various ranks of society will be carefully distinguished, but where the whole people will participate equally, as among the ancients, and where, on certain occasions, young noblemen will test their strength and skill! Bull-fighting has contributed no little to the maintenance of a certain vigour within the Spanish nation. Those amphitheatres in which the youth of Poland formerly took their exercise ought to be carefully re-established; they ought to be made theatres of honour and emulation for these young people. Nothing could be easier than to replace the earlier combats with less cruel exercises in which strength and skill would nevertheless still play a part, and in which the victors would continue to win honours and rewards. Horsemanship, for example, is a highly suitable exercise for Poles, and readily lends itself to brilliant public spectacles.

The heroes of Homer were all distinguished by their strength and skill, and thereby demonstrated in the eyes of the people that they were fit to lead them. The tournaments of the paladins made men not only brave and courageous, but also eager for honour and glory, and ripe for every virtue. The use of firearms, by making the bodily faculties less useful in war, has caused them to fall into discredit. From this it follows that, apart from qualities of the spirit, which are often equivocal and misplaced, on which there are a thousand ways of being deceived, and of which the people are poor judges, a man with the advantage of good birth has nothing to distinguish him from anyone else, to justify his fortune, to demonstrate in his person a natural

right to superiority; and the more these exterior signs
are neglected, the easier it is for those who govern us to
grow corrupt and effeminate with impunity. It is
important, however, and even more important than we
imagine, that those who are one day to command others
should from their youth show themselves to be superior
in all respects, or at least that they should try to do so.
It is good, moreover, that the people should be together
with their leaders on pleasurable occasions, that they
should know them, that they should be accustomed to
seeing them, and that they should often share their
pleasures. Provided that subordination is always
preserved, and that distinctions of rank are not lost
sight of, this is the way to make them love their leaders,
and to combine respect with affection. Finally, a taste
for physical exercise diverts people from dangerous
idleness, effeminate pleasures, and frivolous wit. It is
above all for the sake of the soul that the body should
be exercised: a fact which our petty sages are far from
recognising.

Be sure not to neglect the need for a certain amount
of public display; let it be noble, imposing, with a
magnificence which resides rather in men than in things.
It is hard to believe to what an extent the heart of the
people follows its eyes, and how much it is impressed by
majestic ceremonial. This lends authority an air of
law and order which inspires confidence, and divorces
it from the ideas of caprice and whimsicality associated
with arbitrary power. In preparing these solemnities,
however, you must avoid the frippery, the garishness
and the luxurious decorations usually found in the
courts of kings. The festivals of a free people should
always breathe an air of gravity and decorum, and
objects worthy of esteem should alone be offered for
popular admiration. The Romans, in their triumphs,

displayed enormous luxury, but it was the luxury of the vanquished; the more it shone, the less did it seduce; its very brilliance was an excellent lesson for the Romans. The captive kings were bound with chains of gold and precious stones. That is a proper understanding of luxury. Often it is possible to reach the same goal by two opposite routes. The two woolsacks placed before the seat of the Chancellor in the British House of Lords strike me as a touching and sublime decoration. Two sheaves of wheat similarly placed in the Polish Senate would produce an effect no less pleasing to my taste.

The immense disparities of fortune which divide the magnates from the lesser nobility constitute a great obstacle to the reforms needed to make love of country the dominant passion. As long as luxury reigns among the great, cupidity will reign in all hearts. The object of public admiration and the desires of private individuals will always be the same; and if one must be rich in order to shine, to be rich will always be the dominant passion. This is a great source of corruption, which must be diminished as much as possible. If other attractive objects, if signs of rank, distinguished men in official position, those who were merely rich would be deprived of them; hidden ambitions would naturally seek out these honourable distinctions, that is to say, distinctions of merit and virtue, if they were the only road to success. The consuls of Rome were often very poor, but they had their lictors; the distinction of having lictors was coveted by the people, and the plebeians attained the consulship.

Where inequality reigns, I must confess, it is very hard to eliminate all luxury. But would it not be possible to change the objects of this luxury and thus make its example less pernicious? For instance, the impoverished nobility of Poland formerly attached themselves to the magnates, who gave them education and subsistence as retainers. There you see a truly great and noble form of luxury, the inconveniences of which I fully recognise, but which, far from debasing souls, elevates them, gives them sensibility and resilience; among the Romans, a similar custom led to no abuses as long as the Republic endured. I have read that the Duc d'Épernon, encountering one day the Duc de Sully, wanted to pick a quarrel with him; but that, having only six hundred gentlemen in his entourage, he did not dare attack Sully, who had eight hundred. I doubt that luxury of this sort leaves much room for baubles; and the example it gives will at least not serve to seduce the poor. Bring back the magnates of Poland to the point of desiring no other form of luxury; the result may be divisions, parties, quarrels; but the nation will not be corrupted. In addition, let us tolerate military luxury, the luxury of arms and horses; but let all effeminate adornments be held in contempt; and if the women cannot be persuaded to abandon them, let them at least learn to disdain and disapprove of them in men.

Furthermore, it is not by sumptuary laws that luxury can be successfully extirpated; it is from the depth of the heart itself that you must uproot it by impressing men with healthier and nobler tastes. To forbid things is an inept and vain expedient, unless you begin by making them scorned and hated; and the disapprobation of the law is efficacious only when it reinforces that of the public. Whoever concerns himself with the problem of creating institutions for a people ought to know how to direct opinion, and thus to govern the passions of men. This is true above all in the matter of which I am now speaking. Sumptuary laws serve rather to stimulate desire by constraint than to extinguish it by punishment. Simplicity of manners and adornment is the fruit not so much of law as of education

CHAPTER IV

EDUCATION

THIS is the important question. It is education that must give souls a national formation, and direct their opinions and tastes in such a way that they will be patriotic by inclination, by passion, by necessity. When first he opens his eyes, an infant ought to see the fatherland, and up to the day of his death he ought never to see anything else. Every true republican has drunk in love of country, that is to say love of law and liberty, along with his mother's milk. This love is his whole existence; he sees nothing but the fatherland, he lives for it alone; when he is solitary, he is nothing; when he has ceased to have a fatherland, he no longer exists; and if he is not dead, he is worse than dead.

National education is proper only to free men; it is they only who enjoy a collective existence and are truly bound by law. A Frenchman, an Englishman, a Spaniard, an Italian, a Russian are all practically the same man; each leaves school already fully prepared for license, that is to say, for slavery. At twenty, a Pole ought not to be a man of any other sort; he ought to be a Pole. I wish that, when he learns to read, he should read about his own land; that at the age of ten he should be familiar with all its products, at twelve with all its provinces, highways, and towns; that at fifteen he should know its whole history, at sixteen all its laws; that in all Poland there should be no great action or famous man of which his heart and memory are not full, and of which he cannot give an account at a moment's notice. From this you can see that it is not studies of the usual sort, directed by foreigners and priests, that I would like to have children pursue. The law ought to regulate the content, the order and the form of their studies. They ought to have only Poles for teachers: Poles who are all, if possible, married; who are all distinguished by moral character, probity, good sense and attainments; and who are all destined, after the successful performance of this task for a certain number of years, for employments which, although they are not more important or honourable, for that is impossible, are less arduous and more brilliant. Beware above all of turning teaching into a profession. No public man in Poland should have any other permanent rank than that of citizen. All the positions he fills, and above all those which are as important as this, should be regarded only as testing-places, and as steps in the ladder of advancement by merit. I exhort the Polish people to pay attention to this maxim, on which I shall often insist: I consider it one of the key-points in the organisation of the state. We shall see below how, in my opinion, it is possible to give it universal application.

I do not like those distinctions between schools and academies which result in giving different and separate education to the richer and to the poorer nobility. All, being equal under the constitution of the state, ought to be educated together and in the same fashion; and if it is impossible to set up an absolutely free system of public education, the cost must at least be set at a level the poor can afford to pay. Would it not be possible to provide in each school a certain number of free scholarships, that is to say, supported at state expense, of the sort known in France as bursaries? These scholarships, given to the children of poor gentlemen who have deserved well of the country, given not as an act of charity but as a reward for the merit of the father, would thus become honourable, and might produce a double advantage well worth considering. To accomplish this, nominations should not be arbitrary, but made by a form of selection of which I shall speak hereafter. Those who have been chosen would be called *children of the state*, and distinguished by some honorific insignia which would give them precedence over other children of their own age, including even the children of magnates.

In every school a gymnasium, or place for physical exercise, should be established for the children. This much-neglected provision is, in my opinion, the most important part of education, not only for the purpose of forming robust and healthy physiques, but even more for moral purposes, which are either neglected or else sought only through a mass of vain and pedantic precepts which are simply a waste of breath. I can never sufficiently repeat that good education ought to be negative. Prevent vices from arising, and you will have done enough for virtue. In a good system of public education, the way to accomplish this is simplicity itself: it is to keep children always on the alert, not by boring studies of which they understand nothing and which they hate simply because they are forced to sit still; but by exercises which give them pleasure by satisfying the need of their growing bodies for movement, and which in other ways will be enjoyable.

They should not be allowed to play alone as their fancy dictates, but all together and in public, so that there will always be a common goal toward which they all aspire, and which will excite competition and emulation. Parents who prefer domestic education, and have their children brought up under their own eyes, ought nevertheless to send them to these exercises. Their instruction may be domestic and private, but their games ought always to be public and common to all; for here it is not only a question of keeping them busy, of giving them a robust constitution, of making them agile and muscular, but also of accustoming them at an early age to rules, to equality, to fraternity, to competition, to living under the eyes of their fellow-citizens and to desiring public approbation. Therefore the prizes and rewards of the victors should not be distributed arbitrarily by the games-coaches or by the school-officials, but by the acclamation and judgment of the spectators; and you can be sure that these judgments will always be just, above all if care is taken to make the games attractive to the public, by presenting them with some ceremony and with an eye to spectacular effect. Then we may assume that all worthy people and all good patriots will consider it a duty and a pleasure to attend.

At Berne there is a most unusual exercise for the young patricians who are graduating from school. It is called the Mock State. It is a copy in miniature of everything that goes to make up the political life of the Republic: a senate, chief magistrates, officers, bailiffs, orators, lawsuits, judgments, solemnities. The Mock State has even a small government and a certain income; and this institution, authorised and sponsored by the sovereign, is the nursery of the statesmen who will one day direct public affairs in the same employments which at first they exercised only in play.

No matter what form is given to public education, into the details of which I will not enter here, it is proper to set up a college of magistrates of the first rank who will have supreme authority to administer it, and who will name, dismiss and change at their discretion not only the principals and heads of schools, who themselves, as I have already said, will be candidates for the upper magistracies, but also the games-coaches, whose zeal and vigilance will be carefully stimulated by the promise of higher positions which will be opened or closed to them according to the manner in which they performed these earlier functions. Since it is on these institutions that the hope of the Republic, the glory and fate of the nation depend, I find in them, I must confess, an importance which, I am much surprised to discover, no one has ever thought of attributing to them. For the sake of humanity I am grieved that so many ideas which impress me as being good and useful are always, in spite of their eminent practicality, so far removed from anything that is actually done.

However, my purpose here is only to give a few general suggestions; but that is enough for those I am addressing. These poorly developed ideas give a distant view of the paths, unknown to the moderns, by which the ancients led men to that vigour of soul, to that patriotic zeal, to that esteem for truly personal and properly human qualities, which are without precedent among us; but the leaven exists in the hearts of all men and is ready to ferment if only it is stimulated by suitable institutions. Direct in this sense the usages, the customs, the manners of the Poles; in them you will develop that leaven the very existence of which has not yet been so much as suspected by our corrupt maxims, our outworn institutions, our egoistical philosophy which preaches and kills. The nation will date her second birth from the terrible crisis from which she is emerging; and seeing what her still undisciplined members have accomplished, she will expect and obtain still more from a well-balanced set of institutions, she will respect and cherish laws which flatter her noble pride, which will make and keep her happy and free; plucking from her heart the passions which lead to the evasion of those laws, she will nourish those which cause them to be loved; finally, by renewing herself, so to speak, she will recover in this new age all the vigour of a nation in process of birth. But, without these precautions, expect nothing from your laws. However wise, however far-seeing they may be, they will be evaded and made useless; and you will only have corrected some few abuses that are wounding you, in order to introduce others which you will not have foreseen. So much for the preliminaries which I have thought indispensable. Let us now cast our eyes upon the constitution itself.

CHAPTER V

THE RADICAL DEFECT

If possible, let us from the beginning avoid wandering off into chimerical projects. What is the enterprise, gentlemen, that concerns you at the moment? That of reforming the government of Poland: that is to say, of giving the constitution of a great kingdom the vigour and stability of that of a small republic. Before working toward the execution of this project, we must ask first of all whether it is capable of realisation. The size of nations, the extent of states: this is the first and principal source of the misfortunes of the human race, and above all of the innumerable calamities that sap and destroy civilised peoples. Practically all small states, no matter whether they are republics or monarchies, prosper merely by reason of the fact that they are small; that all the citizens know and watch over one another; that the leaders can see for themselves the evil that is being done, the good they have to do; and that their orders are carried out before their eyes. All great peoples, crushed by their own mass, suffer either from anarchy, like you, or from subordinate oppressors through whom, by the necessities of devolution, the king is obliged to rule. Only God can govern the world; and it would require more than human capacities to govern great nations. It is surprising, it is prodigious, that the vast extent of Poland has not already resulted a hundred times in the conversion of the government into a despotism, that it has not bastardised the souls of the Poles and corrupted the mass of the nation. It is an example unique in history that after the lapse of centuries such a state should even now be merely in a condition of anarchy. The slowness of this progression is due to advantages inseparable from the inconveniences from which you wish to deliver yourselves. Ah! I cannot repeat it often enough; think well before you lay hands on your laws, and above all on those that have made you what you are. The first reform you need is a change in the extent of your country. Your vast provinces will never permit you to enjoy the strict administration of small republics. Begin by contracting your boundaries, if you wish to reform your government. Perhaps your neighbours are thinking of doing you this service. It would no doubt be a great misfortune for the dismembered parts; but it would be a great boon to the body of the nation.

If these retrenchments do not take place, I can see only one means that might perhaps accomplish the same result; and this means, fortunately, is already in harmony with the spirit of your institutions. Let the separation of the two Polands be as complete as that of Lithuania is from them; have three states united in one. If possible, I should like you to have as many states as you now have palatinates. Subdivide each of these in turn into an equal number of particular administrations. Perfect the form of the dietines,[1] extend their authority within their respective palatinates; but define their limits carefully, and be sure that nothing can break the bond of common legislation which unites them, or disturb their common subordination to the body of the republic. In a word, devote yourselves to extending and perfecting the system of federal government: the only one which combines the advantages of large and small states, and thus the only one that can answer your purposes. If you neglect this advice, I doubt whether your work will ever be successful.

Chapter VI

THE QUESTION OF THE THREE ORDERS

I HARDLY ever hear people discussing government without finding an appeal to principles which strike me as being false or ambiguous. The Republic of Poland, it has often been repeated, is composed of three orders: the equestrian order,[2] the senate and the king. I should prefer to say that the Polish nation is composed of three orders: the nobles, who are everything; the burghers, who are nothing; and the peasants, who are less than nothing. If the senate is to be counted as an order in the state, why not also count the chamber of deputies, which is no less distinct, and has no less authority?

[1] [The diet of a province or palatinate, which elected deputies to the national diet.—Tr.]

[2] [i.e. the nobility.—Tr.]

More important still: this division, in the very sense in which it is given, is obviously incomplete; for it would be necessary to add the ministers, who are neither kings, nor senators, nor deputies, and who, in their extreme independence, are equally to be accounted as depositaries of the whole executive power. Can you ever explain to me how the part, which exists only in relation to the whole, can nevertheless form an order independent of that whole? The English peerage, being hereditary, does form, I will admit, an independent order. But in Poland, if you eliminate the equestrian order, there is no longer a senate; for no one can be a senator unless he is already a Polish nobleman. Similarly, there is no king; for it is the equestrian order that elects him, and the king can do nothing without it. But remove the senate and the king: the equestrian order and, through it, the state and the sovereign will remain entire; and the very next day, if the nobles so desire, they will have a senate and a king as before.

Because the senate does not constitute an order within the state, it does not follow, however, that it is of no importance to it; and if it were not the collective depositary of the laws, its members, independent of its collective authority, would nevertheless be depositaries of the legislative power; and to prevent them from voting in plenary sessions of the diet whenever it is a question of enacting or repealing laws would be to deprive them of their birthright; but then they are no longer voting in their capacity as senators, but simply as private citizens. As soon as the legislative power speaks, all return to a position of equality; all other authorities are silent in its presence; its voice is the voice of God on earth. Even the king, when presiding over the diet, has no right to vote, in my opinion, unless he is a Polish nobleman.

It will be said, no doubt, that I am now proving too much, and that if the senators as such have no votes in the diet, they ought not to have them as private citizens either; for the members of the equestrian order do not there vote in person, but solely through their representatives, among whom the senators are not to be reckoned. And why should they vote in the diet as individuals, when no other nobleman, unless he is a deputy, can do so? This objection strikes me as being valid under the existing state of affairs; but when the proposed changes are effected, it will be valid no longer, since then the senators themselves will be perpetual representatives of the nation, but will not be able to act on legislative matters without the concurrence of their colleagues.

It should not be said, therefore, that the concurrence of the king, the senate and the equestrian order is necessary to make a law. This right belongs solely to the equestrian order, of which the senators like the deputies are members, but in which the senate does not enter at all in its corporate capacity. Such is, or ought to be, the law of the state in Poland. But the law of nature, that holy and imprescriptible law, which speaks to the heart and reason of man, does not permit legislative authority to be thus restricted, nor does it allow laws to be binding on anyone who has not voted for them in person, like the deputies, or at least through representatives, like the body of the nobility. This sacred law cannot be violated with impunity; and the state of weakness to which so great a nation now finds itself reduced is the fruit of that feudal barbarism which serves to cut off from the body of the state that part of the nation which is the most numerous, and oftentimes the most wholesome.

God forbid that I should think it necessary at this

point to prove something that a little good sense and compassion will suffice to make everyone feel! And whence does Poland expect to recruit the strength and force that she arbitrarily stifles in her bosom? Noblemen of Poland, be something more: be men. Then only will you be happy and free. But never flatter yourselves that you will be so, as long as you hold your brothers in chains.

I sense the difficulty of the project of freeing your common people. I am afraid not merely of the badly understood self-interest, the self-conceit, and the prejudices of the masters; if these were surmounted, I should also fear the vices and the cowardice of the serfs. Liberty is a food easy to eat, but hard to digest; it takes very strong stomachs to stand it. I laugh at those debased peoples who, allowing themselves to be stirred up by rebels, dare to speak of liberty without having the slightest idea of its meaning, and who, with their hearts full of all the servile vices, imagine that, in order to be free, it is enough to be insubordinate. O proud and holy liberty! if those poor people could only know thee, if they realised at what a price thou art won and preserved; if they felt how much more austere are thy laws than the yoke of tyrants is heavy: their feeble souls, enslaved by passions that would have to be suppressed, would fear thee a hundred times more than slavery; they would flee from thee in terror, as from a burden threatening to crush them.

To free the common people of Poland would be a great and worthy enterprise, but bold, perilous, and not to be attempted lightly. Among the precautions to be taken, there is one which is indispensable and requires time; it is, before everything else, to make the serfs who are to be freed worthy of liberty and capable of enduring it. I shall explain hereafter one of the

VII: MEANS OF MAINTAINING THE CONSTITUTION

means that can be employed to that end. It would be foolhardy of me to guarantee its success, though I myself do not doubt it. If there is any better method, let it be adopted. But whatever happens, remember that your serfs are men like you, that they have in themselves the capacity to become all that you are. Work first of all to develop that capacity, and do not free their bodies until after you have freed their souls. Without this preliminary, you may be sure that your enterprise will fail.

Chapter VII

MEANS OF MAINTAINING THE CONSTITUTION

The laws of Poland, like those of all the rest of Europe, were made by successive bits and pieces. Whenever an abuse was noticed, a law was made to remedy it. From this law arose further abuses, which had in turn to be corrected. This way of acting is endless, and leads to the most terrible of all abuses, which is to deprive all laws of their force by dint of multiplying their number.

The enfeeblement of law occurred in Poland in a way which is most peculiar, and possibly unique, for it lost its force without having been subjugated by the executive power. Even now the legislative power still retains its full authority; it is inactive, but without recognising anything higher than itself. The diet is no less sovereign than it was at the time of its establishment. Nevertheless it is powerless; nothing dominates it, but neither does anything obey it. This state of affairs is remarkable, and deserves consideration.

What has preserved the law thus far? It is the continuous presence of the legislator. It is the frequency of the diets, it is the frequent re-election of the deputies, that has maintained the Republic. England, which enjoys the first of these advantages, has lost her liberty for having neglected the second. A single parliament lasts so long that the court, which would go bankrupt buying it annually, finds it profitable to buy it for seven years, and does not fail to do so. This is your first lesson.

A second means whereby the legislative power has been preserved in Poland is, in the first place, division of the executive power, which has prevented its deposi- taries from taking concerted action against the legislative, and, in the second place, the frequent transfer of this same executive power from hand to hand, which has prevented any consecutive system of usurpation. In the course of his reign each king took some steps toward arbitrary power. But the election of his successor forced the latter to retract instead of pressing forward; the kings, at the beginning of each reign, were all forced by the *pacta conventa*[1] to start from the same point. Thus, in spite of the habitual tendency to despotism, there was no real progress in that direction.

The same was true of the ministers and great officials. All, being independent both of the senate and of one another, had unlimited authority in their respective departments; but these offices, quite apart from the fact that they balanced one another, were not per- petuated in the same families, hence brought them no absolute power; and all power, even when usurped, always returned to its source. The situation would have been different if the whole executive power had been vested either in a single corporate group, like the senate, or in a single family, through inheritance of the crown. This family or corporate group probably would

---

[1] [The Polish coronation oath.—Tʀ.]

188

have oppressed the legislative power sooner or later, and would thereby have placed the Poles under the yoke all other nations bear, and from which they alone are still exempt; for by now I would no longer count Sweden as an exception. This is your second lesson.

Such is the advantage of your situation; it is undoubtedly great. But the following is the disadvantage, which is hardly less great. The executive power, being divided between several individuals, lacks inner harmony, and gives rise to a perpetual wrangling which is incompatible with good order. Each depositary of a portion of this power sets himself, by virtue of that portion, wholly above the magistrates and the law. He does, indeed, recognise the authority of the diet; but since that is the only authority he does recognise, when the diet is dissolved he no longer recognises any; he despises the courts of law and flouts their judgments. Each is a petty despot who, without exactly usurping the sovereign authority, constantly oppresses the citizens in specific cases, and sets a fatal and too frequently imitated example of unscrupulous and fearless violation of the rights and liberties of individuals.

I believe that this is the first and principal cause of the anarchy which reigns in the state. I can see only one way of removing this cause; you should not arm the various law-courts with public power to repress these petty tyrants, for this power, sometimes badly administered and sometimes overwhelmed by superior power, might stir up troubles and disorders which could lead by degrees to civil war; but you should arm with full executive power a respectable and permanent body, such as the senate, which by its firmness and authority would be capable of holding to the line of duty those magnates who are tempted to depart from it. This method strikes me as efficacious, and would surely

189

prove to be so; but the resulting danger would be terrible and very hard to avoid. For as we have shown in the *Social Contract*, any corporation which serves as depositary of the executive power tends strongly and continuously to subjugate the legislative power, and succeeds sooner or later.

To meet this difficulty it has been suggested that you ought to divide the senate into several councils or departments, each under the presidency of the minister in charge of that department; which minister, together with the members of each council, would change at the end of a fixed period, and would rotate with those of the other departments. This idea may be a good one; it was that of the Abbé de Saint-Pierre, and he has well developed it in his *Polysynodie*. If the executive power is thus divided and temporary, it will be more subordinate to the legislative, and the various parts of the administration will be better and more thoroughly handled for being separate. Do not, however, count too much on this device; if the parts remain separate, they will lack integration, and soon, by mutual opposition, will exhaust practically all their energies against each other, until one has gained the ascendant and dominates the rest; or else, if they do agree and act together, they will in reality constitute but a single body with a single spirit, like the houses of a parliament. And in any case, I consider it impossible for independence and equilibrium to be maintained so well between them that there will not always emerge some centre or focal point of administration in which all private and particular forces will ever unite to oppress the sovereign. In almost all our republics, the councils are thus divided into departments which originally were independent of one another, and which soon ceased to be so.

This division into chambers or departments is a

modern invention. The ancients, who knew better than we how to preserve freedom, were wholly unacquainted with this expedient. The Roman senate ruled half the known world, and did not even think of such divisions. This senate never succeeded, however, in oppressing the legislative power, although the senators held office for life. But the laws had censors, the people had tribunes, and the senate did not elect the consuls.

If the administration is to be strong and good, and accomplish its purposes well, the whole executive power should be vested in the same hands. But it is not enough for these hands to change; if possible they should act only under the eyes of the legislator, and with its guidance. That is the real secret of preventing them from usurping its authority.

As long as the estates meet and the deputies change frequently, it will be hard for the senate or for the king to oppress or usurp the legislative authority. It is remarkable that the kings so far have not tried to make the diets more infrequent, although they were not forced, like the kings of England, to convene them often on pain of running short of money. It must be either that affairs were always in a state of crisis which made the royal authority insufficient to deal with them; or that the kings made sure, by their intrigues in the dietines, of having a majority of deputies always at their disposal; or that, by virtue of the *liberum veto*,[1] they were always certain of being able to cut off deliberations which might displease them, and to dissolve the diets at will. When all these motives cease to exist, it is to be expected that the king, or the senate, or both together, will make great efforts to rid themselves of the diets and to make them as infrequent as possible.

[1] [The right of each individual deputy to veto acts of the Diet.—Tr.]

That above all is the thing to be forestalled and prevented. The method I propose is the only one; it is simple and cannot fail to be effective. It is most remarkable that before I set it forth in the *Social Contract*, no one had ever thought of it.

One of the greatest disadvantages of large states, the one which above all makes liberty most difficult to preserve in them, is that the legislative power cannot manifest itself directly, and can act only by delegation. That has its good and its evil side; but the evil outweighs the good. A legislature made up of the whole citizen body is impossible to corrupt, but easy to deceive. Representatives of the people are hard to deceive, but easy to corrupt; and it rarely happens that they are not so corrupted. You have before you the example of the English Parliament and, through the *liberum veto*, that of your own nation. Now, it is possible to enlighten someone who is mistaken; but how can you restrain someone who is for sale? Without being well versed in Polish affairs, I would wager anything in the world that there is more talent in the diet, and more virtue in the dietines.

I see two means of preventing this terrible evil of corruption, which turns the organ of freedom into the instrument of slavery.

The first, as I have already said, is to have the diets elected frequently, for if the representatives are often changed it is more costly and difficult to seduce them. On this point your constitution is better than that of Great Britain; and when you have abolished or modified the *liberum veto*, I can see no other changes to be made in it, unless it would be to add certain obstacles to the sending of the same deputies to two successive diets, and to prevent them from being elected a great many times. I shall return to this point later on.

The second means is to bind the representatives to follow their instructions exactly, and to make them render their constituents a strict account of their conduct in the diet. In this respect I can only marvel at the negligence, the carelessness and, I would even venture to say, the stupidity of the English nation, which, after having armed its deputies with supreme power, has added no brake to regulate the use they may make of that power throughout the seven years of their mandate.

I observe that the Poles are not sufficiently aware of the importance of their dietines, of all they owe to them, nor of all they might get from them by extending their authority and by regularising their form. I myself am convinced that, if the confederations have saved the fatherland, it is the dietines that have preserved it, and that they are the true palladium of liberty.

The instructions of the deputies should be drawn up with great care, not only on the subjects listed in the royal agenda, but also on the other current needs of the state or province; and this should be done by a committee presided over, if you will, by the marshal of the dietine, but otherwise composed of members chosen by majority vote; and the nobility should not disperse until these instructions have been read, debated and approved in plenary session. In addition to the original text of these instructions, handed to the deputies together with their patents of election, a copy signed by them should remain in the archives of the dietine. It is on the basis of these instructions that they ought, on their return, to report on their actions at a session of the dietine convened expressly for that purpose, a custom which must absolutely be revived; and it is on the basis of this report that they should either be excluded from all subsequent candidacy for the deputyship, or else declared eligible, if they have followed their instructions to the satisfaction of their constituents. This examination is of the utmost importance; it would be impossible to pay too much attention to it, or to observe its results too carefully. With each word the deputy speaks in the diet, and with every move he makes, he must already see himself under the eyes of his constituents, and feel the future influence of their judgment both on his hopes of advancement, and on that good opinion of his compatriots which is indispensable to the realisation of those hopes; for, after all, it is not to express their own private sentiments, but to declare the will of the nation, that the nation sends deputies to the diet. This brake is absolutely necessary to hold them to their duty, and to prevent any sort of corruption from any source. Whatever may be said, I cannot see any disadvantage in this limitation, for the chamber of deputies, which does not, or should not, participate in the details of administration, can never have to deal with any unexpected matter; but if such a matter did arise, and a deputy did nothing contrary to the express will of his constituents, they would not blame him for having expressed his opinion, like a good citizen, on a matter they had not foreseen, and on which they had reached no decision. I will add, in conclusion, that if there were actually some disadvantage in holding the deputies thus bound by their instructions, it could not outweigh the immense advantage of preventing the law from ever being anything but the real expression of the will of the nation.

Once these precautions have been taken, furthermore, there should never be a conflict of jurisdiction between the diet and the dietines; and when a law has been passed in the plenary diet, I would not even grant the dietines the right to protest. Let them punish their deputies; let them even, if necessary, cut off their heads, if they have prevaricated; but let them obey fully, continuously, without exception and without protest; let them bear the just penalty of their bad choice; except that, at the next diet, they may, if they think proper, make as vigorous representations as they like.

The diets, being frequent, have less need to be long, and six weeks' duration seems to me quite enough to meet the ordinary needs of the state. But it is inconsistent for the sovereign authority to set limits on itself, especially when it is directly in the hands of the nation. Let the duration of ordinary diets continue to be set at six weeks, right enough; but it will always rest with the assembly to prolong this term by an express decision, when the matters in hand require it. For, after all, if the diet, which by its very nature is above the law, says ' I want to continue,' who is there to tell it ' I do not want you to?' It is only in case a diet wanted to last more than two years that it could not do so; its powers would then terminate, and those of another diet would begin, with the third year. The diet, which can do everything, can undoubtedly prescribe a longer interval between diets; but this new law could only affect subsequent diets, and the one enacting it cannot profit by it. The principle from which these rules are deduced is demonstrated in the *Social Contract*.

So far as extraordinary diets are concerned, good order does indeed require that they should be infrequent, and convened only in cases of urgent necessity. When the king judges that one is necessary, he ought, I would agree, to be believed; but cases of necessity might arise without his admitting it; should the senate then be the judge? In a free state, everything capable of attacking liberty ought to be foreseen. If the confederations continue they can in certain cases take the place of extraordinary diets; but if you abolish the confederations, you must necessarily make provision for such diets.

I consider it impossible for the law to determine in any reasonable way the duration of extraordinary diets, since this depends entirely on the circumstances which cause them to assemble. Ordinarily, speed is necessary in such cases; but since speed is relative to the business at hand, and that business itself is extraordinary, it is impossible to regulate it in advance by legislation; and conditions might arise in which it would be important for the diet to remain assembled until those conditions had changed, or until the term of the ordinary diets had caused its powers to lapse.

To save precious time in the diets, you should try to rid these assemblies of useless discussions which are merely time-consuming. In them there must be, of course, not only rule and order, but also ceremony and majesty. I should even like you to take particular pains in this regard, making people feel, for example, the barbarity and horrible impropriety of seeing the panoply of arms profane the sanctuary of law. Men of Poland, are you more warlike than the Romans? And yet, in the most troubled days of their republic, the sight of a blade never sullied the assemblies or the senate. But I should also wish that, while clinging to important and necessary things, you would avoid doing anything in the diet that could equally well be done elsewhere. The examination of the credentials of the deputies (*rugi*) is a waste of time in the diet; not because this examination is not an important thing in itself, but because it can be done as well or better in the very place where the deputies were elected, where they are best known, and where all their competitors are to be found. It is in their own palatinate, it is in the dietine

196

they represent, that the validity of their election can best and most quickly be determined, as is the present practice with regard to the members of your highest financial and judicial bodies. This done, the diet should admit them without question on the credentials (*laudum*) in their possession, not only to prevent possible obstacles to the prompt election of the marshal,[1] but above all to prevent intrigues whereby the senate or king might interfere with the elections and defraud subjects of whom they disapproved. The recent events in London are a lesson for the Poles. I am well aware of the fact that Wilkes is only a muddlehead; but the precedent of his rejection has smoothed the way, and from now on only those subjects who suit the court will be admitted to the House of Commons.

You should begin by paying more attention to the choice of the members who vote in the dietines. This would make it easier to identify those who are eligible to serve as deputies. The Golden Book of Venice is a model to follow, because of the facilities it offers. It would be very convenient and easy to keep in each election district (*grod*) an accurate register of all the nobles who, under the specified conditions, would be eligible to appear and vote in the dietines; they would be enrolled in the register of their district upon reaching the age prescribed by law; and those who ought to be excluded would be struck off as the case arose, with a statement of the grounds for their exclusion. By these registers, the authenticity of which should be well safeguarded, you would easily identify both the legitimate members of the dietines and the subjects eligible to become deputies; and the length of debates on this topic would be much reduced.

[1] [Presiding Officer.—Tr.]

A better system of discipline in the diets and dietines would surely be most useful; but I can never repeat too often that you must not seek two contradictory things at the same time. Discipline is good, but liberty is better; and the more you hedge in liberty with formalities, the more means of usurpation will these formalities furnish. All the measures you adopt to prevent licence in the legislative order, though good in themselves, will sooner or later be used to oppress it. Long and useless harangues, which waste so much precious time, are a great evil; but it is an even greater evil for a good citizen not to dare speak when he has something useful to say. When it reaches the point where certain mouths only are opened in the diets, and even those are forbidden to speak freely, they soon will say nothing but what is apt to please the powerful.

After necessary changes have been made in the appointment of officials and in the distribution of favours, there will probably be fewer vain harangues, and also fewer flatteries addressed in this form to the king. In order to prune away some of the farragoes of rhetorical nonsense you might, however, require each orator to announce at the beginning of his discourse the proposition he wants to establish and, after presenting his arguments, to summarise his conclusions, as lawyers do in court. If that did not make speeches shorter, it would at least restrain those who merely want to talk for the sake of talking, and waste time to no purpose.

I am none too clear about the forms now prescribed in the diets for the enactment of laws; but I know that, for the reasons already given, these forms should not be the same as those used in the parliament of Great Britain; that the senate of Poland ought to have administrative rather than legislative authority; and that, in all legislative matters, the senators should vote solely as members of the diet, not as members of the senate, and that the individual votes ought to be counted in both chambers alike. Perhaps the custom of the *liberum veto* has prevented this distinction from being made; but it will be very necessary when the *liberum veto* has been abolished; all the more so since this will deprive the chamber of deputies of an immense advantage, for I do not suppose that the senators, far less the ministers, ever shared in this right. The *veto* of the Polish deputies is like that of the tribunes of the people in Rome; the latter did not exercise this right as citizens, but as representatives of the Roman people. Thus the loss of the *liberum veto* affects only the chamber of deputies; and the senate, which loses nothing thereby, will gain in consequence.

Granted this, I see a defect to be corrected in the diet, namely that, since the number of senators is almost equal to the number of deputies, the senate has too much influence in the deliberations of the diet and, by reason of its prestige in the equestrian order, can easily win over the small number of votes it needs to make it constantly preponderant.

I say that this is a defect; for the senate, as a particular corporate group within the state, necessarily has corporate interests which are different from those of the nation, and which may even, in certain respects, be contrary to them. But the law, which is only the expression of the general will, is properly a resultant of all the particular interests combined and balanced in proportion to their number; but corporate interests, because of their too great weight, would upset the balance, and ought not, in their collective capacity, to be included in it. Each individual should have a vote; no corporate group of any kind should have one. But if the senate had too much weight in the diet, it would not only bring its interests to bear upon it, but would make them preponderant.

A natural remedy for this defect suggests itself, namely to increase the number of deputies; but I would fear that this might make too much commotion in the state and approach too near to democratic tumult. If it were absolutely necessary to change the proportion, I would rather decrease the number of senators than increase the number of deputies. And, after all, I cannot really see why, with a palatine at the head of each province, you also need grand castellans. But we should never lose sight of the important principle of making no unnecessary changes, whether by subtraction or by addition.

It is better, in my opinion, to have a less numerous council, and give its members greater freedom, than to increase its size and hamper its freedom of deliberation, as one is always forced to do when the numbers become excessive. To which I will add, if I may be permitted to foresee good as well as evil, that you must avoid bringing the diet up to its maximum possible size in order not to exclude the possibility later on of readily admitting new deputies, in case you ever come to the point of ennobling cities and enfranchising serfs, as is desirable for the power and happiness of the nation.

Let us then look for means of remedying this defect in another way, and with the smallest possible amount of change.

All senators are appointed by the king, and thus are his creatures; what is more, they hold office for life, and for that reason constitute a corporate group which is independent both of the king and of the equestrian order, a corporate group which, as I have said, has separate interests of its own and must tend to usurpation. And here you must not accuse me of inconsistency in admitting the senate as a separate corporation within the republic, while refusing to admit it as a component part of the republic; for this is a very different matter.

First of all, the king must be deprived of the right of appointment to the senate, not so much because of the power he thus retains over the senators, which may not be great, but because of the power it gives him over all those who aspire to that dignity, and through them over the entire body of the nation. Apart from the effect of this change upon the constitution, it would also have the invaluable advantage of killing the spirit of obsequiousness among the nobility, and replacing it with the spirit of patriotism. I can see no disadvantage in having senators appointed by the diet, and I can see many benefits too obvious to be worth describing in detail. Such appointments can be made either by the diet itself, or else on the prior initiative of the dietines, which would nominate a certain number of candidates for each vacancy in their respective palatinates. The diet would choose between these nominees, or perhaps might eliminate some of them and leave the king with the right to choose from the remainder. But, proceeding immediately to the simplest solution of all, why should not each palatine be elected directly by the dietine of his own province? What difficulties have been seen to result from the use of this method in the election of the palatines of Polock and Witebsk, and of the starosta[1] of Samogitia? And what harm would it do to make the privilege of these three provinces the common right of all? Let us not forget how important it is for Poland to turn its constitution in the direction of federalism, in order to avoid as far as possible the

[1] [The holder of a castle and domain bestowed by the Crown.—Tʀ.]

evils that accompany the size, or rather the extensiveness, of the state.

In the second place, if you deprive the senators of life tenure, you will weaken considerably their corporate interest, which tends to usurpation. But this change involves certain difficulties; first, because it is hard for men accustomed to the conduct of public affairs to see themselves suddenly reduced to private life without any fault of their own; second, because senatorial positions are joined with the titles of palatine and castellan and with the local authority attached to them, which means that disorder and discontent would result from the perpetual transfer of those titles and that authority from one individual to another. Finally, this insecurity of tenure cannot be extended to bishops, and perhaps ought not to be extended to ministers, whose positions call for special talents and therefore are not always easy to fill satisfactorily. If the bishops alone held office for life, the authority of the clergy, already excessive, would be considerably increased; and it is important that this authority should be counterbalanced by senators who, like the bishops, enjoy life tenure, and have no more fear than they of being removed.

The following is the remedy I would devise to meet these various difficulties. I should like the positions of first-class senators to continue to be held for life. This would include, in addition to the bishops and the palatines, all the first-class castellans, making eighty-nine irremovable senators.

As to the second-class castellans, I should like to have them serve for a fixed term, perhaps two years, with a new election at each diet, perhaps for a longer period if it were thought proper; but in any case they would leave office at the end of each term, except for those whom the diet might wish to continue in office; and I would place a fixed limit on the number of permissible re-elections, according to a plan which will be described hereafter.

The question of titles would be no great obstacle, since these titles would confer hardly any other function than that of sitting in the senate, and could therefore be eliminated without difficulty; instead of bearing the title of *senatorial castellans* they could simply be called *elective senators*. Since, under our reforms, the senate would be vested with the executive power, a part of its membership would remain in permanent session, and a certain proportion of elective senators would consequently be required to attend in rotation. But this is no place to consider details of this sort.

By this scarcely perceptible change, these castellans or elective senators would really become as many representatives of the diet, which would form a counterweight to the body of the senate, and would strengthen the equestrian order in the assemblies of the nation; with the result that the life senators, though strengthened both by the abolition of the *veto* and by the reduction of the power of king and ministers, and partly merged with the rest of the senate, would be unable to dominate the group consciousness of that body; and the senate, now composed half of life members and half of members for a term, would be as well as possible constituted to serve as an intermediary power between the chamber of deputies and the king, being firm enough to control the administration, and at the same time sufficiently dependent to be subject to law. This arrangement strikes me as a good one, for it is simple and at the same time highly effective.

I shall not pause at this point to consider voting methods. They are not difficult to arrange in an assembly composed of some three hundred members.

In London it is managed successfully in a much larger parliament; in Geneva, where the general council is larger still, and riddled by mutual suspicions; and even in Venice, in a grand council of some twelve hundred noblemen, where vice and rascality are rampant. I have, moreover, discussed this subject in the *Social Contract;* and for anyone who has any regard for my opinions, that is the work to consult.

To moderate the abuses of the *veto*, it is suggested that the deputies should no longer be counted individually, but by palatinates. Although this reform has some advantages, and is favourable to the growth of federalism, you should think it over most carefully before adopting it. Votes taken collectively and in the mass always proceed less directly toward the common interest than do those which are taken individually and separately. It will very often happen that, among the deputies of a palatinate, there is one who, in their private deliberations, will acquire an ascendancy over the others, and will convert to his way of thinking a majority which would have thought otherwise if each had voted independently. Under these conditions, corruptionists will have less to do, and will have a better idea of the men with whom they ought to make contact. Furthermore it is better for each deputy to have to answer individually to the dietine, in order that no one may be able to hide behind others, that the innocent and the guilty may not be confused, and that distributive justice may be better done. There are many arguments to be raised against this arrangement, which would greatly loosen the common bond, and might well expose the state to division at every diet. By making the deputies more dependent on their constituents and their instructions, you will secure almost the same advantages with no disadvantages. This assumes, to be sure, that votes are not to be cast secretly but in public, so that the acts and opinions of each deputy in the diet will be known, and that he may answer for them personally and in his own name. But since this question of voting is among those I have most carefully discussed in the *Social Contract*, it is superfluous to repeat myself here.

With regard to elections, it may perhaps be difficult at first to appoint so many elective senators all at once in each diet; and in general it may be hard to select a large number out of a still larger number, as my constitutional proposals occasionally require. But if, for this purpose, you resorted to balloting, you would easily avoid these difficulties by distributing to the electors, on the eve of election, printed and numbered ballots with the names of all eligible candidates. The next day the electors would come in turn to cast them in the ballot-box, after having marked them, according to the instructions printed thereon, with the names of those chosen and rejected. The counting of these ballots would be done immediately, in the presence of the assembly, by the secretary of the diet, with the assistance of two additional secretaries *ad actum*, to be named forthwith by the marshal from among the deputies present. In this way the operation would become so short and simple that, without clamour or discussion, the whole senate could easily be filled at a single sitting. It is true that further rules will also be needed to determine the list of candidates; but this subject will be remembered and dealt with hereafter.

It remains to speak of the king, who presides over the diet, and who ought, by right of his office, to be the supreme administrator of the laws.

Chapter VIII

THE KING

It is a great misfortune for the head of a nation to be the enemy of freedom, whose defender he should be. This misfortune, in my opinion, is not inherent in the office to such an extent that it cannot be separated from it, or at least considerably diminished. Temptation cannot live without hope. Make your kings incapable of usurpation, and you will prevent them from dreaming of it; and they will apply to the task of governing and defending you well all the energies they now devote to your enslavement. The founders of Poland, as Count Wielhorski has observed, were careful to deny its kings all the instruments of malice, but not those of corruption; and the favours at their disposal are ample for the purpose. The difficulty is that if you deny them the right to grant favours, you would seem to deny them everything. This, however, is precisely the thing to be avoided; for it would be the same thing as saying you did not want a king; and I do not believe that a state as large as Poland could possibly get along without one, that is to say, without a chief of state holding office for life. But unless the leader of a nation is to be a mere cipher, and therefore useless, he must be able to do something; and however little he may be able to do, it must be done either for good or ill.

At the present time the senate is appointed by the king, which is too much. If he has no hand in these appointments, it is not enough. Although the peerage in England is also appointed by the king, it is less dependent on him, since these peerages, once granted, are hereditary; whereas the bishoprics, palatinates and castellanships, being for life only, revert on the death of each holder to the gift of the king.

I have said how, in my opinion, these appointments should be made, namely that the palatines and grand castellans should be named for life by their respective dietines, and the second-class castellans for a specific term by the diet. With regard to the bishops, it seems to me that it would be hard to deprive the king of the right of appointment, unless provision were made to have them elected by their chapters; and I think that this power can well be left to him, except in the case of the archbishop of Gniezno, whose appointment lies naturally within the province of the diet, unless the office be separated from the primacy, which should be at the disposal of the diet only.

As for the ministers, above all the commanders-in-chief and grand treasurers, although their power, which serves as a counter-weight to that of the king, should be diminished in proportion to his own, I do not think it prudent to leave the king with the right to fill these positions with his creatures; and I should like at least to restrict his choice to a small number of nominees presented by the diet. I admit that, since he cannot withdraw these offices after having granted them, he cannot absolutely count on the office-holders. But the power this gives him over office-seekers is sufficient, if not to enable him to change the complexion of the government, at least to give him the hope of doing so; and this is the very hope of which he must be deprived at all costs.

The grand chancellor ought, I think, to be appointed by the king. Kings are the born judges of their people; it was for this office, although they have all abandoned it, that they were first created; it cannot be denied them; and if they do not wish to exercise it themselves, the appointment of proxies for this function is theirs by right, since they will always have to answer for the judgments of those who speak in their name. The nation can, to be sure, give them associate justices, and ought to do so when kings themselves do not give judgment; thus the crown court, which is presided over not by the king but by the grand chancellor, is under the supervision of the nation; and it is right that the dietines should appoint the other members. If the king gave justice in person, I think that he would have the right to be sole judge. In any case, it would always be in his interest to be just; and iniquitous judgments were never a good highway to usurpation.

With regard to other dignities, royal or palatine, which are merely honorific titles, and bring more glitter than credit, you could do no better than to leave them at the full disposal of the king. Let him honour merit and flatter vanity, but do not let him confer power.

The majesty of the throne should be maintained with splendour; but it is important that the king should be left with the smallest possible control over the expenditure necessary for this purpose. It would be desirable for all royal officials to be paid by the Republic, rather than by him, and for the royal revenues to be proportionately reduced, in order to minimise, as far as possible, the handling of money by the king.

It has been suggested that the crown should be made hereditary. I assure you that, at the moment when this law is adopted, Poland can say good-bye for ever to her freedom. You think you can meet the situation by limiting the royal power. You do not realise that these legal limitations will be broken down in the course of time by gradual usurpations, and that a policy adopted and followed without interruption by a royal family is bound in the long run to win out over laws which, by their very nature, tend constantly to relax. If the king cannot corrupt the magnates by favours, he can always corrupt them by promises guaranteed by his successors; and since the plans of the royal family are perpetuated together with the family itself, these obligations will be taken much more seriously, and their fulfilment will be much more relied on, than when an elective crown shows that the plans of the monarch will end with his own life. Poland is free because each reign is preceded by an interval when the nation, renewing all its rights and regaining new vigour, cuts off the progress of abuses and usurpations, when the law revives and recovers its original power. What will become of the *pacta conventa*, the aegis of Poland, if a family, established on the throne in perpetuity, occupies it without interruption, leaving the nation, between the death of the father and the coronation of the son, no more than a vain shadow of ineffective liberty, which soon will nullify the farcical oath sworn by all kings at their coronation, and the moment after forgotten by all forever? You have seen Denmark, you see England, you are about to see Sweden. Profit by these examples to learn once and for all that, no matter how many safeguards may be accumulated, heredity in the crown and freedom in the nation will always be incompatible.

The Poles have always had a tendency to transmit the throne from father to son, or to the nearest heir, though always by election. This inclination, if they continue to follow it, will lead them sooner or later to the misfortune of rendering the throne hereditary; and along these lines they cannot hope to put up as long a struggle against the royal power as have the members of the Holy Roman Empire against the power of the emperor; for Poland does not contain within herself any counterweight which would suffice to keep a

209

hereditary monarch subordinate to law. Despite the power of several members of the Empire, if it had not been for the chance election of Charles VII, the imperial capitulations would already be no more than an empty formality, as they were at the beginning of the century; and the *pacta conventa* will become even more futile when the royal family has had time to establish itself and subordinate all the rest. To summarise my feelings on this subject, I think that it would actually be better for Poland to have an elective crown whose powers were absolute than a hereditary crown whose powers were practically nil.

In place of this disastrous law which would make the crown hereditary, I would suggest a quite different one which, if accepted, would preserve the liberty of Poland; this would be to prescribe by constitutional law that the crown should never pass from father to son, and that every son of a Polish king should forever be excluded from the throne. I say that I would propose this law if it were necessary; but I have in mind another plan which would produce the same effect, and I shall defer until the proper time my explanation of it; but assuming that my plan has the effect of excluding sons from the throne of their father, at least in direct succession, I believe that the ensurance of liberty will not be the only advantage resulting from this exclusion. It will give rise to another even greater benefit; which is that, by depriving kings of all hope of usurping arbitrary power and passing it on to their children, it will direct all their energies toward the glory and prosperity of the state, the sole remaining outlet for their ambitions. It is thus that the ruler of the nation, ceasing to be its hereditary enemy, will become its first citizen; it is thus that he will make it his great concern to render his reign illustrious by useful works, which will endear him to his people, win him the esteem of his neighbours, and make men bless his memory after him; and it is thus that, apart from the means of coercion and seduction, which should never be left in his hands, it will be proper to increase his power in all that pertains to the public welfare. He himself will have little direct and immediate power of action; but he will have great authority, and great powers of supervision and control, to hold each man to his duty, and to guide the government towards its true goal. To preside over the diet, the senate and all corporate groups, to examine strictly the conduct of all office-holders, to take great pains to maintain justice and the integrity of all the law courts, to preserve order and tranquillity in the state, to maintain its position abroad, to command its armies in time of war, to inaugurate useful works in time of peace, these are the duties which particularly pertain to his royal office, and which will give him enough to do if he tries to discharge them in person. For, considering that the details of administration are entrusted to officials created for that purpose, it should be a criminal offence for a king of Poland to entrust any part of his own administrative authority to favourites. Let him ply his trade in person, or abandon it; this is an important point, on which the nation ought never to yield.

Similar principles should be followed in establishing a proper balance and proportion between the legislative and administrative powers. In order to achieve the best possible balance, the power of any given depositary of these powers should be in direct proportion to the number of those who share it, and in inverse proportion to the length of their tenure. The component parts of the diet will come rather close to this ideal relationship. The chamber of deputies, which is the more numerous body, will also be the more powerful; but its entire membership will change frequently. The senate, which is less numerous, will have a smaller share in legislation, but a greater share in the executive power; and its members, standing half-way between the two extremes, will be partly for life and partly for a fixed term, as is appropriate to an intermediary body. The king, who presides over the whole, will continue to hold office for life; and his power, while remaining very great for purposes of supervision, will be limited, with regard to legislation, by the chamber of deputies and with regard to administration by the senate. But in order to maintain equality, the underlying principle of the constitution, nothing therein should be hereditary except the nobility. If the crown were hereditary, it would be necessary to counterbalance it by making the peerage or senatorial order likewise hereditary, as in England. In that case the degraded equestrian order would lose its power, for the chamber of deputies, unlike the house of commons, does not have the annual right of opening or closing the public purse; and the Polish constitution would be overthrown from top to bottom.

Chapter IX

SPECIFIC CAUSES OF ANARCHY

If the diet is thus well balanced and proportioned in all its parts, it will produce good laws and a good government. But this requires that its orders should be respected and obeyed. The anarchy and the contempt for law under which Poland has lived up to now are the result of clearly visible causes. I have already identified the principal one, and indicated the means of curing it. The other contributing causes are

(1) the *liberum veto*, (2) the confederations, and (3) the wrongful use by private citizens of the right to employ armed followers.

The last abuse is such that, if it is not eliminated from the start, all other reforms will be useless. As long as private citizens have the power to resist the force of the executive, they will think they have the right to do so; and as long as they wage petty wars against each other, how can the state live in peace? I admit that fortresses require guardians; but why should there be fortresses which are strong only against citizens, and weak against the enemy? I fear that this reform may encounter difficulties; I do not, however, consider them insuperable, and if a powerful citizen is but reasonable, he will not mind giving up his own armed retainers, provided that all the rest do likewise.

I shall speak hereafter of the military establishment; I shall therefore postpone until then things that might well have been said at this point.

The *liberum veto* is not in itself a pernicious right, but when it oversteps its limits it immediately becomes the most dangerous of abuses. Once it was the guarantor of public freedom; now it is only an instrument of oppression. To eliminate this fatal abuse, it is necessary merely to eliminate the cause. But the heart of man is such that he clings to personal privileges rather than to greater and more general advantages. Only patriotism, enlightened by experience, can learn to sacrifice in the interest of greater goods a spectacular right grown evil by abuse, and henceforth inseparable from that abuse. All Poles should be keenly aware of the evils this unfortunate right has made them suffer. If they love peace and order, they cannot make either prevail among them as long as they allow this right to continue; for although this right was good when the body politic was being formed, or remained in full perfection, it becomes absurd and disastrous as soon as change becomes necessary. And change will always be necessary, above all in a large state surrounded by powerful and ambitious neighbours.

The *liberum veto* would be less absurd if it applied only to the basic principles of the constitution; but that it should be used indiscriminately in all proceedings of the diet is absolutely inadmissible. One of the defects of the Polish constitution is that it fails to make a sufficiently clear distinction between legislation and administration; and that the diet, when it exercises legislative power, combines it with administrative measures, indiscriminately performing acts of sovereignty and acts of government, often actually in the form of mixed actions, in which the members serve simultaneously as magistrates and as legislators.

Our proposed reforms tend to distinguish more clearly between the two powers, and thus to define more accurately the limits of the *liberum veto*. For I do not believe that anyone ever took it into his head to extend it to questions of pure administration, for that would mean abolishing civil authority and all government.

Under the natural law of societies, unanimity was requisite to the formation of the body politic and of the fundamental laws necessary to its existence; such, for example, were the first (as amended), the fifth, the ninth, and the eleventh statutes enacted by the pseudo-diet of 1768. But the unanimity required for the adoption of these laws should equally be required for their abrogation. These, then, are the matters on which the *liberum veto* can continue to operate. And since it is not a question of destroying this right entirely, the Poles who, without too much grumbling, saw it restricted by the diet of 1768, ought easily to see it reduced and limited by a freer and more lawful diet.

The basic points to be established as fundamental laws should be carefully weighed and considered; and these points only should be subject to the *liberum veto*. This will make the constitution as firm and the laws as irrevocable as possible. For it is contrary to the nature of the body politic to be subject to irrevocable laws; but it is contrary neither to nature nor to reason to require that they should be revoked only with the same formalities that brought them into being. That is the only chain with which we can bind the future. This will suffice both to strengthen the constitution, and to satisfy the Poles in their love of the *liberum veto*, without exposing them to the evil consequences to which it has given rise.

As to the multitude of provisions which have been absurdly counted as fundamental articles, and which are nothing more than ordinary acts of legislation, and with regard also to those subsumed under the term questions of state, these are subject, in the natural course of events, to necessary alterations which make it impossible to demand that they be passed unanimously. Furthermore it is absurd that, on each and every question, a single member of the diet should be able to prevent all action, or that the resignation or protest of one or more deputies should be able to dissolve the assembly, and thus cashier the sovereign authority. This barbarous right must be abolished, and the capital penalty decreed against anyone who might be tempted to use it. If there were occasion for protest against the diet, which cannot happen as long as it is free and plenary, it is on the palatinates and dietines that this right might be conferred; but never on the deputies who, as members of the diet, should never have any measure of authority over it, nor any right to challenge its decisions.

Between the *veto*, which is the greatest power individually exercisable by members of the sovereign, and ought never to occur except in the case of truly fundamental laws, and a bare majority, which is the minimum, and has reference to mere acts of administration, there are various intermediary cases in which the extent of agreement should be in proportion to the importance of the matter. For instance, when it is a question of legislation, three-quarters at least of the votes may be required, two-thirds in questions of state, and no more than a bare majority for elections and for other matters of current and temporary interest. I give this only as an illustration of my ideas, and not as a set of figures by which I would be willing to stand.

In a state like Poland, where there is still a great deal of spiritual vitality, it might have been possible to preserve the admirable right of the *liberum veto* in its entirety without much danger, and perhaps even with profit, if the use of that right had been made dangerous and attended by serious consequences for the user. For surely it is inconceivable for anyone who thus prevents the diet from acting, and leaves the state without means of action, to go quietly home and enjoy with impunity the public desolation he has caused.

In the case of a nearly unanimous resolution, therefore, if a single opponent retained the right of veto, I should want him to answer for it with his life, not only to his constituents in the subsequent dietine, but thereafter to the whole of the nation whose misfortune he had been. I should like the law to prescribe that, six months after his negative vote, he should be solemnly tried by an extraordinary court expressly constituted to consider the case, made up of the wisest, most respectable

216

and most illustrious men of the nation; and this court would not be allowed merely to declare him guilty or not guilty, but would have either to condemn him to death without hope of pardon, or to award him compensation and public honours for life, without ever being able to adopt any mean between these two extremes.

Institutions of this sort, favourable as they are to vigorous courage and to the love of liberty, are too far removed from the modern spirit to have any hope of being either adopted or admired. But they were not unknown to the ancients; and that is how the founders of their constitutions were able to uplift the souls of men and inflame them, when necessary, with a truly heroic ardour. In republics where even harsher laws were in force, unselfish citizens were known to dedicate themselves to death when the fatherland was in danger, by offering advice calculated to save it. A *veto* entailing the same danger may occasionally save the republic, and will never cause it much uneasiness.

Dare I speak of the confederations, and go counter to the opinion of the experts? The latter see only the evils they have caused; the evils they prevent should also be recognised. Undoubtedly confederation is a time of violence in the republic; but there are extreme evils which call for violent remedies, and which we must try to cure at any price. Confederation is to Poland what dictatorship was to the Romans. Both cause the laws to be silent in time of pressing danger; but with this great difference, that dictatorship, being directly contrary to the laws of Rome and to the spirit of the Roman government, ended by destroying it, whereas the confederations, being only a very energetic means of confirming and re-establishing the hard-pressed constitution, is capable of tightening and re-enforcing the relaxed vigour of the state, without ever being able to break it. This federative form of action, although it may have arisen by accident, strikes me as a political masterpiece. Wherever liberty reigns it is constantly under attack, and very often in danger. Every free state in which no provision has been made for great crises is in danger of perishing with every storm. Only the Poles have been able to convert their very crises into a new means of safeguarding their constitution. Without the confederations the Polish republic would long since have ceased to exist, and I am afraid that it will not long survive if you decide to abolish them. Consider for a moment the events that have just occurred. Without the confederations the state would have been subjugated, and freedom destroyed forever. Do you want to deprive the republic of the resource that has just preserved it?

And do not suppose that if the *liberum veto* is abolished and majority rule re-established, the confederations would be useless, as if majority rule were their only value. Confederation and majority rule are by no means identical. The executive power implicit in confederations will always give them, in times of extreme need, a degree of vigour, activity and speed impossible in the diet, which is forced to proceed by slower and more formal steps, and which cannot make a single irregular move without overthrowing the constitution.

No, the confederations are the shield, the refuge, the sanctuary of this constitution. As long as they endure, I cannot see how it can be destroyed. They must be left in existence, but also regulated. If all abuses were eliminated, the confederations would become practically unnecessary. The reform of your government should accomplish this result. Violent undertakings alone should then force you to have recourse to them; but such undertakings are among the things for which provision ought to be made. Instead, therefore, of abolishing the confederations, determine the conditions under which they may legitimately occur; and then regulate their composition and powers, so as to give them legal sanction, as far as possible, without hampering their creation or operation. There may even be cases where the facts themselves will call for the immediate confederation of the whole of Poland, as when, for example, on some pretext or other and without open warfare, foreign troops set foot within the state; for after all, whatever the excuse for their entry, and even if the government itself consented to it, confederation at home does not mean enmity abroad. When the diet is prevented, by any obstacle whatsoever, from meeting at the time prescribed by law; when men at arms, at the instigation of no matter whom, are made to appear at the time and place of meeting; if its form is changed, or its activity suspended, or its freedom interfered with in any way; in all such cases a general confederation ought to occur automatically. Meetings and signatures of private citizens are merely offshoots of such a confederation; and all its marshals should accept the commands of whomever it names as leader.

Chapter X

ADMINISTRATION

WITHOUT entering into the details of administration, on which I am lacking equally in knowledge and in ideas, I shall venture simply to express certain views on the two subjects of war and finance, views which I feel I ought to express, because I think them good, although

I am practically certain that they will not be relished. But first of all I shall make an observation on the administration of justice which is not quite so alien to the spirit of the Polish government.

Our distinction between the legal and the military castes was unknown to the ancients. Citizens were neither lawyers nor soldiers nor priests by profession; they performed all these functions as a matter of duty. That is the real secret of making everything proceed toward the common goal, and of preventing the spirit of faction from taking root at the expense of patriotism, so that the hydra of chicanery will not devour a nation. The office of judge, both in the highest and in the local courts, should be a temporary employment by which the nation may test and evaluate the merit and probity of a citizen, in order to raise him thereafter to those more important positions of which he has been found capable. This way of looking at themselves cannot fail to make judges very careful to place themselves absolutely above reproach, and in general to give them all the attentiveness and integrity their office demands. Thus it was, when Rome was at its best, that people passed through the praetorship in order to reach the consulate. In this way it is possible, with a few clear and simple laws, and even with few judges, to have justice well administered, leaving the judges with power to interpret the laws, and when necessary to supplement them in the light of natural justice and common sense. Nothing could be more puerile than the precautions taken on this point by the English. To eliminate arbitrary judgments, they have subjected themselves to a thousand judgments which are iniquitous and even absurd. Hordes of lawyers devour them, endless lawsuits consume them; and with the mad idea of trying to provide for every eventuality, they have turned their laws into an immense labyrinth where memory and reason alike are lost.

You must have three codes, covering constitutional, civil and criminal law respectively; all three as clear, short and precise as possible. These codes will be taught not only in the universities but also in all the secondary schools; and you will need no other body of law. All the rules of natural law are better graven in the hearts of men than in all the rubbish of Justinian. Just make men honest and virtuous, and I assure you that their knowledge of law will be sufficient. But it is necessary for all citizens, and particularly for public figures, to be taught the positive laws of their own country, and the particular rules by which they are governed. They will find them in the codes they are to study; and all noblemen, before being enrolled in the golden book which is to qualify them for admission to a dietine, must pass on the subject of these codes, especially the first, an examination which is no mere formality, and if their knowledge proves not to be sufficient, they will be sent back until it is. As far as Rome and customary law is concerned, all that, if it exists, should be eliminated from the schools and law courts. No other authority than the laws of the state should be recognised; these laws should be uniform in all the provinces, thus drying up one source of litigation; and questions left unanswered by these laws must be settled by the common sense and integrity of the judges. You may be sure that, when the judicial office is nothing more, for those who occupy it, than a place to test their capacity for higher things, they will not abuse their authority as much as you might fear; or that, if there are abuses, they will always be less than those which arise from a mass of laws which are often in conflict, which by their proliferation cause lawsuits to drag on endlessly, and by their contradictions lead also to arbitrary judgments.

What I have been saying of judges should apply *a fortiori* to lawyers. This calling, intrinsically so respectable, grows vile and degrading as soon as it becomes a trade. The lawyer should be the first and severest judge of his client; his job should be, as it was in Rome and still is in Geneva, the first step toward public office ; and in Geneva lawyers are in fact highly respected, and deserve to be. They are candidates for the council, and are very careful to do nothing that will bring them public disapproval. I should like every public function to serve in this way as a stepping-stone to another, so that no one, in the expectation of staying in any one office, will turn it into a lucrative profession, and place himself above the judgment of men. This arrangement would conform perfectly with my desire to have the children of rich citizens pass through the legal calling, now rendered both honorific and temporary. I shall develop this idea further in a moment.

At this point I should say in passing, since it occurs to me, that it is contrary to the principle of equality within the equestrian order for its members to entail their property in any way. Legislation must always tend to diminish those great inequalities of fortune and power which set too great a distance between magnates and simple noblemen, and which always have a natural tendency to increase. With regard to property qualifications, which would determine the amount of land a nobleman would have to own in order to be admitted to the dietines, I can see that there is something to be said both for and against the proposal, and since my knowledge of the country is insufficient to enable me to estimate the consequences, it would be utterly foolhardy for me to reach any conclusion on the matter.

Undoubtedly it would be desirable for a citizen voting in a palatinate to own some land therein, but I should not be too happy to see any fixed quantity prescribed. Granted that possessions are important, are men to count for nothing? What? Does a gentleman, because he has little or no land, cease thereby to be free and noble? And is his poverty alone a crime so grave as to make him forfeit his rights as a citizen?

One final observation: no law should ever be allowed to fall into disuse. Be it bad or indifferent, it should either be formally repealed, or else rigorously enforced. This principle, which is fundamental, will make it necessary to pass all old laws in review, to repeal many of them, and to support with the severest sanctions those you decide to keep. Turning a blind eye toward many things is regarded in France as a basic principle of government; that is what despotism always forces us to do. But in a free government it is a sure means of enfeebling the laws and shaking the constitution. We want few laws, but those well classified, and above all well enforced. All abuses which are not forbidden remain inconsequential; but anyone who utters the word ' law ' in a free state is invoking that before which every citizen, including first of all the king, should tremble. In short, suffer anything to happen rather than to weaken the force of law; for once its power has been exhausted, the state is lost beyond redemption.

Chapter XI

THE ECONOMIC SYSTEM

THE choice of an economic system to be adopted by Poland depends on the purposes she has in view in

THE GOVERNMENT OF POLAND

reforming her constitution. If your only wish is to become noisy, brilliant and fearsome, and to influence the other peoples of Europe, their example lies before you; devote yourselves to following it. Cultivate the arts and sciences, commerce and industry; have professional soldiers, fortresses, and academies ; above all have a good system of public finance which will make money circulate rapidly, and thereby multiply its effectiveness to your great profit; try to make money very necessary, in order to keep the people in a condition of great dependence; and with that end in view, encourage material luxury, and the luxury of spirit which is inseparable from it. In this way you will create a scheming, ardent, avid, ambitious, servile and knavish people, like all the rest; one given to the two extremes of opulence and misery, of licence and slavery, with nothing in between. But you will be counted as one of the great powers of Europe; you will be included in all diplomatic combinations; in all negotiations your alliance will be courted; you will be bound by treaties; and there will be no war in Europe into which you will not have the honour of being plunged. If you are lucky, you will be able to recover your ancient possessions, perhaps to conquer new ones, and you will be able to say, like Pyrrhus or the Russians—in other words, like children—' When the whole world is mine, I shall eat a lot of candy.'

But if, by chance, you would prefer to create a free, wise and peaceful nation, one which has no fear or need of anyone, but is self-sufficient and happy, then you must adopt wholly different methods; you must preserve and revive among your people simple customs and wholesome tastes, and a warlike spirit devoid of ambition; you must create courageous and unselfish souls; devote your people to agriculture and to the most necessary arts and crafts; you must make money contemptible and, if possible, useless, seeking and finding more powerful and reliable motives for the accomplishment of great deeds. I admit that, in following this path, you will not fill the news-sheets with the noise of your celebrations, negotiations, and exploits; the philosophers will burn you no incense, poets will not sing your praises, and you will not be much talked about in Europe; people may even pretend to hold you in contempt. But you will live in true prosperity, justice and liberty; no one will try to pick a quarrel with you; people will fear you without admitting it; and I guarantee that neither the Russians nor anyone else will ever again come to rule over you, or that if, to their own misfortune, they do come, they will leave even more hurriedly. Above all, beware of trying to combine these two objectives, for they are too incompatible; and if you try to divide your forces and march toward both, you are condemning yourselves to a double failure. Choose then ; and if you prefer the first, stop reading me. For all my remaining proposals are directed exclusively to the second.

Excellent economic ideas are undoubtedly to be found in the various papers that have been sent to me. The fault I find with them is that they are more favourable to wealth than to prosperity. In creating new institutions, you must not be content with seeing the immediate effects; you must also correctly foresee the distant but inevitable consequences. The proposal that has been made, for example, for the sale of starosties and for the use of the resulting revenues, strikes me as perfectly normal and feasible under the prevailing European system of using money to accomplish everything. But is this system good in itself, and does it really achieve its purposes? Is it true that money is the sinew of war? Rich peoples have always been beaten and conquered by poor peoples. Is it true that money is the mainspring of good government? Financial systems are modern. I cannot see that anything good or great has come of them. The governments of antiquity did not even know the meaning of the word finance, and what they accomplished with men is prodigious. Money at best is a supplement to men, and the supplement is never worth as much as the thing itself. Men of Poland, leave all this money, I pray you, to other peoples; or content yourselves with what they will have to give you, since they have more need of your wheat than you of their gold. Believe me, it is better to live in plenty than in opulence; be more than pecunious, be rich. Cultivate your fields well, and have no other care; soon you will be harvesting gold, more than enough to buy the oil and wine you need, for Poland abounds, or can abound, in almost everything else. If you want to keep yourselves free and happy, heads, hearts and arms are what you want; it is they that constitute the power of a state and the prosperity of a people. Financial systems make venal souls; and when profit is the only goal, it is always more profitable to be a rascal than to be an honest man. The use of money is devious and secret; it is destined for one thing and used for another. Those who handle it soon learn how to deflect it from its course; and are the overseers appointed to control it anything more than another set of rascals sent to share the spoils? If public and visible riches were the only form of wealth, if the passage of gold left clear traces and could not be concealed, you could ask for no better means of buying services, courage, fidelity and virtue. But since the circulation of money is secret, it is a still better means of making pilferers and traitors, and of putting freedom and the public good upon the auction block. In short, of all the incentives known to me, money is at once the weakest and most useless for the purpose of driving the political mechanism toward its goal, and the strongest and most reliable for the purpose of deflecting it from its course.

I know that men can only be made to act in terms of their own interests; but pecuniary interest is the worst, the basest and the most corrupting of all, and even, as I confidently repeat and shall always maintain, the least and weakest in the eyes of those who really know the human heart. In all hearts there is naturally a reserve of grand passions; when greed for gold alone remains, it is because all the rest, which should have been stimulated and developed, have been enervated and stifled. The miser has no truly dominant passion; he aspires to money only as a matter of foresight, in order to be able to satisfy such passions as may thereafter come to him. Learn how to foment and satisfy them directly, without the use of money, and money will soon lose all its value.

I also admit that public expenditures are inevitable; effect them with anything rather than with money. Even today, in Switzerland, you see officers, magistrates and other public stipendiaries being paid in kind. They receive tithes of wine and wood; these are useful and honorific rights. The whole public service is performed by corvées; the state pays for almost nothing in money. You will say that money is necessary for the payment of soldiers. We shall consider this point in a moment. Payment in kind is not without its disadvantages; there is loss and waste; the administration of this form of wealth is comparatively inconvenient; it is especially irksome to those who are in charge of it, since it gives them fewer opportunities for profit. All that is true;

but the evil is slight in comparison with the host of evils it prevents! A man would like to commit malversation, but he cannot do so without being found out. The example of the bailiffs of the Canton of Berne will be cited against me; but why are they vexatioûs? Because of the money fines they levy. These arbitrary fines are in themselves most objectionable; if they could, however, be paid in kind rather than in money, the evil would be almost negligible. Extorted money can be easily hidden; warehouses would be less easy to conceal. Ten times more money is handled in the single canton of Berne than in all the rest of Switzerland, and its administration is iniquitous in the same proportion. Look at every country, every government, every part of the world; nowhere will you find a great evil in morals and politics where money is not involved.

You will say that the equality of fortunes which reigns in Switzerland makes it easy for the administration to be economical; whereas the great families and magnates of Poland require great expenditures, and great financial resources to meet them. Not at all. These magnates are rich in their own right; and their expenditures will diminish when luxury ceases to be esteemed in the state, without distinguishing them any the less from men of inferior fortune, whose expenditures will diminish in the same proportion. Pay for their services with authority, honours and exalted positions. In Poland, inequality of rank is compensated by the privilege of noble birth, which makes office-holders jealous rather of honour than of profit. The republic, by appropriately gradating and distributing these purely honorific rewards, will husband a treasure which will never ruin it, and which will give it heroes for citizens. The treasure of honours is an inexhaustible resource for a people which has a sense of honour; and would to God that Poland could hope to exhaust it! How happy the nation which cannot possibly find in its bosom any further distinctions for virtue!

Pecuniary compensation has the defect not only of being an unworthy reward for virtue, but also of being insufficiently public, of failing to make a continuous impression on the minds and hearts of men, of disappearing as soon as it is awarded, and of leaving no visible trace to excite emulation by perpetuating the honour which should accompany it. I should like to have all ranks, offices, and honorific awards distinguished by external signs, so that no public figure would ever be allowed to go *incognito*, but would be followed everywhere by the marks of his rank or dignity; this would make people respect him at all times, and at all times make him keep his own self-respect; it would enable him to dominate over opulence; for a man who was rich and nothing more would constantly find himself cast in the shade by poor but titled citizens, and would find no pleasure or esteem in his own country; this would force him to serve his country in order to cut a figure in it, to be a man of integrity for reasons of ambition, and to aspire, in spite of his wealth, to ranks attainable only through public approbation, and liable at all times to be lost through disapproval. That is the way to sap the strength of wealth, and to create men who are not for sale. I lay great emphasis on this point, for I am sure that your neighbours, particularly the Russians, will spare no efforts to corrupt your officials, and that the great problem of your government is to strive to make them incorruptible.

If it should be said I am trying to turn Poland into a nation of mendicant friars I should first retort that this is only a Frenchman's sort of argument, and that a witticism is not a rational procf. I should also reply that my maxims ought not to be stretched beyond the limits either of my own intentions, or of reason; that my object is not to prevent the circulation of specie, but merely to slow it down, and above all to show how important it is for a good economic system not to be a system of money and public finance. To eradicate cupidity in Sparta, Lycurgus did not abolish money, but had it made of iron. I myself have no intention of banning gold or silver, but merely of making them less necessary, and of arranging things so that a man who has none can be poor without being a beggar. Basically, money is not wealth, but only a token thereof; it is not the token but the thing it represents that ought to be multiplied. I have seen, in spite of travellers' tales, that the English, in the midst of all their gold, are individually no less needy than other peoples. And what does it matter to me, after all, to have a hundred guineas instead of ten, if the hundred do not bring me a more comfortable living? Pecuniary wealth is only relative; and as relations change through the operation of a thousand possible causes, you may find yourself successively rich and poor with the same sum of money; but this is not true of natural goods; for they, being immediately useful to man, always have an absolute value which in no way depends on the operations of trade. I will grant you that the English people is richer than the others; but it does not follow that a citizen of London lives more comfortably than a citizen of Paris. As between peoples, the advantage rests with the one which has the more money. But that has nothing to do with the lot of private individuals; and the prosperity of a nation does not lie therein.

Encourage agriculture and the useful arts, not by enriching the farmers, which would only incite them to leave their calling, but by making that calling pleasant and honourable. Establish the most necessary manufactures; multiply your wheat and men unceasingly, and do not worry about the rest. The surplus produce of your soil, produce which, as a result of increasing monopolies, will be lacking in the rest of Europe, will necessarily bring you more money than you need. Apart from this necessary and certain produce, you will be poor as long as you want more; and as soon as you learn how to get along without more, you will be rich. The prevailing spirit of your economic system, if I had my way, would be as follows: pay little attention to foreign countries, give little heed to commerce; but multiply as far as possible your domestic production and consumption of foodstuffs. The inevitable and natural result of a free and just government is increased population. The more you perfect your government, therefore, the more will you multiply your people even without intending to do so. You will thus have neither beggars nor millionaires. Luxury and indigence together will insensibly disappear; and the citizens, cured of the frivolous tastes created by opulence, and of the vices associated with poverty, will devote their best efforts to serving the country, and will find their glory and happiness in doing their duty.

I should like you always to lay heavier charges on the personal services than on the purses of men, using corvées and not money payments to provide roads, bridges, public buildings, and the service of prince and state. This sort of tax is basically the least onerous, and above all it is the one least subject to abuse. For money disappears when it leaves the hands of those who are paying; but everyone can see what work men are doing, and they cannot be overburdened to no purpose. I know that this method is impractical where luxury, commerce and the arts are in the ascendant; but nothing is easier among a simple and virtuous people, and nothing is more useful in keeping them so. This is yet another reason for preferring it.

I will return now to the question of starosties; and once again I admit that the idea of selling them for the benefit of the public treasury is good and natural so far as the economic aspect is concerned. But in its political and moral aspects, this idea is so little to my taste that, if the starosties were sold, I should want you to buy them back and use them to endow the salaries and rewards of those who might serve or deserve well of the fatherland. In short I should like, if it were possible, for there to be no public treasury, and for the exchequer to know nothing of money payments. I feel that this can never be strictly realised; but the spirit of the government should always tend in that direction; and nothing could be more contrary to this spirit than the sale of offices now under discussion. It would make the republic richer, to be sure; but the vigour of the government would be correspondingly weakened.

I admit that the administration of public property would become more difficult, and above all less agreeable for the administrators, if all this property were in kind rather than in money; but in that case you must make this administration, and its superintendence, an occasion to test the common sense, the vigilance and above all the integrity of those who aspire to more eminent positions. In this respect you will simply be imitating the municipal administration of Lyons, where men must begin as administrators of the charity hospital before proceeding to positions of civic trust; and it is by the way they acquit themselves in the former position that their worthiness for the latter is judged. The integrity of the quaestors of the Roman army was unsurpassed, for the quaestorship was the first step towards the curule offices. In positions which may tempt cupidity, things must be so arranged that ambition this repress it. The greatest good which results from will lies not in saving funds from rascals, but in making unselfishness appear honourable, and rendering poverty respectable when it is the fruit of integrity.

The revenues of the republic do not meet its expenses. I can well believe it; the citizens do not want to pay anything at all. But men who want to be free should not be the slaves of their purses; and where is the state where liberty does not have to be paid for, often very dearly? You will cite Switzerland; but, as I have already said, in Switzerland the citizens themselves perform the functions which people everywhere else prefer to pay for, and have others perform. They are soldiers, officers, magistrates, labourers, anything in the service of the state, and since they are always ready to pay with their persons, it is not necessary for them also to pay with their purses. If the Poles want to do likewise, they will have no more need of money than the Swiss. But if a great state refuses to conduct itself on the principles of a small republic, it must not look for the same benefits, nor should it reject the cause while desiring the consequence. If Poland were, as I should like it to be, a confederation of thirty-three small states, it would combine the power of a great monarchy with the freedom of a small republic; but this would mean renouncing ostentation, and I am afraid that this would be the hardest thing of all.

Of all the bases on which to levy a tax, the easiest and least expensive is undoubtedly capitation; but it is also the most forced and arbitrary; and that no doubt is why Montesquieu considers it servile, although it was the only form of taxation practised by the Romans, and still exists at the present time in several republics;

233

under other names, it is true, as in the case of Geneva, where it is called ' paying the guards,' and is paid only by citizens and burghers, while the inhabitants and natives pay other taxes. All this is exactly opposite to Montesquieu's idea.

But since it is unjust and unreasonable to tax people who have nothing, taxes on property are always better than taxes on persons. You must simply avoid those which are difficult and costly to levy, and above all those which can be avoided by smuggling, for this is unproductive, fills the state with defrauders and brigands, and corrupts the fidelity of the citizens. Assessments should be so well apportioned that the difficulties of fraud will be greater than its benefits. There should never be a tax, therefore, on anything that can be hidden easily, like lace and jewels; it is better to forbid the wearing of them than to ban their importation. In France the temptation to smuggle is wantonly encouraged; and this makes me believe that the tax administration derives a profit from the existence of smugglers. This system is abominable, and wholly contrary to common sense. Experience shows that stamp taxes are particularly hard on the poor, and burdensome to commerce; that they greatly increase chicanery, and cause the people to cry out wherever they are established. I should not advise you to consider them. Taxes on animals strike me as being much better, provided that fraud is avoided, for every possible fraud is always a source of evils. But in so far as the payments must be made in money, they may be burdensome to the taxpayers; and the proceeds of this sort of tax are unduly subject to misappropriation.

In my opinion the best and most natural tax, and one which is in no way open to fraud, is a proportional tax on land, on all land without exception, as was suggested by Marshal de Vauban and the Abbé de Saint-Pierre; for after all, it is that which produces that ought to pay. All lands, whether owned by the king, noblemen, ecclesiastics or commoners, should pay equally, that is to say in proportion to their extent and productivity, no matter who the proprietor may be. This levy would seem to require a preliminary operation, namely a general land census, which would be long and costly. But this expense can be avoided easily, and even advantageously, by levying the tax not on the land directly but on its products, which would be even fairer; this could be done by establishing a tithe, as large or small as seemed proper, which would be levied on the harvest in kind, like the ecclesiastical tithe. And to avoid the difficulties of administration and storage, you would farm out these tithes, as the curates do, to the highest bidder; with the result that private individuals would have to pay the tithe out of their harvest only, and would not pay it out of their purses unless they preferred to do so, at a tariff fixed by the government. The accumulated receipts could be made an object of commerce by selling the foodstuffs thus collected, which could be sent abroad by way of Riga or Danzig. In this way you would also eliminate all the expenses of collection and administration, and all those swarms of clerks and employees who are so odious to the people and troublesome to the public; and most important of all, the republic would have money without the citizens being obliged to give any. For I shall never tire of repeating that what makes tallages and imposts burdensome to the farmer is the fact that they are pecuniary, and that he is first obliged to sell in order to be able to pay them.

Chapter XII

THE MILITARY SYSTEM

Of all the expenses of the republic, the maintenance of the royal army is the most considerable; and the services this army renders are certainly not in proportion to the cost. You will immediately say, however, that troops are necessary to defend the state. I would agree, if these troops actually defended it; but I cannot see that this army ever guaranteed it against any invasion, and I am afraid that it will do no better in the future.

Poland is surrounded by warlike powers which constantly maintain large standing armies of perfectly disciplined soldiers, armies which she herself could never match without soon exhausting herself, particularly in the deplorable condition in which she will be left by the brigands who are now ravaging her. Furthermore, she would not be allowed to rearm; and if, with the resources of a most vigorous administration, she attempted to raise a respectable army, her neighbours, alert to prevent it, would quickly crush her before she had been able to carry out the plan. No, if she seeks merely to imitate them, she will never resist them.

The Polish nation is different by nature, government, customs and language, not only from her neighbours, but also from all the rest of Europe. I should like her also to be different in her military organisation, tactics and discipline, being always herself, not someone else. Only then will she be all she is capable of becoming, and draw forth from her bosom all the resources she is capable of having.

The most inviolable law of nature is the law of the strongest. No laws, no constitution can be exempted from this law. If you look for means of guaranteeing yourselves against invasion by a neighbour stronger than you, you are chasing a will-o'-the-wisp. It would be even more absurd for you to want to make conquests and to acquire offensive power; this is incompatible with the form of your government. Anyone who wants to be free ought not to want to be a conqueror. The Romans were such by necessity and, you might say, in spite of themselves. War was a necessary remedy for the defect of their constitution. Constantly attacked and constantly victorious, they were the only disciplined people in a sea of barbarians, and became the masters of the world by constantly defending themselves. Your position is so unlike theirs that there is no one against whose attacks you would even be able to defend yourselves. You will never have offensive power; it will be a long time before you have defensive power. But you will soon, or more accurately speaking, you already have the power of self-preservation, which will guarantee you, even though subjected, against destruction, and will preserve your government and your liberty in its one true sanctuary, the heart of the Polish people.

Regular troops, the plague and depopulators of Europe, are good for two purposes only, to attack and conquer neighbours, or to bind and enslave citizens. Both of these ends are equally foreign to you; renounce, then, the means which lead to them. I know that the state should not remain without defenders; but its true defenders are its members. Each citizen should be a soldier by duty, none by profession. Such was the military system of the Romans; such is that of the Swiss today; such ought to be that of every free state, and particularly of Poland. In no position to hire an army sufficient for her defence, she must find that army, when necessary, in her inhabitants. A good militia, a genuine, well-drilled militia, is alone capable of satisfying this need. This militia will cost the republic little, will always be ready to serve it, and will serve it well, for after all, we always defend our own goods better than the goods of others.

Count Wielhorski suggests that a regiment should be raised by each palatinate, and kept constantly on an active footing. This supposes that the royal army, or at least the royal infantry, would be disbanded; for I believe that the maintenance of these thirty-three regiments would unduly overburden the republic if it had, in addition, the royal army to pay for. This change would not be without value, and strikes me as being easy to effect; but it can also become burdensome, and its abuses will be difficult to forestall. I should not advise scattering the soldiers as a police force in the towns and villages; that would be bad for discipline. Soldiers, above all professional ones, ought never to be left without a check on their conduct; still less should they be entrusted with any sort of control over citizens. They ought always to march and live together as a body; constantly subordinated and supervised, they should be nothing but blind instruments in the hands of their officers. If they were entrusted with any sort of control, however small, innumerable acts of violence, vexations and abuses without number, would ensue; the soldiers and the inhabitants would become mutual enemies. This is a misfortune that occurs wherever regular troops are found; the proposed regiments, being on continuous service, would acquire the spirit of regular troops, and this spirit is never favourable to freedom. The Roman republic was destroyed by its legions, when the remoteness of its conquests forced it to keep some on continuous service. Once again, the Poles ought not to look about them for

238

things to imitate, not even when those things are good. This goodness, being relative to wholly different constitutions, would be an evil in their own. They should look exclusively to what is suitable to them, not to what others do.

Why not, then, instead of regular troops, a hundred times more burdensome than useful to any people uninterested in conquests, establish a genuine militia in Poland exactly as in Switzerland, where every inhabitant is a soldier, but only when necessary? The institution of serfdom in Poland makes it impossible, I admit, for the peasants to be armed immediately; arms in servile hands will always be more dangerous than useful to the state. Pending the happy moment of emancipation, however, Poland teems with cities, and their inhabitants, if conscripted, could in time of need furnish numerous troops whose upkeep, except during the period of that same need, would cost the state nothing. The majority of these inhabitants, having no land, would thus pay their taxes in service; and this service could easily be distributed in such a way as not to be at all burdensome to them, even though they were sufficiently drilled.

In Switzerland every individual who marries must be furnished with a uniform, which becomes his festive dress, with a rifle, and with all the equipment of a foot-soldier; he is enrolled in the company of his district. During the summer, on Sundays and holidays, these militias are drilled by formations, first by squads, next by companies, then by regiments; until finally, when their turn has come, they assemble in the country, and in succession form small encampments, in which they are drilled in all the manoeuvres appropriate to infantry. As long as they do not leave their place of residence, and thus are little or not at all interrupted in their work, they receive no pay; but as soon as they go out into the country they receive rations and are paid by the state; and no one is allowed to send another in his place, in order that each may receive training and that all may see service. In a state like Poland, with its vast provinces, it is easy to find the wherewithal to replace the royal army with a sufficient number of militiamen, who would be kept constantly mobilised, but changed once a year at least, and drawn in small detachments from all the corps, which would not be seriously burdensome to the individuals, whose turn would come hardly more often than once in twelve or fifteen years. In this way, the whole nation would be given military training, a good and numerous army would always be ready when needed, and it would cost far less, especially in peacetime, than the royal army costs to-day.

To make a real success of this operation, however, it would be necessary to begin by changing public opinion regarding a vocation which will in fact be wholly altered, and to make the Polish people look on the soldier no longer as a bandit who, in order to live, sells himself for five cents a day, but as a citizen who is doing his duty in the service of his country. This vocation must be restored to the honour which it formerly enjoyed, and which it still enjoys in Switzerland and in Geneva, where the best citizens are as proud of being in their corps and under arms as in the town hall and in the sovereign council. To accomplish this, it is important that, in the choice of officers, consideration should be given not at all to rank, credit and fortune, but solely to experience and talent. Nothing is easier than to make skill in the use of arms a point of honour, which will make everyone drill zealously for the service of his country before the eyes of his family and his people; a zeal which cannot be awakened to the same extent in a mob of riffraff which has been enlisted by chance, and is conscious only of the hardships of drill. I can remember the time when the citizens of Geneva manoeuvred much better than regular troops; but the magistrates, finding that this inspired the citizen body with a martial spirit alien to their own purposes, have taken care to suppress this sort of emulation, and have succeeded only too well.

In the execution of this plan, you could, with perfect safety, restore to the king the military authority which naturally belongs to his office; for it is inconceivable that the nation could be used to oppress itself, at least when all those who comprise it are given a share of freedom. It is only with regular and standing armies that the executive power can ever enslave a state. The great Roman armies were unabusive as long as they changed with each consul; and down to the time of Marius, it did not so much as enter the head of any consul that he might use them in any way to enslave the republic. It was not until the great remoteness of their conquests forced the Romans to keep the same armies mobilised for a long time, to man them with ruffianly recruits, and to perpetuate command over them by the proconsuls, that the latter began to feel their independence and to want to use it to establish their own power. The armies of Sulla, Pompey and Caesar became true regular forces, which replaced the republican spirit with the spirit of military government; and this to such an extent that the soldiers of Caesar considered themselves grossly insulted when, in a moment of mutual friction, he called them citizens, *quirites*. In the plan I envisage, and shall soon have finished outlining, all Poland will become warlike in defence of her liberty against the undertakings no less of the prince than of her neighbours; and I will venture to say that, once this plan has been well executed, the office of commander-in-chief could be abolished and its functions reunited with the crown, without placing liberty in the slightest danger, unless the nation should allow itself to be beguiled by plans of conquest; in which case I would no longer answer for anything. Whoever wants to deprive others of their freedom almost always ends by losing his own; this is true even of kings, and very much more true of peoples.

Why should not the equestrian order, in which the republic really resides, itself follow a plan like that here suggested for the infantry? Establish in all the palatinates cavalry corps in which the whole nobility will be enrolled, each with its own officers, general staff, banners, its own designated emergency quarters, and its fixed annual times of meeting. Let these brave noblemen learn how to drill in formation, to perform all sorts of movements and evolutions, to give order and precision to their manoeuvres, to recognise military discipline. I should not want them to imitate slavishly the tactics of the other nations. I should like them to evolve tactics of their own, tactics which would develop and perfect their own natural and national dispositions; I should like them above all to practice for lightness and speed, learning how to break off, disperse and regroup without difficulty or confusion; to excel in what is called guerilla warfare, in all the manoeuvres appropriate to light troops, in the art of inundating a country like a torrent, of striking everywhere without ever being struck, of continuing to act in concert though separated, of cutting communications, of intercepting convoys, of charging rear-guards, of capturing vanguards, of surprising detachments, of harassing large bodies of troops marching and camping together; I should like them to adopt the methods of the ancient

Parthians, whose valour they already possess, and learn like them to conquer and destroy the best disciplined armies without ever joining battle and without leaving them a moment's respite. In short, have infantry, since it is necessary, but rely only on your cavalry, and leave no stone unturned in devising a system which will place the entire outcome of the war in its hands.

A free people is not well advised to have fortresses; they are not at all suited to the Polish genius, and sooner or later they everywhere become nests for tyrants. The places you think you are fortifying against the Russians you will inevitably be fortifying for them; and for you they will become shackles from which you will never deliver yourselves. Neglect even the advantages of fortified outposts, and do not bankrupt yourselves for artillery; such things are not what you need. A sudden invasion is a great misfortune, no doubt; but permanent enslavement is a far greater one. You will never be able to make it difficult for your neighbours to enter your territory; but you can make it difficult for them to withdraw with impunity; and that should be your sole concern. Antony and Crassus invaded the territory of the Parthians easily, but to their own misfortune. A land as vast as yours always offers its inhabitants places of refuge and great resources for eluding its aggressors. No human art could prevent sudden action by the strong against the weak; but the weak can provide themselves with means of retaliation; and when experience teaches how hard it is to retire from your country, people will be in less of a hurry to enter it. Leave your country wide open, then, like Sparta, but build, like her, strong citadels in the hearts of the citizens; and just as Themistocles carried Athens away in her fleet, carry off your cities, when need be, on your horses. The spirit of imitation seldom produces

243

anything good, and never anything great. Each country has advantages which are peculiar to itself, and which should be extended and fostered by its constitution. Husband and cultivate those of Poland, and she will have few other nations to envy.

A single thing suffices to make it impossible to conquer her, namely love of country and of liberty, animated by the virtues inseparable from that love. You have just given an ever-memorable example of it. As long as this love burns in your hearts, it may not ensure you against a temporary yoke; but sooner or later it will burst forth, shake off the yoke, and set you free. Work, therefore, without pause or relaxation, to bring patriotism to the highest pitch in every Polish heart. I have already indicated some of the means appropriate to that end. At this point it remains only for me to discuss the one which I believe to be the strongest, the most powerful of all, one which is even infallible in its effects if properly executed; this is to arrange things so that every citizen will feel himself to be constantly under the public eye; that no one will advance or succeed save by the favour of the public; that no office or position shall be filled save by the will of the nation; and finally that, from the lowliest nobleman, even from the lowliest peasant, up to the king, if possible, all shall be so dependent on public esteem that nothing can be done, nothing acquired, no success obtained without it. Out of the effervescence excited by this mutual emulation will arise that patriotic intoxication which alone can raise men above themselves, and without which liberty is but an empty word, and laws but a chimera.

In the equestrian order this system is easy to establish, if you are careful throughout to make it follow a fixed sequence of official promotions, admitting no one to the honours and dignities of the state unless he has previously passed through the inferior grades, which will serve both as a qualification and as a test for those seeking a higher degree of eminence. Since equality among noblemen is a fundamental law of Poland, the career of public service in that country ought always to begin with subordinate positions; that is the spirit of the constitution. These positions should be open to every citizen who is zealous enough to seek them, and who believes himself able to fill them successfully; but they should be the indispensable first step for anyone, great or small, who wishes to advance in this career. Each is free to present himself or not; but once he has done so, he must, unless he retires voluntarily, either advance or be rebuffed with disapprobation. All his conduct must be seen and judged by his fellow-citizens; he must know that his every step is being watched, that all his acts are being weighed, that a faithful account is being kept of all his good and evil deeds, and that this account will influence the whole subsequent course of his life.

Chapter XIII

PLAN FOR A SEQUENCE OF OFFICIAL PROMOTIONS EMBRACING ALL MEMBERS OF THE GOVERNMENT

The following is a plan for the establishment of such a sequence of official promotions, a plan which I have tried to adapt as far as possible to the existing form of government, with the sole exception of the nomination of senators, which is reformed in the manner and for the reasons already given.

All active members of the republic, by which I mean those who participate in the administration, shall be divided into three classes, each distinguished by visible insignia to be worn on the person of its members. The orders of knighthood, which formerly were proofs of virtue, are now no more than signs of royal favour. The ribbons and jewels which distinguish them have an air of frippery and of feminine adornment which must be avoided in our reforms. I should like the insignia of my proposed three orders to consist of plaques of various metals, the material value of which should be inversely proportional to the rank of the wearer.

Before entering upon an official career, young men shall pass through a preliminary trial period as lawyers, assessors and even as judges in the lower courts, as managers of some part of the public funds, and in general in all those inferior posts which give the holders a chance to show their merit, their capacity, their thoroughness, and above all their integrity. This trial period should continue for at least three years, at the end of which time, armed with certificates from their superiors and with evidence of public approbation, they shall present themselves to the dietine of their province, where, after a rigorous examination of their conduct, those who are found worthy shall be honoured with a plaque of gold inscribed with their name, province and date of reception, and bearing underneath in larger characters the inscription *Spes patriae*. Those who have received this plaque shall wear it constantly on their right arms or over their hearts; they shall be called *servants of the state* ; and they alone, of all the equestrian order, shall be qualified for election as deputy to the diet, as associate justice, or treasury commissioner, or entrusted with any public function which appertains to sovereignty.

To reach the second grade it will be necessary to have been elected three times as deputy to the diet, and to have obtained each time, in the immediately subsequent dietine, the approval of the constituents; and no one may be elected deputy a second or third time unless he has a certificate to this effect with regard to his preceding deputyship. Service as associate justice or as treasury commissioner shall be equivalent to a deputyship; and it will suffice to have sat three times in any of these bodies, but always with approbation, in order to have the right to enter the second grade. Upon presenting his three certificates to the diet, therefore, the servant of the state who has obtained them will be honoured with the second plaque and with the title of which it is the token.

This plaque shall be of silver, of the same size and shape as the preceding one; it shall bear the same inscriptions, except that the words *Spes patriae* shall be replaced by *Civis electus*. Those who wear these plaques shall be called *citizens elect*, or simply electees, and are no longer eligible to serve as simple deputies, associate justices or treasury commissioners; but they shall all be candidates for senatorships. No one may enter the senate until he has entered the second grade and wears its insignia; and all the elective senators who, according to our plan, will be drawn immediately from this group, shall continue to wear the same insignia until they reach the third grade.

It is from the members of the second category that I should like to have chosen the principals of secondary schools and the inspectors of primary education. They might be required to fill these posts for a certain time before being admitted to the senate, and to present the diet a certificate of approval from the college of administrators of education; without forgetting that this certificate, like all the rest, must always be confirmed by the voice of the public, which may be consulted in a thousand different ways.

The choice of elective senators shall be made in the chamber of deputies at each ordinary session of the diet, so that their term shall be for two years only; but they may be continued in office, or re-elected after an interval, for two additional terms, provided that, at the expiration of each term, they have first obtained from the aforesaid chamber a certificate of approval similar to that required from the dietines for re-election to a second or third deputyship. For unless a like certificate is obtained for each mandate, it will be impossible to proceed to further office; and in order not to be excluded from the government, the only recourse will be to go back and begin again in the lower grades, a recourse which should be permitted in order not to deprive a zealous citizen, no matter what faults he may have committed, of all hope of erasing them and achieving success. Furthermore, no special committee should ever be entrusted with the giving or withholding of these certificates or acts of approbation; these judgments must always be made by the whole chamber. This will be done without difficulty or loss of time if, in judging outgoing elective senators, you follow the same method of balloting that I have suggested for their election.

At this point you will say, perhaps, that all these acts of approbation, given first by particular bodies, then by the dietines, and finally by the diet, will be not so much accorded to merit, justice and truth, as extorted by intrigue and credit. To that I have but one answer to make. I thought I was speaking to a people which, without being wholly free from vices, still had a certain amount of resilience and virtue; and on that supposition, my plan is good. But if Poland has already reached the point where everything is radically venal and corrupt, it is vain for her to try to reform her laws and preserve her freedom; she must abandon such hopes, and bow her neck to the yoke. But let us return to the matter in hand.

Each elective senator who has held office three times with approbation shall pass by right into the third grade, the highest in the state; and its insignia shall be conferred on him by the king on the nomination of the diet. This shall take the form of a plaque of blue steel similar to the preceding ones, and shall bear the following inscription: *Custos legum.* Those who have received it shall wear it all the rest of their lives, no matter how eminent the positions they may subsequently attain, and even on the throne itself, if they succeed in ascending it.

The palatines and grand castellans can be drawn only from the body of the law guardians, and in the same way that the latter were chosen from the citizens elect, that is, by the choice of the diet. And since these palatines occupy the most eminent positions in the republic, and hold them for life, in order that their spirit of emulation may not slumber in offices where they no longer see anything above them save the throne, access to the latter shall be open to them, but in such a way that here again they shall be able to advance only on the strength of virtue, and by the voice of the people.

Let us observe in passing ᴛhat the career I am laying down for citizens to follow, in rising by successive stages to the head of the republic, seems quite well proportioned to the stages of human life, so that those who hold the reins of government, although past the first flush of youth, nevertheless may still be in the prime of life, and so that, after fifteen or twenty years of continuous testing under the eyes of the public, they will still have a sufficiently large number of years

249

during which to give the fatherland the benefit of their talents, experience and virtues, and themselves to enjoy, in the leading positions of the state, the respect and honours they have so well deserved. Assuming that a man begins his public career at twenty, it is possible for him to become a palatine by thirty-five; but since it is very hard, and not even suitable, for this sequence of offices to be accomplished so quickly, this eminent post will seldom be reached before the forties; and this, in my opinion, is the age most likely to combine all the qualities desirable in a statesman. At this point we may also observe that this sequence of offices also seems, as far as possible, to be appropriate to the needs of the government. In calculating the probabilities, I would estimate that every two years there would be at least fifty new citizens elect and twenty law guardians; and these numbers are more than sufficient to recruit the two parts of the senate to which these grades respectively lead. For it is easy to see that although the first rank of the senate is the more numerous, the fact that it is held for life means that it will need fewer replacements than the second, which, under my plan, is renewed at each ordinary diet.

You have already seen, and soon will see again, that I do not leave the supernumerary citizens elect to stand idle while waiting to enter the senate as elective senators. In order that the law guardians also shall not be left idle while waiting for new service as palatines and castellans, it is from this body that I would form the college of the administrators of education, of which I have already spoken. This college could be placed under the presidency of the primate or another bishop, with the proviso that no other ecclesiastic, whether bishop or senator, could be admitted to it.

The sequence of promotions strikes me as being

adequate to the needs of the essential and intermediary part of the state, namely, the nobility and the magistrates. But we have not yet provided for the two extremes, namely the common people and the king. Let us begin with the former, which so far has been accounted nothing, but which in the end must count for something if you want to give a certain power and solidity to Poland. Nothing could be more delicate than the operation of which we are now speaking; for although everyone feels how unfortunate it is for the republic that the nation should be in a sense confined to the equestrian order, and that all the rest, peasants and burghers, should be nil, both in the government and in legislation, such, after all, is the ancient constitution. At the present moment it would be neither prudent nor possible to change it all at once. But it may be prudent and possible to effect this change by degrees, and make the more numerous part of the nation, without any perceptible revolution, attach its affections to the fatherland and even to the government. This will be effected by two methods, the first being to administer justice scrupulously, so that the serf and commoner, never having to fear unjust vexation by the nobleman, will be cured of the aversion in which they must naturally hold him. This calls for a great reformation of the courts of law, and for particular care in the formation of the corps of advocates.

The second method, without which the first is useless, is to open the way to the serfs to become free, and to the burghers to become noblemen. Even if the thing were in fact impracticable, it would be necessary at least for it to be seen as a possibility. But it seems to me that more can be done, and without running the slightest risk. The following, for example, is a means which seems to me to lead safely to the proposed end.

Every other year, in the interval between diets, an appropriate time and place would be set in each province for a meeting of all the citizens elect of that province who were not yet elective senators. They would meet, under the presidency of a law guardian who was not yet a life senator, in a *censorial* or *benevolent* committee, to which would be invited not all the curates, but only those deemed most worthy of the honour. I even think that this distinction, by constituting a tacit judgment in the eyes of the people, might also arouse a certain spirit of emulation among the village curates, and preserve a large number of them from that dissolute way of life to which they are all too prone.

The business of this assembly, to which old men and notables from all walks of life could also be invited, would be to examine proposals for innovations useful to the province; reports would be heard from the curates on the condition of their own and neighbouring parishes, and from the notables on the condition of agriculture and of the families of their canton. These reports would be carefully verified; each member of the committee would add his own observations to them; and a faithful record would be kept of the whole, from which would be drawn succinct memorials to be addressed to the dietines.

The needs of hard-pressed families, of the disabled, of widows and orphans, would be considered in detail, and would be proportionately met from a fund formed by voluntary contributions from the well-to-do people of the province. These contributions would be the less burdensome inasmuch as they would become the only charitable assessment, for beggars and poorhouses ought not to be tolerated anywhere in Poland. The priests will no doubt raise a great outcry for the preservation of poorhouses; and this outcry is simply one more reason for destroying these institutions.

In this same committee, which would never concern itself with reprimands and penalties, but solely with benefits, praise and encouragement, accurate lists would be made, on the basis of reliable information, of individuals in all walks of life whose conduct was worthy of honour and recompense.[1] These lists would be forwarded to the senate and king, to be considered on the appropriate occasion, and to help them make their choices and preferences wisely; and it is on the evidence supplied by these same assemblies that the free secondary-school scholarships already mentioned would be awarded by the administrators of education.

But the principal and most important function of this committee would be to draw up, on reliable depositions and on the well-verified report of public opinion, a roster of those peasants who were distinguished for good conduct, education and morals, for their devotion to their families and for the proper fulfilment of all the duties of their station. This roster would then be presented to the dietine, which would elect therefrom a legally prescribed number for manumission, and would provide, by agreed means, for the compensation of their owners by granting them exemptions, prerogatives, and other advantages proportionate to the

[1] In making these judgments much more attention should be paid to persons than to isolated actions. True goodness acts with little fanfare. It is by uniform and sustained conduct, by private and domestic virtues, by the proper fulfilment of all the duties of one's station, by actions, in short, which flow from character and principles, that a man can merit honours, rather than by a few great, theatrical gestures which are already sufficiently rewarded by the admiration of the public. The ostentation of philosophers is very fond of dazzling actions. But a man who performs five or six actions of this sort, brilliant, noisy and well-advertised, has no other purpose than to accumulate credit to his account, so that he can with impunity be hard and unjust all his life. ' Give us the small change of great deeds.' This quip, first uttered by a woman, is very wise.

number of their peasants who had been found worthy of freedom. For it is absolutely necessary to arrange things so that, instead of being burdensome to the master, the manumission of the serf should bring him honour and profit; with the understanding that, to avoid abuses, these manumissions should be made not by the master, but in the dietines, by a formal judgment, and in no more than the numbers prescribed by the law.

When a certain number of families in a canton had been successively freed you could proceed to free whole villages, to unite them gradually into communes, to assign them a certain amount of communal property, like the communal lands in Switzerland, and to give them communal officers; and when you had gradually brought things to the point where, without perceptible revolution, it was possible to complete the operation on a large scale, you would finally be able to give them back their natural right to participate in tne administration of their country by sending deputies to the dietines.

All this having been done, you would arm all these peasants, now converted into free men and citizens; you would enrol them in the army, you would drill them; and you would end up with a truly excellent militia, more than sufficient for the defence of the state.

A similar method could be followed for the ennoblement of a certain number of burghers and, even without ennobling them, for the awarding to them of certain outstanding positions which they alone could fill, to the exclusion of the nobles; and this would be following the example of the Venetians, who, for all their jealous insistence on noble privileges, always give a commoner, in addition to other subordinate positions, the second office in the state, that of grand chancellor, to which no nobleman can ever aspire. In this way, by opening to the burghers the road to nobility and honours, you would attach their affections to the fatherland and to the maintenance of the constitution. You might also, without ennobling individuals, ennoble certain towns collectively, with preference to those where commerce, industry and the arts were most flourishing, and where the municipal administration was consequently the best. These ennobled cities could, like the free cities of the Empire, send deputies to the diet; and their example would not fail to excite in all the rest a keen desire to obtain the same honour.

The censorial committees entrusted with this work of beneficence, a work which, to the shame of kings and peoples, has never yet existed anywhere, would be composed, without being elective, in the manner most suited to the zealous and honest performance of their functions; for their members, as aspirants to the senatorial positions open to their respective grades, would be very careful to deserve by public approbation the suffrage of the diet. And this work would be sufficient to keep these aspirants on their mettle and to hold them in the public eye during the intervals which might occur between their successive elections. Observe, however, that this would be done without raising them, during these intervals, above the rank of private citizens of a particular grade; for this type of tribunal, useful and respectable as it is, would never have any other task than to confer benefits, and hence would be vested with no coercive power whatsoever. Thus I am not at this point increasing the number of magistracies; but I am making use of the passage from one magistracy to another to enlist the temporary services of those who are to become magistrates.

In executing this plan of official promotions by successive stages, a process which could be accelerated, decelerated, or even halted according to its good or ill success, you would proceed just as you saw fit, guided by experience; you would enkindle in all the lower orders an ardent zeal to contribute to the public welfare; you would finally succeed in animating all parts of Poland, and in binding them together in such a way that they would no longer be anything more than a single corporate group, whose vigour and strength would be at least ten times greater than is now possible; and this with the inestimable advantage of having avoided all abrupt and rapid changes, and the danger of revolution.

You have a fine opportunity to begin this operation in a striking and noble fashion, one which should produce the greatest effect. In the misfortunes Poland has just been undergoing, it is not possible that the confederates should have failed to receive aid, and tokens of attachment, from certain burghers, and even from some peasants. Imitate the magnanimity of the Romans, who were so careful, after the great calamities of their republic, to shower evidences of their gratitude upon foreigners, subjects, slaves and even animals who, during their misfortunes, had rendered them some signal services. What a fine beginning, in my opinion, it would be solemnly to confer nobility on these burghers, and freedom on these peasants; and this with all the pomp and circumstance needed to make the ceremony august, touching and memorable! And do not stop with this beginning. The men thus distinguished should ever remain the favourite children of the fatherland. They must be watched over, protected, aided and sustained, even if they are bad characters. At all costs they must be made to prosper all their lives, in order that, by giving this example to the public view,

Poland may show all Europe what, in her time of victory, may be expected by anyone who dares aid her in her distress.

This gives a rough idea, intended merely as an illustration, of the way to proceed in order that everyone may see the road to any attainment open before him; to make all, while serving the country well, move by degrees toward the most honourable ranks; and to enable virtue to open all the doors that fortune is pleased to shut.

But all is not yet done; and the part of this plan that still remains to be described is undoubtedly the most embarrassing and difficult. It attempts to surmount obstacles against which the wisdom and experience of the most consummate statesmen have always failed. Nevertheless it seems to me that, if my plan were adopted, the very simple method I am about to suggest would remove all difficulties, prevent all abuses, and would in practice turn what seems to be a new obstacle into an actual advantage.

Chapter XIV

THE ELECTION OF KINGS

ALL these difficulties come down to the single one of giving the state a ruler whose selection will not cause trouble, and who will make no attempts against liberty. What makes this difficulty all the worse is that the ruler himself should be endowed with those great qualities needed by anyone who ventures to govern free men. An hereditary crown avoids trouble, but leads to slavery; election preserves freedom, but shakes the state with each new reign. This alternative is unfortunate;

but before I speak of the means of avoiding it, allow me to reflect for a moment on the way in which the Poles ordinarily dispose of their crown.

I ask, first of all, why must they give themselves foreign kings? What singular blindness has led them thus to adopt the surest means of enslaving their nation, of abolishing their customs, of making themselves the playthings of foreign courts, and of wantonly increasing the tumult of interregnums? What an injustice to themselves, what an affront to their fatherland! As if, despairing of finding among their own a man worthy to command them, they were forced to seek him from afar! How have they failed to sense, how have they failed to see, that this was entirely contrary to fact? Open the annals of your nation, and you will never see it illustrious and victorious save under Polish kings; you will almost always see it oppressed and debased under foreigners. Let experience finally come in support of reason! See what ills you are bringing on yourselves, and what benefits you are losing!

For how does it happen, I ask again, that the Polish nation, having taken such trouble to make its crown elective, has not thought to make use of this law to throw the members of the administration into a competition of zeal and glory which by itself would have been able to do more for the good of the country than all the rest of the laws put together? What a powerful inspiration to great and ambitious spirits this crown would have been if it had been destined for the worthiest, and held prospectively before the eyes of every citizen capable of deserving public esteem! What virtues, what noble efforts ought not the hope of acquiring its highest prize inspire within the nation! What a ferment of patriotism in every heart, if it were well known that patriotism alone was the means of obtaining

258

this position, now become the secret ambition of every private citizen, and if it only depended on himself, on the strength of merit and services, to approach ever nearer to it and, with good luck, to obtain it in fact! Let us seek the best means of putting into operation this great motive, so powerful and hitherto so much neglected in the Republic. You will say that restricting the crown to Poles alone will not suffice to eliminate all the difficulties involved; we shall consider this point in a few moments, after I have proposed my solution. This plan is simple; but when I say that it consists of introducing the drawing of lots into the election of kings, it would seem at first glance that it fails to meet the purpose I myself have just been prescribing. I beg that you will be good enough to give me time to explain myself, or at least to re-read attentively what I have already written.

For if you say, 'What assurance is there that a king chosen by lot will have the qualities needed to fill the office worthily?' you are raising an objection I have already met; since it is sufficient for this purpose to provide that the king can only be drawn from the life senators. For, considering that they themselves will be drawn from the order of law guardians, and will have passed with honour through all the grades of the republic, the evidence of their whole lives, and the public approbation they have received in all the positions they have filled, will be sufficient guarantee of the merit and virtue of every one of them.

I do not intend, however, that even as between life senators the lot alone should determine the preference; this would still fail in part to achieve the great purpose which ought to be kept in mind. It is necessary that the lot should do something, and that choice should do a great deal, in order, on the one hand, to frustrate the intrigues and manoeuvres of foreign powers and, on the other hand, to give all the palatines this very great motive not to allow their conduct to grow slack, but to continue serving their country zealously, that they may deserve the preference over their competitors.

I admit that the class of competitors strikes me as being rather large, if you include the grand castellans who, under the present constitution, are almost equal in rank to the palatines. But I cannot see what disadvantage there would be in restricting immediate access to the throne to the palatines alone. This would create within the same order yet another rank, through which the grand castellans would have to pass before becoming palatines, and thus yet another means of keeping the senate dependent on the legislator. You have already seen that I consider the grand castellans a superfluous part of the constitution. If you decide, nevertheless, in order to avoid all great changes, to leave them their offices and senatorial rank, I approve of the decision. But in the sequence I am suggesting, nothing requires them to be placed on the same level as the palatines; and since nothing prevents it, either, you will be able without untoward consequences to decide the matter whichever way you think best. I shall assume here that the decision will be to reserve immediate access to the throne exclusively to the palatines.

Immediately after the death of the king, therefore, that is to say within the shortest possible interval, as determined by law, the election diet shall be solemnly convened; the names of all the palatines shall be placed in competition; and of these, three shall be drawn by lot, with all possible precautions to prevent any sort of fraud from affecting the result. These three names shall be declared aloud to the assembly which, at the same sitting and by majority vote, shall choose the one it prefers; and he shall be proclaimed king that very day.

You will find, I admit, that this form of election has one great disadvantage, namely that the nation cannot choose freely that one of the whole body of palatines whom she most honours and cherishes, and whom she judges worthiest of the kingship. But this disadvantage is not new to Poland. where it has been seen in several elections, and above all in the last, that without regard for those whom the nation favours, she has been forced to choose the one she would have rejected. But in return for this advantage, which she no longer has and now sacrifices, how many more important ones does she gain by this form of election!

In the first place, the use of the lot immediately frustrates the factions and intrigues of foreign nations, which cannot influence this election, being too uncertain of success to devote much effort to it, since even fraud would be insufficient to favour a subject whom the nation can always reject. The greatness of this advantage alone is such that it ensures the peace of Poland, stifles venality in the republic, and leaves the election with almost all the tranquillity of hereditary succession.

The same advantage also operates against intrigue by the candidates themselves. For who among them would want to put himself to any expense to ensure himself a preference which does not depend on men, and sacrifice his fortune for an event which involves so many unfavourable chances as against a single chance of success? And we may add that those whom fortune has favoured will no longer have time to bribe the electors, since the election must take place at the same session.

The free choice of the nation between three candidates saves it from the disadvantages of the lot, which might conceivably light on an unworthy person. For if this should happen, the nation will be careful not to choose him; and among thirty-three illustrious men, the élite of the nation, among whom it is inconceivable that there should be even one unworthy person, it is impossible that the three favoured by the lot should all be unworthy.

By this form of selection, therefore, and this is a very important consideration, we shall combine all the advantages of election and inheritance.

For in the first place, since the crown does not pass from father to son, there will never be any continuous and systematic attempt to enslave the republic. In the second place, the lot itself, in this form, is the instrument of an informed and voluntary election. From the estimable corps of law guardians, and among the palatines who are selected from it, no choice whatsoever can be made that has not already been made by the nation.

But observe what a spirit of emulation this prospect must introduce into the corps of palatines and grand castellans, who otherwise, as holders of life offices, might grow slack in the assurance of being no longer removable. They can no longer be constrained by fear; but the hope of occupying a throne, which each of them sees to be so near to him, is a fresh spur to keep them constantly at watch over themselves. They know that the lot would favour them in vain if they were refused election, and that the only way to be chosen is to deserve it. This advantage is too great, too obvious, to require elaboration.

Let us assume for a moment, taking the darkest possible view, that it is impossible to prevent fraud in the drawing of lots, and that one of the candidates has succeeded in outwitting the vigilance of all the rest, despite their interest in the matter. This fraud would be a misfortune for the excluded candidates. But the effect on the republic would be the same as if the results of the lottery had been honest; for the advantages of election would nevertheless remain, and the disturbances of an interregnum and the dangers of inheritance would still be avoided; the candidate whose ambition had tempted him to the point of resorting to this fraud would still be, in addition, a man of merit, capable in the judgment of the nation of wearing the crown with honour; and finally, even after this fraud, he would still, in order to profit by it, have to depend on the subsequent and formal choice of the republic.

By this plan, adopted in its entirety, the whole state is knit together; and from the lowliest individual to the premier palatine, there is no one who can see any other way of advancing than by the road of duty and public approval. The king alone, once elected, sees nothing above him but the law, and has no other curb to restrain him; and since he has no further need of public approval, he can safely dispense with it if his plans so require. I can hardly see more than one means of remedying this, and this one means is unthinkable; it would be to make the crown in some way revocable, and to require the kings to be confirmed in office at fixed intervals. But, I repeat, this expedient cannot be suggested; by keeping the throne and the state in a condition of continuous turmoil, it would never leave the administration in a sufficiently strong position to be able to devote itself solely and effectively to the public welfare.

The ancients had a custom which has never been practised save by a single people, but the success of which was such that it is astonishing no other has been tempted to imitate it. It is true that it is hardly appropriate to any but an elective monarchy, although it was invented and practised in a hereditary kingdom. I am referring to the trial of Egyptian kings after their death, and to the judgment which granted or refused them burial and royal honours, according as they had governed the state well or ill during their lives. The indifference of the moderns to all moral objects, and to everything capable of strengthening the soul, will no doubt make them think it madness to consider reviving this custom for the kings of Poland; and I should not dream of trying to persuade Frenchmen, particularly philosophers, to adopt it; but I think it can be suggested to Poles. I even venture to maintain that this institution would bring them great advantages obtainable in no other way, and not one disadvantage. With regard to our present problem, it is impossible, except for a base soul insensible of posthumous reputation, that the justice of an inevitable judgment should not impress the king, and impose on his passions a curb which will, I admit, vary in strength, but which will always be capable of restraining them up to a point; above all when it also involves the interests of his children, whose lot will be determined by the judgment passed on the memory of the father.

After the death of each king, therefore, I should like to have his body deposited in a suitable place, until the verdict on his memory had been pronounced; the tribunal authorised to determine and decree his burial should be convened as rapidly as possible; his life and reign should be rigorously examined by that tribunal; and after hearing evidence, in which every citizen would be allowed both to accuse and to defend, the trial should, on the basis of this evidence, be followed by a judgment handed down with the greatest possible solemnity.

As a consequence of this judgment, if favourable, the late king would be declared a good and just prince, his name inscribed with honour in the list of the kings of Poland, his body ceremoniously interred in their burial-place, the epithet *of glorious memory* added to his name in all public acts and speeches, and a dowry assigned to his widow; and his children, declared royal princes, would be honoured for the rest of their lives with all the advantages associated with that title.

But if, on the contrary, he was found guilty of injustice, violence, malversation and above all of having made attempts against the public liberty, his memory would be condemned and stigmatised; his body, denied royal burial, would be interred without honour, like that of a private citizen, and his name stricken from the public register of kings; and his children, deprived of the title and prerogatives of royal princes, would return to the class of private citizens, without honorific or stigmatising distinctions.

I should like this judgment to be made with the greatest possible formality, but also, if possible, to be handed down before the election of a successor, in order that the influence of the latter might not affect the sentence, the severity of which he would have a personal interest in mitigating. I know that it would be desirable to have more time to uncover hidden truths thoroughly, and to place more evidence before the court. But if it were delayed until after the election, I should be afraid that this important act might soon become no more than an empty ceremony and, as would infallibly happen in a hereditary kingdom, a funeral oration for the deceased king rather than a just and rigorous judgment of his conduct. It is preferable on this occasion to give greater scope to public opinion, and lose some scraps of evidence, in order to preserve the integrity

265

and austerity of a judgment which would otherwise become futile.

With regard to the tribunal which would pass this sentence, I should like it to be neither the senate, nor the diet, nor any body vested with any sort of governmental authority, but an entire order of citizens, which cannot easily be either deceived or corrupted. It seems to me that the citizens elect, better informed and more experienced than the servants of the state, and less prejudiced than the law guardians, who are already too close to the throne, would be just the intermediary body in which you would find the largest amount both of intelligence and of integrity, which would be most likely to give none but reliable judgments, and which would therefore be preferable to the other two on this occasion. Even if it should happen that this body was not large enough to render a judgment of such importance, I should prefer to see it supplemented by members drawn from the servants of the state rather than from the law guardians. Finally, I should not like the presiding officer of this tribunal to be an office-holder, but a marshal chosen from their own number, and elected by themselves, like the presiding officers of the diets and confederations; so important is it to prevent any particular interest from influencing this act, which can become very august or very ridiculous according to the manner in which it is carried out.

In concluding this subject of the election and judgment of kings, I should here speak of one of your customs which has struck me as being most shocking, and quite contrary to the spirit of your constitution, namely the way in which that constitution is seen to be virtually overthrown and annulled at the death of the king, to the point even of suspending and closing all the courts of law; as if this constitution were so dependent on the prince that the death of the one was the destruction of the other. Great heavens! Precisely the reverse should be true. With the death of the king, everything should proceed as if he were still alive; you should hardly be able to perceive that a piece of the machine is missing, that piece being so little essential to its solidity. Fortunately this inconsistency is an isolated thing. You have only to declare that it no longer exists, and nothing else need be changed. But this strange contradiction must not be allowed to continue; for if it is already inconsistent with the present constitution, it will be still more so after the constitution has been reformed.

Chapter XV

CONCLUSION

My plan has now been sufficiently outlined. I shall stop. No matter what plan is adopted, you should not forget what I have said in the *Social Contract* regarding the state of weakness and anarchy in which a nation finds itself as soon as it establishes or reforms its constitution. In this moment of disorder and effervescence, it is incapable of putting up any sort of resistance, and the slightest shock is capable of upsetting everything. It is important, therefore, to arrange at all costs for an interval of tranquillity, during which you may be able without risk to work upon yourselves and rejuvenate your constitution. Although the changes to be made in yours are not fundamental, and do not seem very great, they are sufficient to require this precaution; and a certain length of time will inevitably be needed before the effects even of the best reforms can be felt, and the firmness which should result from them can be acquired.

It is only on the assumption that your success will be proportionate to the courage of the confederates and to the justice of their cause that you can dream of undertaking such an enterprise. You will never be free as long as a single Russian soldier remains in Poland; and you will always be in danger of losing your freedom as long as Russia interferes in your affairs. But if you succeed in forcing her to deal with you as one power with another, and no longer as protector and protectorate, then profit by the exhaustion into which the Turkish war will have thrown her to accomplish your task before she is able to disturb it. Although I set no store by the security to be gained by foreign treaties, this unique circumstance may perhaps force you to lean, as far as possible, on this support, if only for the purpose of learning the present disposition of those who will treat with you. But with this one exception, and perhaps a few trade treaties later on, do not waste your energies in vain negotiations; do not bankrupt yourselves on ambassadors and ministers to foreign courts; and do not account alliances and treaties as things of any moment. All this is useless with the Christian powers, who recognise no other bonds than those of self-interest. When they find it advantageous to fulfil their obligations, they will fulfil them; when they find it advantageous to break them, they will do so; such promises might as well not be made at all. Furthermore, if this self-interest were always real, knowledge of what it would profit them to do would make it possible to predict what they would do. But it is almost never reason of state that guides them; it is the momentary interest of a minister, of a mistress, of a favourite; it is the motive no human wisdom has been able to predict which determines them, sometimes for, sometimes against their true interests. What assurance can you

268

have in dealing with people who have no fixed system, and who are led only by chance impulses? Nothing could be more frivolous than the political science of courts. Since it has no certain principles, no certain conclusions can be drawn from them; and all this fine theorising about the interest of princes is a child's game which makes sensible men laugh.

Do not rely with confidence, therefore, either on your allies or on your neighbours. There is only one of them on whom you can count in some small measure, namely the Sultan of Turkey, and you should spare no efforts to gain his support. Not that his statecraft is much more reliable than that of the other powers; with him, too, everything depends on a vizier, a favourite, a harem intrigue. But the interest of the Porte is clear and simple; it is a matter of life and death to it; and although the Porte has much less enlightenment and finesse, it generally shows more honesty and common sense. With it, as contrasted with the Christian powers, you at least have the added advantage that it likes to fulfil its obligations and ordinarily respects treaties. You should try to make a treaty with it for twenty years, as clear and strong a one as possible. As long as another power conceals its plans, this treaty will be the best, perhaps the only guarantee available to you; and in the condition in which Russia will probably be left by the present war, I think that it may be enough to enable you to undertake your work in safety; the more so since the common interest of the powers of Europe, and above all of your other neighbours, is to leave you to continue as a barrier between themselves and the Russians; and by dint of changing follies they must, at least now and then, be wise.

One thing makes me believe that, in general, they will watch without jealousy your work of constitutional reform: the fact that this work tends only to increase the power of legislation, and consequently of liberty; and that this liberty is regarded in all the courts as a visionary madness which tends rather to weaken than to strengthen a state. That is why France has always favoured the liberties of Germany and Holland; and that is why Russia now favours the present government of Sweden, and blocks the projects of the king with all her strength. All these great ministers, who judge mankind in general by themselves and their entourage, and thus think that they know men, are very far from imagining the vigour which love of country and the impulse of virtue can impart to free souls. It makes no difference that they are the gulls of their own low opinion of republics, and that the latter show in all their enterprises an unexpected power of resistance; these men will never abandon a prejudice founded on the contempt they feel that they themselves deserve, and in terms of which they appraise the human race. In spite of the rather striking experience the Russians have just had in Poland, nothing will make them change their minds. They will always regard free men as they themselves must be regarded, namely as human ciphers moved only by the twin instruments of money and the knout. If they see, therefore, that the republic of Poland, instead of trying to fill its coffers, to increase its revenues and to raise large forces of regular troops, is thinking, on the contrary, of disbanding its army and dispensing with money, they will believe that she is striving to weaken herself; and in the belief that, in order to conquer her, they will have only to appear whenever they like, they will let her reform herself at leisure, laughing the meanwhile among themselves at her labours. And it must be admitted that a state of liberty deprives a people of offensive power, and that in following my plan you should renounce all hope of conquest. But twenty years from now, when your work has been done, if the Russians try to overrun you, they will learn what sort of soldiers in defence of their hearths are these men of peace who do not know how to attack the hearths of others, and who have forgotten the value of money.

For the rest, when you are rid of these cruel guests, take care not to make any sort of compromise with the king they tried to give you. You must either cut off his head, as he deserves, or else, disregarding his first election, which is absolutely void, you must elect him afresh with new *pacta conventa*, in which you will make him renounce the right of appointment to high official positions. The second alternative is not only the more humane, but also the wiser; I even find in it a certain generous pride which will perhaps mortify the court of St Petersburg much more than as if you elected someone else. Poniatowski was very wicked, without doubt; now, perhaps, he is no longer anything more than unfortunate; for in the present situation, at least, he seems to me to be behaving very much as he ought, by taking no part in anything at all. Naturally, at the bottom of his heart, he must fervently desire the expulsion of his hard masters. It would, perhaps, have been an act of patriotic heroism for him to have joined the confederates to expel the Russians; but it is well known that Poniatowski is no hero. Furthermore, quite apart from the fact that he would not have been allowed to do so, and that, as a man who owes everything to the Russians, he is constantly watched, apart from all this, I frankly declare that, if I were in his place, I should not want, for anything in the world, to be capable of that kind of heroism.

I realise that he is not the king you will need when your reforms have been completed; but he may be the one you need to effect them peaceably. If he lives but eight or ten years more, and if your system has then begun to operate, and several palatinates are already filled with law guardians, you need not be afraid of giving him a successor like himself; but I myself am afraid that, if you simply dispossess him, you will not know what to do with him, and will expose yourselves to new troubles.

Nevertheless, no matter what difficulties are to be avoided by electing him freely, you must not dream of doing so until you have made very sure of his real intentions, and unless you find that he still retains some common sense, some feeling of honour, some love of country, some knowledge of his real interests, and some desire to pursue them. For at all times, and above all in the sad situation in which Poland will be left by her misfortunes, there would be nothing more fatal for her than to have a traitor at the head of the government.

As for the manner of broaching the work in question, I have no taste at all for the subtle schemes that have been suggested to you for the purpose of surprising and, in a sense, deceiving the nation with regard to the changes to be introduced into its laws. I should only advise that, while revealing your plan in its full extent, you should not abruptly begin putting it into operation in such a way as to fill the republic with malcontents; that you should leave most office-holders in possession; that you shall fill posts under the new dispensation only as they fall vacant. Never shake the machine too brusquely. I have no doubt that a good plan, once adopted, will change the spirit even of those who played a part in government under another system. Since new citizens cannot be created all at once, you must begin by making use of those who exist, and to offer a new road for their ambition is the way to make them want to follow it.

If, in spite of the courage and constancy of the confederates, and in spite of the justice of their cause, fortune and all the powers abandon them, and deliver the fatherland to its oppressors . . . . But I have not the honour of being a Pole, and in a situation like that in which you find yourselves it is not permissible to give advice otherwise than by example.

I have now finished, within the limits of my powers, and would to God that it were with as much success as ardour, the task set me by Count Wielhorski. Perhaps all this is only a lot of nonsense; but these are my ideas. It is not my fault if they bear so little resemblance to those of other men; and it has not lain within my power to organise my mind in another fashion. I even admit that, singular as these ideas may be considered, I myself cannot see anything in them that is not good, well adapted to the human heart, and practicable, above all in Poland; I have tried to make my views follow the spirit of this republic, and to propose only the minimum of changes needed to correct its faults. It seems to me that a government based on such motives ought to proceed to its true goal as directly, as surely and as long as possible; without forgetting, however, that all the works of men are as imperfect, transitory and perishable as man himself.

I have purposely omitted several very important topics on which I did not feel myself qualified to express an opinion. I shall leave this task to men wiser and more enlightened than I; and I shall end this long rigmarole by making my apologies to Count Wielhorski for having taken up so much of his time with it. Although I think differently from other men, I do not flatter myself that I am wiser than they, nor that he will find anything in my reveries that can really be useful to his country. But my wishes for her prosperity are too real, pure and disinterested to make it possible for my zeal to be increased by the pride of contributing to her cause. May she triumph over her enemies, become and remain peaceful, happy and free, may she serve as a great example to the universe and, profiting by the patriotic labours of Count Wielhorski, may she find and form in her bosom many citizens who resemble him!

CONSTITUTIONAL PROJECT
FOR CORSICA

Drafted 1765

You ask for a plan of government suitable for Corsica. It is asking for more than you think. There are peoples who, do what you may, are incapable of being well governed, for the law has no hold over them, and a government without laws cannot be a good government. I do not say that the Corsican people is in that condition; on the contrary, no people impresses me as being so fortunately disposed by nature to receive a good administration. But even this is not enough, for all things lead to abuses, which are often inevitable; and the abuse of political institutions follows so closely upon their establishment that it is hardly worth while to set them up, only to see them degenerate so rapidly.

Attempts are made to overcome this difficulty by mechanical devices designed to keep the government in its original condition; it is bound with a thousand chains and fetters to prevent it from declining, and is hampered to such an extent that, dragged down by the weight of its irons, it remains inactive and motionless and, if it does not go downhill, neither does it advance toward its goal.

All this is the consequence of an undue separation of two inseparable things, the body which governs and the body which is governed. In the original constitution of government, these two bodies are but one; they become separate only through the abuse of that constitution.

Really shrewd men, in such cases, follow the line of expediency, and shape the government to fit the nation. There is, however, something far better to be done, namely to shape the nation to fit the government. In the first case, to the extent that the government declines while the nation remains unchanged, expediency vanishes. But in the second case, everything changes simultaneously; the nation, carrying the government with it, supports it while it itself remains stable, and causes it to decline when it itself declines. Both remain at all times suited to each other.

The Corsican people are in that fortunate condition which makes possible the establishment of a good constitution; they can begin at the beginning, and take steps to prevent degeneration. Full of health and vigour, they can give themselves a government which will keep them healthy and vigorous. But even now the establishment of such a government will have certain obstacles to overcome. The Corsicans have not yet adopted the vices of other nations, but they have already adopted their prejudices; these prejudices are what will have to be combated and destroyed in order to create good institutions.

PART I

THE advantageous location of the island of Corsica, and the fortunate natural qualities of its inhabitants, seem to offer them a reasonable hope of being able to become a flourishing people and to make their mark in Europe if, in the constitution they are thinking of adopting, they turn their sights in that direction. But the extreme exhaustion into which they have been plunged by forty years of uninterrupted warfare, the existing poverty of the island, and the state of depopulation and devastation in which it finds itself, will not allow them immediately to provide for an expensive form of administration, such as would be needed if they were to organise with such an end in view. Furthermore, a thousand insuperable obstacles would stand in the way of the execution of such a plan. Genoa, still mistress of a part of the sea-coast and of almost all the seaports, would repeatedly crush their rising merchant marine, constantly exposed as it is to the double danger of the Genoese and of the Barbary pirates. The Corsicans would be able to control the seas only with the aid of warships, which would cost them ten times more than they could earn by trade. Exposed on land and sea, forced to defend themselves on all sides, what would become of them? At the mercy of everyone, unable in their weakness to make a single advantageous trade treaty, they would be dictated to by one and all; surrounded by so many risks, they would earn only such profits as others would not deign to take, profits which would always shrink to nothing. And if, by incredible good fortune, they were to overcome all these difficulties, their very prosperity, by attracting the attention of their neighbours, would be a new source of danger to their ill-established freedom. A constant object of covetousness to the great powers and of jealousy to the small, their island would never for a moment cease to be threatened with a new enslavement from which it could never again be extricated.

No matter what object the Corsican nation may have in view in forming a constitution, the first thing it has to do is to give itself, by its own efforts, all the stability of which it is capable. No one who depends on others, and lacks resources of his own, can ever be free. Alliances, treaties, gentlemen's agreements, such things may bind the weak to the strong, but never the strong to the weak.

Leave negotiations, then, to the powers, and depend on yourselves only. Worthy Corsicans, who knows better than you how much can be done alone? Without friends, without support, without money, without armies, enslaved by formidable masters, single-handed you have thrown off the yoke. You have seen them ally against you, one by one, the most redoubtable potentates of Europe, and flood your island with foreign armies; all this you have surmounted. Your fortitude alone has accomplished what money could never have done; if you had sought to preserve your wealth, you would have lost your liberty. Do not draw conclusions about your own nation from the experience of others; rules drawn from your own experience are the best by which to govern yourselves.

It is not so much a question of becoming different as of knowing how to stay as you are. The Corsicans have improved greatly since becoming free; they have added prudence to courage, they have learned to obey their equals, they have acquired virtue and morality, and all this without the use of laws; if they could continue thus, I would see little need to do more. But when the danger that has united them grows distant, the factions which are now repressed will revive among them; and instead of joining forces for the maintenance of their independence, they will wear out those forces against one another, and will have none left for self-defence if the attack upon them is renewed. That even now is what you must forestall. The divisions of the Corsicans have ever been a trick of their masters to make them weak and dependent; but this trick, incessantly used, has finally resulted in a propensity to dissension, and has made them naturally restless, turbulent and hard to govern, even by their own leaders. Good laws and a new constitution are needed to re-establish that concord the very desire for which has hitherto been destroyed by tyranny. Corsica, when subject to foreign masters whose hard yoke was never patiently borne, was in constant turmoil. Her people must now reconsider its position, and look in freedom for peace.

The following, then, are the principles which ought, in my opinion, to serve as the basis for their laws: to make use of their own people and their own country as far as possible; to cultivate and regroup their own forces; to depend on those forces only; and to pay no more attention to foreign powers than as if they did not exist.

Let us proceed on this basis to establish the fundamental rules of our new constitution.

The island of Corsica, being incapable of growing rich in money, should try to grow rich in men. The power derived from population is more real than that derived from finance, and is more certain in its effects. Since the use of manpower cannot be concealed from view, it always reaches its public objective. It is not thus with the use of money, which flows off and is lost in private destinations; it is collected for one purpose and spent for another; the people pay for protection, and their payments are used to oppress them. That is why a state rich in money is always weak, and a state rich in men is always strong.[1]

To multiply men it is necessary to multiply their means of subsistence; hence agriculture. By this I do not mean the art of theorising on agriculture, of setting up academies to talk about it, or of writing books on the subject. I mean a constitution which will lead a people to spread out over the whole extent of its territory, to settle there, and to cultivate it throughout; this will make it love country life and labour, finding them so replete with the necessaries and pleasures of life that it will have no wish to leave them.

A taste for agriculture promotes population not only by multiplying the means of human subsistence, but also by giving the body of the nation a temperament and a way of life conducive to an increased birth-rate. In all countries, the inhabitants of the countryside have more children than city-dwellers, partly as a result of the simplicity of rural life, which creates healthier bodies, and partly as a result of its severe working-conditions, which prevent disorder and vice. For, other things being equal, those women who are most chaste, and whose senses have been least inflamed by habits

[1] Most usurpers have used one of the following two methods to consolidate their power: the first is to impoverish and barbarise the conquered peoples; the second is, on the contrary, to make them effeminate under the pretext of educating and enriching them. The first of these means has always defeated its own purpose; it has always led, on the part of the oppressed peoples, to acts of vigour, revolutions, republics. The second means has always been successful; and the peoples, grown soft, corrupt, feeble and disputatious, making fine speeches on liberty in the depths of slavery, have all been crushed by their masters, then destroyed by conquerors.

of pleasure, produce more children than others; and it is no less certain that men enervated by debauchery, the inevitable fruit of idleness, are less fit for generation than those who have been made more temperate by an industrious way of life.

Peasants are much more attached to their soil than are townsmen to their cities. The equality and simplicity of rural life have, for those acquainted with no other mode of existence, an attraction which leaves them with no desire to change it. Hence that satisfaction with his own way of life which makes a man peaceful; hence that love of country which attaches him to its constitution.

Tilling the soil makes men patient and robust, which is what is needed to make good soldiers. Those recruited from the cities are flabby and mutinous; they cannot bear the fatigues of war; they break down under the strain of marching; they are consumed by illnesses; they fight among themselves and fly before the enemy. Trained militias are the best and most reliable troops; the true education of a soldier is to work on a farm.

Agriculture is the only means of maintaining the external independence of a state. With all the wealth in the world, if you lack food you will be dependent on others; your neighbours can set any value they like on your money, since they can afford to wait. But the bread we need has an indisputable value for us; and in every kind of commerce, it is always the less eager party who dictates to the other. I admit that in a system based on financial power, it would be necessary to operate on different principles; it all depends on the final goal you have in view. Commerce produces wealth, but agriculture ensures freedom.

You may say that it would be better to have both; but they are incompatible, as we shall show presently.

In all countries, it will be added, the land is cultivated. True, just as there is more or less trade and commerce in all countries; but that is not to say that agriculture and commerce flourish everywhere. I am not concerned here with the consequences which flow from natural necessities, but with those which result from the nature of the government and general spirit of the nation.

Although the form of government adopted by a people is more often the work of chance and fortune than of its own choice, there are nevertheless certain qualities in the nature and soil of each country which make one government more appropriate to it than another; and each form of government has a particular force which leads people toward a particular occupation.

The form of government we choose must be, on the one hand, the least expensive, since Corsica is poor; and it must be, on the other hand, the most favourable to agriculture, since agriculture is, at the present time, the only occupation which can preserve to the Corsican people the freedom it has won, and give it the firmness it requires.

The least costly administration is that which has the shortest chain of command, and requires the smallest number of official categories. It is in general the republican, and in particular the democratic state.

The administration most favourable to agriculture is the one where power, not being entirely concentrated at any one point, does not carry with it an unequal distribution of population, but leaves people dispersed equally throughout the territory: such is democracy.

Switzerland illustrates these principles in a most striking fashion. Switzerland is, for the most part, a poor and sterile country. Her government is everywhere republican. But in those cantons, like Berne,

Solothurn, and Freiburg, which are more fertile than the rest, the government is aristocratic. In the poorest, where agriculture is less productive and requires more effort, the government is democratic. Even under the simplest administration, the state has no more than it needs to subsist. Under any other it would exhaust itself and die.

You may say that Corsica, being more fertile and having a milder climate, can support a more onerous form of government. In other times that would be true; but now, crushed by long years of slavery, and devastated by long wars, the nation first of all must recover its health. When it has put its fertile soil into production, it can dream of becoming rich and of adopting a more brilliant administration. Indeed, if the constitution we are about to establish is successful, further constitutional change will become necessary. Cultivation of the land cultivates the spirit; all agricultural peoples multiply; they multiply in proportion to the product of their soil; and when that soil is fertile, they finally multiply to such an extent that it no longer suffices to support them; then they are forced either to found colonies or to change their form of government.

When the country is saturated with inhabitants, the surplus can no longer be employed in agriculture, but must be used in industry, commerce, or the arts; and this new system demands a different type of administration. Let us hope that the institutions Corsica is about to establish will soon require her to make such changes! But as long as she has no more men than she can use in agriculture, as long as an inch of fallow land remains on the island, she should cleave to the rural system, and change it only when the island no longer suffices.

The rural system, as I have said, involves a democratic state; we have therefore no choice as to the form of government to be adopted. It is true that this form must be somewhat modified in practice by reason of the size of the island, for a purely democratic government is suitable rather to a small town than to a nation. It would be impossible to bring together the whole people of an island like those cf a city; and when the supreme authority is entrusted to delegates, the government changes and becomes aristocratic. What Corsica needs is a mixed government, where the people assemble by sections rather than as a whole, and where the repositories of its power are changed at frequent intervals. This was well understood by the author of the Vescovado Report of 1764, an excellent report, to be consulted with confidence on all matters which have been omitted from the present discussion.

The firm establishment of this form of government will produce two great advantages. First, by confining the work of administration to a small number only, it will permit the choice of enlightened men. Secondly, by requiring the concurrence of all members of the state in the exercise of the supreme authority, it will place all on a plane of perfect equality, thus permitting them to spread throughout the whole extent of the island and to populate it uniformly. This is the fundamental principle of our new constitution. If we make it such that it will keep the population everywhere in equilibrium, we shall by that fact alone have made it as perfect as possible. If this principle is correct, our regulations become clear, and our work is simplified to an astonishing degree.

A part of this work has already been done. We have fewer institutions than prejudices to destroy; the task is not so much to alter as to perfect the existing state of affairs. The Genoese themselves have prepared the way for your new constitution; and, with a care worthy of

Providence, they have laid the foundations of freedom while trying to consolidate tyranny. They have deprived you of practically all commerce; and now is not in fact the time for you to engage in it. If foreign trade existed, it would be necessary to prohibit it until your constitution had become firmly established, and domestic production was supplying all it could. They have hindered the export of your agricultural produce; your interest is not that it should be exported, but that enough men should be born upon the island to consume it.

The counties and regions they have formed or initiated to facilitate the collection of taxes are the only possible means of establishing democracy among a people which cannot assemble all together at any one time and place. They are also the sole means of keeping the country independent of the cities, which can thus more easily be held in subjection. The Genoese have also applied themselves to the task of destroying your nobility, of taking away its dignities and titles, and of extinguishing the great fiefs. You are fortunate that they have taken upon themselves the odium of this enterprise, which you might not have been able to do if they had not done it before you. Have no hesitation in completing their work; when they thought they were labouring for themselves they were labouring for you. Only the purpose is different; for the Genoese were interested in the operation for its own sake, while you are interested in its results. They sought only to degrade the nobility, while you seek to ennoble the nation. This is a point on which I can see that the ideas of the Corsicans are not yet sound. In all their official protests, such as the Remonstrance of Aix-la-Chapelle, they have complained that Genoa has repressed, or rather destroyed, their nobility. It was a grievance, no doubt, but it

287

was not a misfortune; on the contrary, it is an advantage without which it would be impossible for the Corsicans to remain free.

It is confusing shadow with substance to identify the dignity of a state with the titles of some of its members. When the kingdom of Corsica belonged to Genoa, it may have been useful for it to have had marquesses, counts and other titled noblemen to serve, so to speak, as mediators between the Corsican people and the Republic. But against whom would the Corsicans now require such protectors, protectors less apt to guarantee them against tyranny than themselves to usurp it; protectors who would afflict them with their own vexations and disputes until one of them, victorious over the others, had turned all his fellow-citizens into subjects?

We must distinguish between two types of nobility: feudal nobility, which appertains to monarchy, and political nobility, which appertains to aristocracy. The first has several orders or degrees, titled and untitled, from the great vassals down to simple gentlemen; its rights, though hereditary, are in a manner of speaking individual, remaining attached to each individual family; and, since they are wholly independent of each other, they are also independent of the constitution and sovereignty of the state. The second, on the contrary, being united in a single indivisible body, whose rights all reside in the body rather than in the members, constitutes so essential a part of the body politic that neither one can subsist without the other; and all the individuals who compose it, equal by birth in titles, privileges and authority, are known without distinction as patricians.

It is clear from the titles of the ancient Corsican nobility, and from the fiefs it possessed, with rights

approaching those of sovereignty itself, that it belonged
to the first of these two types, and owed its origin
either to Moorish or French conquerors, or to the
princes in whom the popes had vested the island of
Corsica. Now this sort of nobility, far from being
capable of participating in a democratic or mixed
republic, is not even capable of participating in an
aristocracy; for aristocracy admits only of corporate,
and not of individual rights. Apart from virtue,
democracy recognises no other nobility than that of
freedom; and aristocracy likewise recognises no other
nobility than that of authority. Everything foreign to
the constitution should be carefully banished from the
body politic. Leave then to other states all such titles
as count and marquess, titles which degrade ordinary
citizens. The fundamental law of your new constitution must be equality. Everything must be related to
it, including even authority, which is established only
to defend it. All should be equal by right of birth;
the state should grant no distinctions save for merit,
virtue and patriotic service; and these distinctions
should be no more hereditary than are the qualities on
which they are based. We shall soon see how it is
possible to establish different gradations of rank among
a people without letting birth or nobility enter into the
question at all. All fiefs, allegiances, quit-rents and
feudal rights hitherto abolished shall therefore remain
abolished forever; and the state shall repurchase those
which still remain, in order that all titles and seigneurial
rights may continue extinguished and suppressed
throughout the island.

In order that all parts of the state may retain between
themselves, as far as possible, the same equality we are
trying to establish between individuals, the boundaries
of the districts, counties and regions shall be regulated

in such a way as to diminish the extreme inequalities that now exist between them. The province of Bastia and Nebbio alone contains as many inhabitants as the seven provinces of Capo Corso, Aleria, Porto-Vecchio, Sartene, Vico, Calvi and Algagliola. That of Ajaccio contains more than the four neighbouring provinces. Without removing all existing boundaries and upsetting all established relationships, it is possible with a few slight changes to modify these enormous discrepancies. For example, the abolition of fiefs makes it easy to unite the fiefs of Canari, Brando and Nonza to form a new region which, with the addition of the county of Pietra-bugno, will nearly equal the region of Capo Corso. The fief of Istria, joined to the province of Sartene, will still not make it equal to the province of Corte; and that of Bastia and Nebbio, although reduced by a county, can be divided at the line of the Guolo and still form two very populous regions. This is meant simply as an example to illustrate my meaning; for I do not know the local situation well enough to reach any final conclusions.

By these slight changes, the island of Corsica, which I assume to have been wholly liberated, would be divided into twelve regions which would not be entirely disproportionate to one another; especially after the municipal rights of the cities, as is proper, had been reduced, thus leaving them with less weight in their respective regions.

Cities are useful in a country in so far as they foster commerce and manufacture; but they are harmful under the system we have adopted. Their inhabitants are either idlers or agriculturists. But tillage is always better performed by countrymen than by city-dwellers; and idleness is the source of all the vices which have thus far ravaged Corsica. The stupid pride of the burghers serves only to debase and discourage the farm-worker. A prey to indolence and its attendant passions, they plunge themselves into debauchery and sell themselves for pleasure. Selfishness makes them servile, and idleness makes them restless; they are either slaves or mutineers, never free men. This difference has been clearly felt throughout the present war, ever since the nation has broken its fetters. It is the vigour of your counties that made the revolution; it is their firmness that has sustained it; your unshakable courage, proof against all reverses, comes from them. Cities, inhabited by mercenary men, have sold their nation to preserve some petty privileges for themselves, privileges by which the Genoese have well known how to profit; and these cities, justly punished for their baseness, still remain the strongholds of tyranny, while the Corsican people already rejoices gloriously in the freedom it has gained at the price of its blood.

An agricultural people must not look on life in the city as a thing to be coveted, or envy the lot of the idlers who dwell therein; consequently city-dwelling must not be favoured with advantages harmful to the population at large or to the freedom of the nation. An agriculturist must not be inferior by birth to anyone; let him see above him laws and magistrates only; and let him become a magistrate himself if his talents and probity make him worthy of it. In short, cities and their inhabitants should not, any more than fiefs and their possessors, retain exclusive privileges of any sort. The whole island should enjoy equal rights, bear equal burdens, and become in equal measure what, in local parlance, is known as *Terra di commune.*

But if cities are harmful, capital cities are still more so; a capital is an abyss in which virtually the whole nation loses its morals, its laws, its courage and its freedom. It is imagined that large cities are favourable to agriculture because they consume much farm produce; but they consume even more farmers, partly through the attraction of the idea of finding a better job, and partly because the natural race-suicide of city populations necessitates constant recruitment from the country. The environs of capital cities have an air of vitality; but the farther they are left behind, the more desolate everything becomes. The capital breathes forth a constant pestilence which finally saps and destroys the nation.

Nevertheless, the government needs a centre, a meeting-place to which everything will be referred; to make the central administration itinerant would be unduly inconvenient. In order to have it rotate from province to province, it would be necessary to divide the island into a number of small confederated states, each of which would assume the presidency in turn; but this system would complicate the operation of the machine, and its parts would be less closely knit.

Although the island is not large enough to require any such division, it is too large to be able to dispense with a capital. But this capital must provide a means of communication between the various regions without attracting their inhabitants; all should communicate with it, but stay where they are. In short, the seat of the central government should be more like a county-town than a capital.

In this connexion, pure necessity has already led the choice of the nation to the same conclusion that reason herself would have reached. By keeping their mastery of the seaports, the Genoese have left you with only one city, Corte, which is no less fortunately located for the Corsican administration than Bastia was for the Genoese. Corte, located in the middle of the island, is almost equidistant from all its coasts. It is precisely on the dividing line between the two great regions *di quà* and *di là de' monti*, and equally accessible to all. It is far from the sea, which will keep the morality, simplicity, uprightness and national character of its inhabitants intact longer than if it were subject to foreign influences. It is in the highest part of the island, with a very healthy climate, but with soil of low fertility; and the fact that it is located near the source of its rivers, by making difficult the importation of foodstuffs, will serve to prevent it from growing over-large. If you take the still further precaution of making none of the great offices of state hereditary, or even tenable for life, it may be assumed that public men, being no more than transient residents of the capital, will not soon give it that fatal splendour which is the ornament and ruin of states.

These are the first reflexions suggested to me by a rapid survey of local conditions on the island. Before going on to discuss the government in greater detail, we must first see what that government ought to do, and on what principles it ought to be conducted. On this must rest our final decision as to the form of government; for each form has a spirit which is natural and peculiar to it, and from which it will never depart.

We have already done our best to level the site of the future nation; let us now try to sketch upon this site a plan of the building to be erected. The first rule to be followed is the principle of national character; for each people has, or ought to have, a national character; if it did not, we should have to start by giving it one. Islanders above all, being less mixed, less merged with other peoples, ordinarily have one that is especially marked. The Corsicans in particular are naturally endowed with very distinct characteristics; and if this character, disfigured by slavery and tyranny, has become hard to recognise, it is also, on the other hand, because of their isolated position, easy to re-establish and preserve.

The island of Corsica, says Diodorus, is mountainous, well-wooded, and watered by large rivers. Its inhabitants live on meat, milk and honey, with which their country supplies them in abundance; in their relations with one another they observe the rules of justice and humanity with greater strictness than do other barbarians; the first to find honey in the mountains and in the hollow trunks of trees is assured that no one will challenge his possession. They are always sure of recovering their sheep, each of which is marked by the owner, and then allowed to graze unguarded over the countryside. This same spirit of equity seems to guide them in all the circumstances of life.

Great historians, in the simplest narratives and without introducing explanations of their own, know how to make the reader aware of the causes of each fact they report.

When a country is not peopled by colonists, it is the nature of the soil that gives rise to the original character of the inhabitants. A terrain that is rough, broken, and hard to cultivate is bound to provide more nourishment for animals than for men; fields are necessarily rare, and pastures abundant. Hence pastoral life, and the multiplication of cattle. The herds of individual owners, wandering in the mountains, will be mixed and intermingled. Honey can be distinguished in no other way than by the mark of the first occupier; ownership of it can neither be created nor preserved save through public good faith; and it is necessary for everyone to be just, for otherwise no one would have anything, and the nation would perish.

Mountains, woods, rivers, pastures; would you not think you were reading a description of Switzerland? And in the past the same character ascribed by Diodorus to the Corsicans was also to be found in Switzerland: equity, humanity, good faith. The only difference was that, dwelling in a more severe climate, they were more industrious; buried in snow for half the year, they were forced to make provision for the winter; sparsely scattered over their rocky land, they cultivated it with an effort that made them robust; continuous labour left them no time to become acquainted with the passions; communications were always difficult, and when snow and ice closed them altogether, each in his own hut was forced to be sufficient unto himself and his family, which led to crude but happy industry. Each in his own household practised all the necessary arts and crafts; all were masons, carpenters, cabinet makers, wheelwrights. The rivers and torrents that divided them from one another gave each, by way of compensation, the means of getting along without his neighbours; saws, forges, and mills multiplied; they learned to regulate the flow of the waters, both for the purpose of turning wheels and of improving irrigation. Thus it is that, in the midst of their precipices and valleys, each, living on his own land, succeeded in making it satisfy all his needs; being well off on what he had, he desired nothing further. Since needs and interests did not conflict, and no one depended on anyone else, their only relations with one another were those of benevolence and friendship; peace and concord reigned in their numerous families. Marriages were almost the only subjects of negotiation between them, and here inclination alone was consulted, no marriage ever being contracted for reasons of ambition, or prevented on grounds of interest and inequality.

This people, poor but not needy, and enjoying the most perfect independence, thus multiplied in unshakable unity; they had no virtues, since, having no vices to overcome, it cost them nothing to do good; and they were good and just without ever knowing what justice and virtue were. This hard-working and independent life attached the Swiss to their fatherland with a strength which gave them two great means of defending it, namely, harmony in council and courage in battle. When you consider the constant unity that prevailed among men who had no masters and practically no laws, and whom the neighbouring princes tried to divide with all the strategems known to politics; when you see the unshakable firmness, the constancy, the very fury with which these fearsome men fought their battles, resolved to conquer or die, and not even conceiving of the idea of disjoining their life from their liberty, it is no longer difficult to understand the prodigies they performed in defence of their country and independence; it is no longer surprising to see the three greatest powers and the most warlike troops of Europe fail successively in their designs against this heroic nation, whose simplicity could no more be overcome by trickery than their courage by valour. Corsicans, this is the model you should follow in order to return to your original estate.

But these rustic men, whose knowledge at first did not extend beyond themselves, their mountains and their huts, learned to know other nations by defending themselves against them; their victories opened the neighbouring frontiers to them; their reputation for bravery gave princes the idea of employing them. They began to pay the troops they had been unable to conquer; these worthy men, who had so well defended their own liberty, became the oppressors of the liberty of others.

It was surprising to see them bring to the service of princes the same valour they had devoted to resisting them, the same fidelity they had shown toward their own fatherland; to see them sell for money those virtues which can least be bought and which money most quickly corrupts. But in this early period they brought to the service of princes the same pride they had taken in resisting them; they looked upon themselves less as their satellites than as their defenders, and believed that they had sold not so much their services as their protection.

Imperceptibly they were debased, and were no longer anything more than mercenaries; a taste for money made them feel poor; contempt for their way of life gradually destroyed the virtues that same life had engendered, and the Swiss became hirelings, like the French, though asking a penny more. Another less obvious cause also corrupted this vigorous nation. Their isolated and simple life made them independent as well as robust; each recognised no other master than himself; but all, having the same tastes and interests, found it easy to unite in pursuit of the same objects; the uniformity of their life served them in place of law. But when association with other peoples had made them love what they should have feared, and admire what they should have scorned, the ambition of their leading men made them change their principles; they felt that, the better to rule the people, they would have to give them less independent tastes. Hence the introduction of commerce, industry and luxury which, by tying the occupations and needs of private citizens to public authority, made them far more dependent on their rulers than they had been in the original state.

Poverty did not make itself felt in Switzerland until

money began to circulate there; money created inequalities both in resources and in fortunes; it became
a great instrument of acquisition which was inaccessible
to those who had nothing. Commercial and manu-
facturing establishments were multiplied; the arts and
crafts diverted a multitude of hands from agriculture.
Men multiplied and, no longer distributed evenly
throughout the country, concentrated in regions whose
location was comparatively favourable and whose
resources were comparatively rich. Some deserted
their fatherland; others became parasites upon it, con-
suming without producing anything; large numbers of
children became a burden. The rate of population
growth declined appreciably; and while the cities grew,
the increasing neglect of agriculture and the rising cost
of living had the effect of making imported foodstuffs
ever more necessary, thus placing the country in a
position of increasing dependence on its neighbours.
Idle habits introduced corruption and multiplied the
number of pensioners dependent on foreign powers;
love of country, extinguished in all hearts, was replaced
by an exclusive love of money; all those sentiments
which give strength to the soul having been stifled,
firmness was no longer to be seen in conduct, nor
vigour in council. Formerly an impoverished Switzerland laid down the law to France; now a rich Switzerland trembles at the frown of a French minister.

These are important lessons for the Corsican people ;
let us see how it ought to apply them to its own case.
The Corsican people retains many of its original virtues,
which will greatly facilitate the establishment of our
constitution. In servitude it has contracted many
vices which will have to be corrected. Of these vices,
some will disappear together with the cause that
engendered them; others will require a contrary cause

to uproot the passion which is responsible for their existence.[1]

In the first category I would place that indomitable and ferocious temper with which the Corsicans are credited. They are accused of being mutinous; who can tell, considering that they have never been justly governed? Those who constantly incited them against one another ought to have foreseen that this animosity would often be turned against its makers.

In the second category I would place that inclination to theft and murder which has made them odious. The source of these two vices is idleness and impunity. This is self-evident with regard to the former, and easily demonstrable with regard to the latter, for family feuds and schemes of vengeance, with the satisfaction of which the Corsicans were constantly occupied, are the product of idle encounters, and reinforced by gloomy meditation, and are made easy of execution through assurance of impunity.

Who could fail to be struck with horror at a barbarous government which, in order to see these luckless people cut each other's throats, spared no pains to incite them to it? Murder was not punished; nay, rather, it was rewarded; blood-money was one of the revenues of the Republic. The unhappy Corsicans were forced, in

[1] There is in all states a progression, a natural and necessary development, from birth to destruction. To make their life as long and excellent as possible, it is better to emphasise the period before rather than the period after they have attained maximum vigour. It is not desirable for Corsica all at once to be all that she is capable of becoming; it is better for her to ascend toward this point than to reach it immediately, and then do nothing but decline; her state of decay is such that if her state of maximum vigour occurred now it would be a very feeble state; whereas placing her in a position to reach it in the future will make it very good when it arrives.

order to avoid total destruction, to pay tribute for the privilege of being disarmed.

May the Corsicans, once again restored to an industrious mode of life, lose the habit of wandering over the island as bandits; may their regular and simple occupations, by keeping them in the bosom of their own families, leave them few issues to settle between them! May their labour provide them easily with the means of subsistence for themselves and their families! May those who have all the necessaries of life be not also obliged to have cash, either to pay taxes and other assessments, or to satisfy the requirements of a capricious luxury which, without contributing to the well-being of him who flaunts it, serves merely to excite the envy and hatred of others!

It is easy to see how these advantages are brought about by the system for which we have expressed our preference; but that is not enough. It is a question of causing the people to adopt these practices, to love the way of life we want to give them, to make it the centre of their pleasures, desires and tastes, and in general to render it their only happiness in life, and the only goal of their ambitions.

The Genoese boasted of having fostered agriculture on the island; the Corsicans seem to agree. I do not share their opinion; for the ill-success of the Genoese proves that their methods were ill-chosen. In this enterprise, the Republic did not seek to multiply the inhabitants of the island, since she so openly favoured murder; nor to make them prosperous, since she ruined them by her exactions; nor even to facilitate the collection of taxes, since she burdened the sale and transport of various farm products with customs duties and forbade their exportation. Her object was, on the contrary, to make more burdensome the very taxes she did not

300

dare to increase; to keep the Corsicans perpetually degraded, by attaching them, in a manner of speaking, to the soil, by turning them away from commerce, manufacture and all the lucrative professions, and by preventing them from improving, educating or enriching themselves. Her object was to secure all their produce at a low price through official monopolies. She used every means to drain the island of money, to make the island need money, and at the same time to prevent money from returning to it. Tyranny could not have used a more subtle device; for by appearing to favour agriculture, she succeeded in crushing the nation; she wished to reduce it to a mass of degraded peasants living in the most deplorable poverty.

What was the consequence? The Corsicans were discouraged and gave up work, since work held no hope for them; they preferred to do nothing rather than weary themselves to no purpose. Their industrious and simple life gave way to idleness, laziness and every sort of vice; thievery procured them the money they needed to pay their taxes, money that their farm produce could never have brought them; they left their fields to work on the highways.

I can see no quicker or surer means of remedying this situation than the two following: the first is to attach men to the land, in a manner of speaking, by making it the basis of their status and rights; the second is to reinforce this bond with family ties, by making land a necessary condition of paternity.

With this in mind, it has seemed to me that it would be possible, basing constitutional law on distinctions drawn from the nature of the case, to divide the whole Corsican nation into three classes; the resulting inequalities, being wholly personal, would be a fortunate substitute for the hereditary or local inequalities created by the system of municipal feudalism we are abolishing. The first class will be that of the *citizens*, and the second that of the *patriots*, the third that of the *aspirants*. We shall consider later the conditions of enrolment in each of these classes, and the privileges to be enjoyed by each.

This class division should not be effected by a census or enumeration at the outset of the new constitution, but should be established gradually and automatically through the simple operation of the passage of time.

The first act in the establishment of the projected system should be a solemn oath sworn by all Corsicans twenty years old or older; and all those who swear it should without distinction be enrolled as citizens. It is quite proper that all these brave men, who have delivered their nation at the price of their blood, should enter in possession of all these advantages, and in the foremost rank enjoy the freedom they have won her.

But once the union has been formed and the oath solemnly taken, all those who, although born on the island, have not yet come of age will remain in the class of aspirants until they are able, on the following conditions, to rise into the two higher classes.

Every legally married aspirant who has some property of his own, apart from his wife's dowry, shall be enrolled in the class of patriots.

Every patriot, married or widowed, who has two living children, a house of his own, and land enough to live on, shall be enrolled in the class of citizens.

This first step, though sufficient to make land honourable, is not enough to ensure its cultivation, unless we eliminate that dependence on money which caused the poverty of the island under the Genoese government. We must set it down as a safe rule that wherever money is a prime necessity, the nation will abandon agriculture to throw itself into more lucrative professions; the farm-worker's way of life is then either an article of commerce and a species of manufacture for the powerful farmer, or else the last resource of poverty for the mass of the peasantry. Those who grow rich in commerce and industry invest their money, when they have made enough, in landed properties which others cultivate for them; thus the whole nation finds itself divided into rich idlers, who own the land, and wretched peasants, who starve while tilling it.

The more necessary money is to private citizens, the more necessary is it to the government; whence it follows that the more commerce flourishes, the higher the taxes; and in order to pay these taxes, the peasant must sell the produce of the land if he is to get any good out of tilling it. It is no use for him to have wheat, wine, oil, he absolutely must have money; he must carry his produce here and there in the cities; he must turn himself into a petty trader, petty salesman, petty rascal. His children, brought up in the debauching atmosphere of trade grow attached to the cities and lose all taste for their calling; they become soldiers or sailors rather than follow in the footsteps of their fathers. Soon the country is deserted, and the city teems with vagrants; there is a gradually increasing shortage of bread; the poverty of the general public increases along with the opulence of private individuals; and both of these lead in conjunction to all those vices which cause the ultimate ruin of a nation.

I am so fully convinced that any system of commerce is destructive to agriculture that I do not even make an exception for trade in agricultural products. If agriculture were to maintain itself under this system, the profits would have to be shared equally between the merchant and the tiller of the soil. But that is the very thing that cannot be; for the bargaining of the one being always free, and that of the other always forced, the former will always dictate to the latter, a relationship which, by destroying the balance, cannot lead to a solid and permanent state of affairs.

It should not be imagined that the island will be the richer for having a great deal of money. This will be true in relation to other peoples and in matters of foreign trade; but in itself a nation is neither richer nor poorer for having more or less money; or, which comes to the same thing, for having the same quantity of money circulate with greater or lesser velocity. It is not only that money is a token, but also that it is a relative token, in practice effective merely by reason of its unequal distribution. For whether we assume that each individual on the island of Corsica has ten crowns only, or that each has a hundred thousand, the relative condition of all in both cases is absolutely the same; no one is either poorer or richer in relation to his fellows; and the only difference is that on the second hypothesis trading becomes more cumbersome. If Corsica needed the services of foreigners, she would need money; but since she is capable of self-sufficiency, she does not need it; and since it is useful only as a token of inequality, the less it circulates within the island, the greater its real prosperity will be. We must see whether the things done with money cannot be done without it; and if they can, these alternative methods must be compared with reference to our purposes.

Facts prove that the island of Corsica, even in its present fallow and exhausted state, is sufficient to support its inhabitants, for even during thirty-six years of war, when their hands have been more often put to arms than to the plough, not a single shipload of provisions or foodstuffs of any kind has been landed for their use; and even apart from foodstuffs, the island has everything it needs to keep the population in a flourishing condition without borrowing anything from abroad. It has wool for textiles, hemp and flax for rope and canvas, leather for shoes, timber for ships, iron for its forges, copper for utensils and small change. It has salt enough for home consumption; it will have a surplus by restoring the salt works of Aleria, which the Genoese went to so much trouble and expense to destroy, and which still yield salt in spite of them. Even if they wanted to, the Corsicians could not carry on foreign trade in kind without buying superfluities; even in this case, therefore, money would not be necessary to their commerce, since money is the sole commodity they would be seeking. From this it follows that, in her relations with other nations, Corsica has no need for money.

The island itself is fairly large and divided by mountains; its great and numerous rivers are largely unnavigable; there is no natural communication between its several parts; but the variety of their products keeps these parts in mutual dependence by making each necessary to the others. The province of Capo Corso, which produces almost nothing but wine, needs the wheat and oil supplied to it by Balagna. Similarly Corte, on its heights, produces grain, and lacks all else; Bonifazio, on the outskirts of the marshes at the other extremity of the island, needs everything and supplies nothing. Thus the project of equalising the population calls for a circulation of agricultural produce, for the facilitation of payments from region to region, and thus for internal trade.

On this point, however, I have two comments to make: first, that this trade can, with government assistance, be effected largely by barter; second, that with this same assistance, and as a natural consequence of our new arrangements, this trade and barter ought steadily to diminish, and in the end to be reduced to very little.

You know that, in the state of exhaustion to which the Genoese had reduced Corsica, money was constantly flowing out and never returning, and thus became at last so rare that, in some cantons of the island, it was no longer known, and no buying or selling was done except by barter.

In their official protests the Corsicans have cited this fact as one of their grievances; they were right, for these poor people needed money to pay their taxes, and when they no longer had any they were seized and distrained in their homes, and saw themselves stripped of their most necessary utensils, their furniture, their poultry, their rags, all of which had then to be transported from place to place and sold at less than a tenth of the true value; with the result that, for lack of money, they paid the tax tenfold.

But since, under our system, no one will be forced to pay taxes in specie, lack of money will not be a token of poverty and will not serve to increase it; exchange can thus be effected in kind, without intermediary assets, and it will be possible to live in abundance without ever handling a penny.

I see that under the Genoese governors, who banned and in a thousand ways harassed the movement of produce from province to province, the communes set up warehouses to store wheat, wine and oil until the moment when trade would be both favourable and licit, and that these warehouses served the Genoese officials as pretext for a thousand odious monopolies. Since the idea of such warehouses is not new, it would be all the easier to put it into execution, and it would provide a means of exchange which would be simple and convenient both for the nation and for private individuals, without the danger of disadvantages which would make it burdens(me to the people.

Even without having recourse to actual warehouses and depots, it would be possible in each county town to set up a public double-entry register, where private individuals each year would have recorded, on one side, the nature and quantity of their surplus products, and on the other side those they lacked. By balancing and comparing these registers from province to province, the price of produce and the volume of trade could be so regulated that each county would dispose of its surplus and satisfy its needs without deficiency or excess, and almost as conveniently as if the harvest were measured to its needs.

These operations can be performed with the greatest nicety and without the use of real money; either by way of direct exchange, or with the aid of a purely imaginary monetary unit which could serve as a term of comparison, as pistoles are used in France; or else by using as money some concrete form of denumerable property, like oxen among the Greeks and sheep among the Romans, and by reckoning it at its average value. For then an actual ox may be worth more or less than an ox, and a sheep more or less than a sheep, an anomaly which makes the imaginary unit preferable, since the latter is conceived only as an abstract number and is therefore always accurate.

As long as you confine yourselves to this, trade will remain in balance; and exchange, being regulated solely according to the relative abundance or scarcity of produce, and the greater or lesser facility of transport, will everywhere and at all times remain on a basis of proportionate equality; and all the products of the island, being equally distributed, will adjust themselves automatically to the level of the population. I will add that the public administration will be able without difficulty to preside over these transactions and exchanges, to keep account of them, to regulate their volume and to effect their distribution; for in so far as transactions are in kind, public officials will not be able, and will not even feel any temptation, to abuse them. Whereas the conversion of produce into money opens the way to all those exactions, monopolies and rascalities which in such cases are typical of office-holders.

Many difficulties are to be expected at the beginning; but these difficulties are inevitable in any system which is new and runs counter to established usage. I may add that this system of administration, once established, will become easier every year, not only as a result of experience and practice, but also by reason of the progressive diminution of trade which must necessarily follow, until it has been reduced of its own accord to the smallest possible volume, which is the final goal we ought to envisage.

Everyone should make a living, and no one should grow rich; that is the fundamental principle of the prosperity of the nation; and the system I propose, so far as in it lies, proceeds as directly as possible toward that goal. Since superfluous produce is not an article of commerce, and is not retailed for money, it will be cultivated only to the extent that necessaries are needed; and anyone who can procure directly the things he lacks will take no interest in having a surplus.

As soon as the products of the earth cease to be merchandise, their cultivation will gradually be proportioned in each province, and even on each farm, to the general requirements of the province and the particular requirements of the farmer. Each will try to have everything he needs by producing it directly on his own land, rather than by exchange, which will always be less convenient and less certain, however greatly it may be facilitated.

It cannot be denied that it is advantageous to have each sort of land produce the things for which it is best suited; by this arrangement you get more out of a country, and with less effort, than in any other way. But this consideration, for all its importance, is only secondary. It is better for the land to produce a little less and for the inhabitants to lead better-regulated lives. With any movement of trade and commerce it is impossible to prevent destructive vices from creeping into a nation. The lack of certain advantages in the choice of land can be compensated by labour; and it is better to make bad use of fields than to make bad use of men. Furthermore, each farmer can and should have this in mind in selecting his own land, and each parish or commune in selecting its community property, as we shall see hereafter.

It may be feared that this economic system would produce an effect contrary to my expectations; that it would tend to discourage rather than to encourage agriculture; that the farmers, deriving no profit from their produce, would neglect their work, that they would confine themselves to mere subsistence farming, and that, without seeking prosperity and content with raising an absolute minimum for their own use, they would let the remainder of their land lie fallow. This is apparently confirmed by the experience of the Genoese government, under which the ban on the exportation of agricultural produce had precisely this effect.

But it must be remembered that, under this administration, money was the prime necessity, and thus the immediate object of labour; and that in consequence all labour incapable of earning money was necessarily neglected; that the farmer, overwhelmed by contempt, vexations and poverty, regarded his calling as the worst of misfortunes; and that, seeing he could not grow rich following it, he either went looking for another or else grew discouraged. But the whole basic tendency of our new constitution is to make this calling happy in its mediocrity, and respectable in its simplicity. Providing all the necessaries of life, all the means of acquiring social recognition and of discharging public obligations, and all this without sale or traffic, it will leave men incapable even of imagining a better or nobler way of life. Those who succeed in it, seeing nothing above them, will glory in it, and on making their way to the highest offices, will fill them as successfully as the early Romans. Being unable to leave this way of life, they will want to distinguish themselves in it, outdoing the rest by harvesting larger crops, by supplying the state with a stronger military contingent, by earning popular votes in the elections. Large families, well nourished and well clad, will bring honour to their fathers; and real abundance being the only known form of luxury, each will want to distinguish himself by luxury of this sort. As long as the human heart remains as it is, such institutions will not breed idleness.

What local magistrates and heads of families should do in each region, parish and household to make themselves independent of the rest, the central government of the island should do to make itself independent of neighbouring peoples.

An exact tabulation of the goods imported into the island during a certain number of years will give a good and reliable list of things that cannot be dispensed with; for the present situation is not one in which luxury and superfluity can occur. By careful observation of what the island both does and can produce, you will find that necessary foreign imports amount to very little; and this is fully confirmed by the facts; for in the years 1735 and 1736, when the island, under blockade by the Genoese navy, had no communication with the mainland, there was not only no lack of anything in the way of foodstuffs, but there were no unbearable shortages of any sort. The most appreciable deficiencies were in munitions of war, in leather, and in cotton for candle-wicks; and a substitute for the last was found in the pith of certain reeds.

From this small number of necessary imports must also be subtracted everything the island does not now provide, but could provide if it were better cultivated and more vigorously industrialised. Although we must be careful to reject the idle arts, the arts of pleasure and luxury, we must be equally careful to favour those which are useful to agriculture and advantageous to human life. We have no need for wood-carvers and goldsmiths, but we do need carpenters and blacksmiths; we need weavers, good workers in woollens, not embroiderers or drawers of gold thread.

We shall begin by making sure of having the most necessary raw materials, namely wood, iron, wool, leather, hemp and flax. The island abounds in wood both for construction and for fuel; but we must not rely on this abundance to abandon the use and cutting of forests to the sole discretion of the proprietors. As the population of the island increases and new land is brought under cultivation, the woods will suffer a rapid deterioration which can only be repaired very slowly.

Switzerland was formerly covered with woods so abundant that they were an encumbrance; but as a result both of the multiplication of pasturage and of the establishment of manufactures, they were cut without rule or measure; now these immense forests have nothing to show but nearly naked rock. Fortunately the Swiss, warned by the example of France, have seen the danger, and have brought it under control to the best of their abilities. It remains to be seen whether their precautions are not too late; for if, in spite of these precautions, their woods diminish daily, it is clear that they must end in destruction.

Corsica, by starting earlier, would not have the same danger to fear; a strict system of forest control must be set up in good season, and cutting so regulated that production equals consumption. It should not be done as in France, where the water and forest wardens receive a fee for cutting rights, and have therefore an interest in destroying everything; a task they fulfil to the best of their abilities. The future must be provided for long in advance; and so, although now may not be the right moment to establish a navy, the time will come when it will be necessary to do so; and then you will appreciate the advantage of not having handed over to foreign navies the fine forests which lie by the sea. Old and no longer profitable woods should be exploited or sold; but those which are vigorous should be left standing; they will be used when their time has come.

It is said that a copper mine has been found on the island; that is good; but iron mines are worth still more. There must surely be some on the island; the location, the mountains, the nature of the terrain, the thermal springs found in the province of Capo Corso and elsewhere, all this makes me believe that many such mines will be found if you look carefully with the aid of competent experts. Assuming this to be so, you will not allow them to be exploited indifferently; but in setting up forges you will choose those sites which are most favourable, most accessible to woods and rivers, and most capable of being opened to convenient lines of transport.

The same attention will be paid to manufactures of all sorts, each with reference to its own particular needs, in order to facilitate labour and distribution as far as possible. Care will be taken, however, not to set up establishments of this sort in the most populous and fertile sections of the island. On the contrary, other things being equal, you will choose the most arid sites, sites which, unless they were peopled by industry, would remain desert. This will cause some difficulties in the matter of supplying necessary provisions; but the advantages gained and the disadvantages avoided ought infinitely to outweigh this consideration.

In this way, above all, we are following our great and primary principle, which is not only to extend and multiply the population, but to equalise it as far as possible throughout the island. For if the sterile places were not peopled by industry, they would remain desert; and so much would be lost for the possible increase of the nation.

If you were to found such establishments in fertile places, the abundance of provisions and the profits of labour, profits necessarily greater in the arts and crafts than in agriculture, would divert farmers or their families from rural cares, and would gradually depopulate the countryside, making it necessary to attract new settlers from afar to cultivate it. Thus, by overloading some points of territory with inhabitants, we should depopulate others, and in thus destroying the balance we should be going directly counter to the spirit of our new constitution.

The transportation of foodstuffs, by rendering them more costly in the factories, will diminish the profit of the workers and, by keeping their condition closer to that of the farmers, will better maintain the balance between them. This balance can never be such, however, that the advantage will not still lie with industry, partly because it attracts a larger share of the money circulating in the state, partly because wealth provides opportunities for the effects of power and inequality to be felt, and partly because increased strength accrues to large numbers of men gathered together in one place, a strength which the ambitious know how to combine to their own advantage. It is, therefore, important that this too-favoured part should remain dependent for its livelihood on the rest of the nation; in the case of internal conflict, it is in the nature of our new constitution that the farmer should be the one to lay down the law to the worker.

With these precautions, there will be no danger in favouring the establishment of useful arts and crafts upon the island; and I suspect that these establishments, if well managed, will be able to ensure all the necessaries without requiring any foreign imports at all, with the possible exception of some trifles for the sake of which a proportionate export will be permitted, the balance being at all times carefully maintained by the administration.

So far, I have shown how the Corsican people could subsist in ease and independence with very little trade; how of the little that is necessary the greater part can easily be effected by barter; and how the need for imports from outside the island can be reduced to practically nothing. Thus we have seen that if the use of money and currency cannot be absolutely destroyed in private transactions, it can at least be reduced to so small a matter that it will be hard for it to give rise to abuses; that no fortunes will be made in this way;

and that if they could be made, they would become practically useless and would give their possessors little advantage.

But the question of public finance remains; how shall we regulate it? What revenues shall we assign to the administration? Shall its officials be paid or unpaid? How shall we arrange for its upkeep? That is the next point to be considered.

Systems of public finance are a modern invention; the word finance was no more known to the ancients than the words tithe and capitation. The word *vectigal* was used in a different sense, as we shall explain hereafter. The sovereign laid imposts on conquered or vanquished peoples, never on its own immediate subjects; this was especially true of republics. The people of Athens, far from being taxed, was paid by the government; and Rome, whose wars must have cost her so much, often made distribution of wheat, and even of land, to the people. The state none the less subsisted, and maintained large armed forces on land and sea, and constructed considerable public works which were at least as expensive, proportionately, as those of modern states. How was this done?

Two periods are to be distinguished in the life of states, the period of origins, and the period of growth. In the beginning, a state had no other revenue than the public domain, and this domain was considerable. Romulus reserved for it one third of all the land; he assigned the second third for the maintenance of priests and holy things; the third only was divided among the citizens. It was little, but this little was free. Do you think that a French farmer would not willingly reduce himself to a third of the land he now cultivates, on condition that this third be held free of all tallages, corvées and tithes, and that no taxes of any kind be levied on it?

Thus the public revenue in Rome was collected not in money, but in foodstuffs and other products. Expenditures were of the same nature as receipts. Magistrates and soldiers were not paid, but fed and clothed; and in cases of urgent need, the extraordinary levies imposed on the people were corvées, not money taxes. Its onerous public works cost the state practically nothing; they were the labour of those redoubtable legions which worked as they fought, and were made up not of riff-raff but of citizens.

When the Romans began to expand and turned into conquerors, they placed the burden of maintaining their troops upon the conquered peoples; when soldiers were paid, it was the subjects, never the Romans, who were taxed. In moments of pressing danger the senate assessed itself; it raised loans which were faithfully repaid; and during the whole life of the Republic, I do not know of the Roman people ever paying money taxes, either on real estate or by capitation.

Corsicans, this is a fine model! Be not surprised that there were more virtues among the Romans than elsewhere; money was less necessary to them; the state had small revenues and did great things. Its treasure was in the strength of its citizens. I would say that owing to the situation of Corsica and the form of its government, no administration in the world will be less costly; for, being an island and a republic, it will have no need of standing armies; and the chiefs of state, since all return to the equality of private life, will be unable to withdraw anything from the common mass that will not very soon return to it.

But it is not thus that I envisage the sinews of public power. On the contrary, I want to see a great deal spent on state service; my only quarrel, strictly speaking, is with the choice of means. I regard finance as the fat of the body politic, fat which, when clogged up in certain muscular tissues, overburdens the body with useless obesity, and makes it heavy rather than strong. I want to nourish the state on a more salutary food, which will add to its substance; food capable of turning into fibre and muscle without clogging the vessels; which will give vigour rather than grossness to the members, and strengthen the body without making it heavy.

Far from wanting the state to be poor, I should like, on the contrary, for it to own everything, and for each individual to share in the common property only in proportion to his services. Joseph's acquisition, on behalf of the king, of all the property of the Egyptians, would have been a good thing if he had not done too much or too little. But, without entering into speculations which would take me too far afield, it is sufficient here to explain my idea, which is not to destroy private property absolutely, since that is impossible, but to confine it within the narrowest possible limits; to give it a measure, a rule, a rein which will contain, direct, and subjugate it, and keep it ever subordinate to the public good. In short, I want the property of the state to be as large and strong, that of the citizens as small and weak, as possible. That is why I avoid embodying it in things over which the private possessor has too much control; such as money and currency, which can be readily hidden from public inspection.

The setting up of a public domain is not, I admit, as easy to do in present-day Corsica, which is already divided among its inhabitants, as it was at the birth of Rome, when its conquered territory did not as yet belong to anyone. However, I know that there is a large quantity of excellent land still lying fallow on the island, land of which the government could easily make use, either by alienating it for a certain number of years to those who will put it under cultivation, or by having it brought under the plough by corvées in the several communities. It would be necessary to have been on the spot to judge regarding the possible distribution of these lands, and the possible use to be made of them; but I have no doubt that by means of a few exchanges and by certain fairly easy adjustments it will be possible in each region, and even in each parish, to procure community property which can even be augmented in a few years by the system of which we shall speak in dealing with the law of succession.

Another method which is even simpler, and which should provide clearer, more certain and much more considerable revenues, is to follow an example which I find close at hand in the Protestant cantons of Switzerland. At the time of the Reformation these cantons seized the ecclesiastical tithes; and these tithes, on which they worthily support their clergy, have constituted the main revenue of the state. I do not say that the Corsicans ought to touch the revenues of the church, God forbid! But I think that the people will not be greatly vexed if the state demands as much of them as do the clergy, who are already sufficiently endowed with real estate. The levying of this tax will be carried out without difficulty and inconvenience, and almost without cost, since it will only be necessary to double the ecclesiastical tithe and then take half of it.

I derive a third sort of revenue, the best and surest of all, from men themselves, using their labour, their arms and their hearts, rather than their purses, in the service of the fatherland, both for its defence, in the militia, and for its utility, in corvées on public works.

Do not let the word corvée frighten republicans! I

know that it is held in abomination in France; but is it so held in Switzerland? The roads there are also built by corvées, and no one complains. The apparent convenience of money payment can delude none but superficial minds; and it is a sure principle that the fewer the intermediaries between need and service, the less onerous the service should be.

Without venturing to express my thoughts in their entirety, without arguing here that corvées and all other forms of personal service by citizens are an absolute good, I would agree, if you wish, that it would be better to have all that done on a paid basis, if the means of payment did not introduce an infinity of measureless abuses and of evils greater and more unlimited than those which can result from this form of constraint; especially when this constraint is imposed by one whose walk of life is the same as that of those on whom he imposes it.

Finally, in order that the contribution should be shared equally, it is just that those who, having no lands, cannot pay a tithe of their produce, should pay with their own labour; thus the corvées ought to fall especially on the order of aspirants. But citizens and patriots ought to lead them to the work and set them an example. Let everything done for the public good be at all times honourable! Let the magistrate himself, though occupied with other cares, show that the rest are not beneath him, like those Roman consuls who, to set an example to their troops, were the first to put their hands to the construction of field-works.

With regard to fines and confiscations, which constitute a fourth type of revenue in republics, I hope that our new constitution will render such revenue practically non-existent among us; I therefore shall not take it into account.

All these public revenues, being in kind rather than in money, would seem hard to collect, to store, and to use; and this is true in part. But we are less concerned here with ease than with soundness of administration; and it is better for it to be a bit more troublesome if it engenders fewer abuses. The best economic system for Corsica and for a republic is certainly not the best for a monarchy and for a large state. The one I suggest would certainly not work in France or England, and could not even be established there; but it is most successful in Switzerland, where it has been established for centuries, and it is the only one that country could have endured.

In Switzerland, taxes in each district are farmed out; they are collected either in kind or in money, as the contributors may elect; magistrates and officials everywhere are likewise paid for the most part in wheat, wine, fodder, wood. In this way collection is neither embarrassing to the public nor burdensome to private citizens; but the disadvantage of the system, as I see it, is that there are men whose profession it is to cheat the prince and vex the subjects.

It is most important not to allow any professional tax-farmers in the Republic, not so much because of their dishonest profits as because of the fatal example they set; an example which, all too promptly diffused throughout the nation, destroys all worthy feelings by making illicit wealth and its advantages respectable, and by casting unselfishness, simplicity, morality and all the virtues under a cloud of scorn and opprobrium.

Let us beware of increasing our pecuniary at the expense of our moral treasure; it is the latter that puts us truly in possession of men and of all their power, whereas the former gives only the appearance of service, since the will cannot be bought. It is better that the

administration of the public treasury should be like
that of the father of family, and lose something, than
for it to gain more and be like that of a usurer.

Let us, then, leave tax collections in the hands of the
state, even though it may bring in much less. Let us
even avoid making tax-collecting a profession, for this
would lead to nearly the same disadvantages as tax-
farming. What is most pernicious in a system of
public finance is the employment of professional tax-
gatherers. At any price we must avoid having a
single publican in the state. Instead of making the
collection of taxes and public revenues a lucrative
career, we must make it, on the contrary, a test of
ability and integrity for the younger citizens; we must
make this branch of administration the novitiate, so to
speak, for public employment, and the first step toward
the winning of magistracies. This idea was suggested
to me by a comparison of the administration of the
Charity Hospital of Paris, whose depredations and
robberies are notorious, with that of the Charity
Hospital of Lyons, which is a model of unselfishness
and good management possibly unequalled anywhere
on earth. Whence comes this difference? Are the
people of Lyons intrinsically better than Parisians? No.
But in Lyons the office of hospital administrator is
temporary. You must begin by properly discharging
the duties of this office in order to become a municipal
magistrate and a merchant provost; whereas in Paris
the administrators serve for life; they manage to derive
the greatest possible advantage from an office which
for them is not a proving-ground, but a profession, a
reward, a privileged position attached, so to speak, to
other privileges. There are certain offices where it is
agreed that the income should be augmented by the
right to rob the poor.

Nor should it be thought that this work requires more experience and training than young people are able to have; it simply demands a kind of activity for which they are peculiarly suited; and since they are ordinarily less avaricious, less hard-hearted in their exactions than their elders, since they are sensitive, on the one hand, to the sufferings of the poor, and strongly interested, on the other hand, in discharging well the duties of an office in which they are being tested, they will conduct themselves in that office exactly as the situation requires.

The collector of each parish shall render his accounts to the county, that of each county to its region, that of each region to the chamber of accounts, which will be composed of a certain number of councillors of state. The public treasure will thus consist, for the most part, of agricultural produce and other products, scattered in small warehouses throughout the republic, and in part of money which will be remitted to the general treasury, after the deduction of such minor disbursements as have to be made locally.

Since private citizens will always be at liberty to pay their assessments in money or in kind, at a rate to be established annually in each region, the government, once it has calculated the optimum proportion to be maintained between these two types of contribution, will be in a position to perceive immediately any change in this proportion as soon as it occurs, and to look for its cause and cure.

This is the keystone of our political system, the only point that requires skill, calculation, and thought. That is why the chamber of accounts, which everywhere else is only a very minor tribunal, will be for us the centre of affairs, the motive power behind the whole administration, and will be composed of the leading persons in the state.

322

When collections in kind exceed their due proportion, and those in money are deficient, it will be a sign that agriculture and population are doing well, but that useful industries are being neglected; it will be proper to re-animate them somewhat, lest the private citizens, by becoming too isolated, wild and independent, no longer place sufficient value on the government.

But this defect, an infallible sign of prosperity, will always be little to be feared and easily remedied. It will not be the same with the opposite defect, which, as soon as it becomes perceptible, is already a matter of the highest consequence, and cannot be too quickly corrected. For when the tax-payers supply more money than agricultural produce, it is a sure sign that too much is being exported abroad; that trade is becoming too easy, that lucrative arts and crafts are growing on the island at the expense of agriculture, and consequently that simplicity and all its attendant virtues are beginning to degenerate. The abuses this alteration produces indicate the remedies to be brought to bear upon them. But these remedies call for great wisdom in their manner of application, for in this matter it is much easier to forestall the evil than to eradicate it.

If you did no more than to impose taxes on objects of luxury, close the ports to foreign commerce, suppress manufactures, and halt the circulation of specie, you would simply plunge the people into idleness, poverty and discouragement. You would make money disappear without increasing agricultural production; you would eliminate the resources of wealth without re-establishing those of labour. Changing the value of money is also a bad policy in a republic: first because then it is the public which robs itself, which is absolutely meaningless; secondly, because there is between the quantity of tokens and the quantity of things a proportion which always regulates their respective values in the same way, with the result that, when the sovereign tries to change the tokens, he does no more than change the names, since the value of things then necessarily changes in the same proportion. With kings it is a different matter; and when the sovereign inflates the currency, he derives therefrom the real advantage of robbing his creditors. But if ever this operation is repeated, this advantage is compensated and wiped out by the loss of public credit.

Enact sumptuary laws, therefore, but make them always more severe for the leaders of the state, and more lenient for the lower orders; make simplicity a point of vanity, and arrange things so that a rich man will not know how to derive honour from his money. These are not impractical speculations; thus do the Venetians reserve for their noblemen the right to wear the plain, rough, black cloth of Padua, so that the best citizens consider it an honour to receive the like permission.

When manners are simple, agrarian laws are necessary, for then the rich, being unable to invest their wealth in anything else, accumulate real estate. But neither agrarian laws, nor any other law, can ever be retroactive; and no lands legitimately acquired, no matter how great the quantity, can be confiscated by virtue of a subsequent law forbidding the ownership of so much. No law can despoil any private citizen of any part of his property; the law can merely prevent him from acquiring more. Then, if he breaks the law, he deserves punishment; and the illegitimately acquired surplus can and ought to be confiscated. The Romans saw the necessity of agrarian laws when the time to enact them had already passed; and through their failure to make the distinction just stated, they finally destroyed the Republic by a means which ought to have preserved it. The Greeks wanted to deprive their patricians of their lands; they should have prevented them from acquiring them. It is very true that, later on, these same patricians acquired still more, in defiance of the law; but that was because the evil was already inveterate when the law was passed, and there was no longer time to cure it.

Fear and hope are the two great instruments for the governance of men; but instead of using both indiscriminately, you must use each according to its own nature. Fear does not stimulate, it restrains; and its use in penal laws is not to make men do good, but to prevent them from doing evil. We do not even find that fear of poverty makes idlers industrious. To excite men to vie with one another in labour, therefore, you should present it to them not as a means of avoiding hunger, but as a means of advancing toward well-being. Let us take it, then, as a general rule that no one should be punished for having failed to act, but only for having acted.

To stimulate the activity of a nation, therefore, you must offer it great hopes, great desires, great motives for positive action. The great springs of human conduct come down, on close examination, to two, pleasure and vanity; and what is more, if you subtract from the first all that appertains to the second, you will find in the last analysis that everything comes down to practically pure vanity. It is easy to see that all public voluptuaries are merely vain; their pretended pleasure is pure ostentation, and consists rather in showing or describing pleasure than in enjoying it. True pleasure is simple and peaceable, it loves silence and meditation; he who enjoys it is entirely absorbed in the thing itself, and finds no amusement in saying ' I am enjoying myself.' But vanity is the fruit of opinion; it arises from it and feeds upon it. Whence it follows that the arbiters of a people's opinion are also arbiters of its actions. It seeks things in proportion to the value it places upon them; to show it what it ought to respect is to tell it what it ought to do. This word vanity is not well chosen, since vanity is only one of the two branches of self-esteem. I must explain my meaning. Opinion which lays great store by frivolous objects produces vanity; but that which lights on objects intrinsically great and beautiful produces pride. You can thus render a people either proud or vain, depending on the choice of the objects to which you direct its judgments.

Pride is more natural than vanity, since it consists in deriving self-esteem from truly estimable goods; whereas vanity, by giving value to that which is valueless, is the work of prejudices which are slow to arise. It takes time to bedazzle the eyes of a nation. Since there is nothing more truly beautiful than power and independence, every people in process of formation begins by being proud. But no new people was ever vain; for vanity, by its very nature, is individual; it cannot be the instrument of so great an enterprise as the creation of a national body.

Two contrary conditions plunge men into the torpor of idleness: the first is that peace of soul which makes men content with what they possess; the second is an unlimited covetousness which makes them see the impossibility of satisfying their desires. He who lives without desire, and he who knows he cannot obtain what he desires, remain equally in a state of inaction. To act you must both aspire to something and be able to have hopes of achieving it. Any government which tries to stimulate activity among the people must first take care to place within its reach objects capable of tempting it. Arrange things so that work will offer citizens great advantages, not only in your own estimation, but also in theirs; infallibly you will make them industrious. Among these advantages, it is true not only that wealth is not always the most attractive, but that it may even be the least attractive of all, as long as it does not serve as a means to the attainment of those which are desired.

The most general and certain of all possible means to the satisfaction of your desires, whatever they may be, is power. Thus, to whatever passions a man or a people inclines, if those passions are vigorous they will vigorously aspire to power, either as an end, if they are proud or vain, or as a means, if they are vindictive or pleasure-loving.

It is, therefore, in the skilful and economical management of civil power that the great art of government consists; not only to preserve the government itself, but also to diffuse life and activity throughout the state, and to render the people active and industrious.

Civil power is exercised in two ways: the first legitimate, by authority; the second abusive, by wealth. Wherever wealth dominates, power and authority are ordinarily separate; for the means of acquiring wealth and the means of attaining authority are not the same, and thus are rarely employed by the same people. Apparent power, in these cases, is in the hands of the magistrates, and real power in those of the rich. In such a government everything proceeds in response to the passions of men; nothing aims toward the goal set by the original constitution.

Under these conditions the goal of ambition becomes twofold: some aspire to authority in order to sell the use thereof to the rich and thus themselves grow rich; the rest, the majority, go directly after wealth, with which they are sure one day of having power, either by buying authority for themselves, or by buying those who are its depositaries.

Let us assume that, in a state so constituted, honours and authority, on the one hand, are hereditary; and that, on the other hand, the means of acquiring wealth, being beyond the reach of all but a minority, depend on credit, favour, friends; it is then impossible, while a few adventurers go on to fortune and thence, by easy stages, to public office, for universal discouragement not to overcome the bulk of the nation and to plunge it into a state of listlessness.

Generally speaking, therefore, the government of all rich nations is weak, and I apply this term indiscriminately both to one which always acts weakly and, which comes to the same thing, to one which must use violent means to maintain itself.

I can explain my meaning in no better way than by the example of Carthage and Rome. The first massacred and crucified its generals, its magistrates and its citizens, and was only a feeble government, frightened of everything and increasingly unstable. The second deprived no one of his life, and did not even confiscate his property; an accused criminal could depart in peace, and that was the end of the proceedings. The vigour of this admirable government had no need of cruelty; the greatest of misfortunes was to be excluded from its membership.

* * *

[1] Peoples will be industrious when work is honoured; and it always depends on the government to make it so. When esteem and authority are within the reach of the citizens, they will try to attain them ; but if they see

[1] [The following are disconnected fragments.—Tr.]

that they are too far removed, they will not stir a step. What plunges them into discouragement is not the greatness of the work, but its futility.

* * *

You will ask if it is by tilling a field that one acquires the talents needed for governing. I answer yes, in a government as simple and upright as ours. Great talents are a substitute for patriotic zeal; they are necessary to lead a people which does not love its country and does not honour its leaders. But make the people love the commonwealth, seek virtue, and do not concern yourself with great talents; they would do more harm than good. The best motive force for a government is love of country, and this love is cultivated together with the land. Common sense suffices to govern a well-constituted state; and common sense develops quite as much in the heart as in the head, since men who are not blinded by their passions always behave well.

* * *

Men are naturally lazy: but ardour in labour is the first-fruit of a well-regulated society; and when a people relapses into laziness and discouragement, it is always a result of the abuse of that same society, which no longer gives labour the reward it has a right to expect.

* * *

Wherever money reigns, the money the people gives to maintain its liberty is always the instrument of its enslavement; and what it pays voluntarily today is used tomorrow to compel it to pay.

* * *

When a country becomes overpopulated, it will be necessary to employ the excess population in industry and the arts in order to draw from abroad those things that so numerous a people requires for its subsistence. Then, little by little, the vices inseparable from these establishments will also arise and, gradually corrupting the nation in its tastes and principles, will alter and at last destroy the government. This evil is inevitable; and since it is necessary that all human things should come to an end, it is well that a state, after a long and vigorous existence, should end by excess of population.

*   *   *